THE VICER

Emeritus Associate Professor at C
arts institutions, Anindyo Roy has had a thirty-ye—
teacher and writer. Roy's main area of interest is imperialism and
literature, with special focus on nineteenth- and early twentieth-century
Britain and India.

Praise for the Book

The Viceroy's Artist is story at a human scale: a man, caught between
his past and the arc of a sweeping historical drama unfolding around
him. Roy's storytelling carries the reader with Lear in a quietly thrilling
undertow, far from the familiar shores of colonial history as we think we
know them.

**Tilar J. Mazzeo, *New York Times* bestselling author of
*The Widow Clicquot***

Edward Lear [...] is the most engaging and unusual of Victorian literary
and artistic travellers and Anindyo Roy brings him to life with delicate
detail [...] This lovely book has captured with compelling intimacy
not only the singular character of Lear himself but also the nineteenth-
century moment in which he lived.

Lucy Lethbridge, prize-winning author of *Who Was Ada Lovelace?*

Anindyo Roy's richly visual novel [...] marvellously enables us to follow
Edward Lear's experience of India [...] Visual beauty and verbal comedy
alternate with the artist's memories of personal sorrows, perception of
historic cruelties and liking for a good meal.

Janet Montefiore, editor of the *Kipling Journal*

A very clever fictionalized re-creation of Lear's own meticulous record of his travels on the subcontinent [...] all in a colourful style which Lear himself would surely have approved.

Michael Montgomery, author of *Lear's Italy* and *The Owl and the Pussy Cats: Lear in Love, the Untold Story*

In this entertaining and touching story, Anindyo Roy has captured the voice and imagination of the beloved poet of nonsense, Edward Lear [...] Lear comes alive as poignantly human [...] yet we also see Lear, despite ill health, seeking joy though his art, delighting in travel, and finding companionship by making children and their families laugh.

Mary Ellis Gibson, author of *Indian Angles: English Verse in Colonial India from Jones to Tagore*

A very good read indeed and one that Lear himself would have chuckled about.

Derek Johns, president of the Edward Lear Society

A spellbinding novel! Anindyo Roy has written a graceful and mesmerizing fiction, an expansive yet distilled portrait of 19th-century India and its 'men of Empire'. Haunting, funny, and undeniably original *The Viceroy's Artist* is a book about Empire, art-making, and the relationships that sustain us.

Sarah Braunstein, author of *The Sweet Relief of Missing Children*

THE VICEROY'S ARTIST

A Novel

ANINDYO ROY

First published in 2023 by Hachette India
(Registered name: Hachette Book Publishing India Pvt. Ltd)
An Hachette UK company
www.hachetteindia.com

1

Copyright © 2023 Anindyo Roy

Anindyo Roy asserts the moral right to be identified as the
author of this work.

Inside illustrations by Saurav Roy.

All rights reserved. No part of the publication may be copied, reproduced,
downloaded, stored in a retrieval system, or transmitted in any form or by any
means without the prior written permission of the publisher, nor be otherwise
circulated in any form of binding or cover or digital format other than that in
which it is published and without a similar condition being imposed on the
subsequent purchaser.

Subsequent edition/reprint specifications may be subject to change,
including but not limited to cover or inside finishes, paper, text colour,
and/or colour sections.

This is a work of fiction. Names, characters, places and incidents (other than
those obviously genuine) are fictitious and any resemblance to real persons,
living or dead, or actual events or locales is purely coincidental.

ISBN 978-93-5731-542-5

Hachette Book Publishing India Pvt. Ltd
4th & 5th Floors, Corporate Centre,
Plot No. 94, Sector 44, Gurugram 122003, India

Typeset in Arno Pro 11/15
by R. Ajith Kumar, New Delhi

Printed and bound in India
by Manipal Technologies Limited

MIX
Paper from
responsible sources
FSC™ C043100

To the memory of my late mother, Meena Roy, who first introduced me to the world of nonsense by reading from Sukumar Ray's Abol Tabol, *the collection of poems inspired by Edward Lear's* A Book of Nonsense.

Contents

Dramatis Personae

Edward Lear: The nineteenth-century poet of nonsense, author of *A Book of Nonsense* (1846) and *Nonsense Songs* (1872), an inveterate world traveller, a draughtsman who made striking illustrations of birds and animals and a painter of landscapes.

Giorgi Kokalis: The Albanian who served Lear as manservant from 1856 to 1883 was often referred to as the 'Suliot' by Lear. A faithful and ever-vigilant friend, a trustworthy travelling companion, he was, according to Lear, a thoroughly unsatisfactory chef.

Franklin Lushington: A judge at the Supreme Court of Justice in the Ionian Islands, Lear first met him in Malta in 1849, and later in Corfu, Lear's home for nearly seventeen years, where they met frequently, dined together and went for long walks.

Chichester Fortescu: A close friend of Lear, born in County Louth, Ireland, he was a Member of Parliament. Admitted to the Irish Privy Council and president of the Board of Trade, he was married to Countess Waldergrave.

Lady (Countess) Waldergrave: One of London's leading society hostesses, wife of Fortescu and one of Lear's closest friends. Lear was often invited to the parties she threw at Strawberry Hill.

Alfred Tennyson: Poet Laureate of Britain and part of Lear's upper-class circle of friends. Lear also illustrated an edition of Tennyson's poems.

Emily Tennyson: Alfred Tennyson's wife, she remained Lear's loyal friend even after the friendship between her husband and Lear had cooled.

Holman Hunt: The Pre-Raphaelite painter, Lear's close friend, he and Lear shared a steady correspondence over the years. Lear admired Hunt for his sense of light.

Ann: Edward Lear's oldest sister, she was the firstborn in the Lear family of twenty children, of which Lear was the youngest. Ann took care of Lear after their father was sent to debtors' prison and also helped him to recover from fits of epilepsy that afflicted him since he was a child. A painter herself, it was under her guidance that Lear's artistic talents first developed.

Eleanor and Harriet: Lear's other sisters.

Charles: Lear's brother who became a missionary in West Africa.

Lord Northbrook (Thomas Baring): Viceroy of India, appointed by Gladstone, met Lear in 1848 in Rome. As Lear's patron, he commissioned the painting of Kanchenjunga, which enabled Lear to travel in India for fourteen months, a journey chronicled in his *Indian Journals*.

Evelyn Baring: Cousin of Lord Northbrook and his personal secretary in India.

Archibald Campbell: Assistant surgeon in the East India Company, a resident of Darjeeling from 1840 to 1862, and superintendent of the Darjeeling sanitorium.

Joseph Hooker: English botanist, once a resident of Darjeeling, who studied the fauna of the eastern Himalayan foothills and was imprisoned by the Chogyal after he strayed into the Kingdom of Sikkim without obtaining a permit. Hooker later served as director of the Royal Botanic Gardens at Kew from 1865 to 1885.

Edgar Ware: The assistant commissioner of the town of Kurseong, located close to Darjeeling.

Queen Victoria: Queen Victoria took lessons in drawing from Lear for several weeks in 1846 when the latter was only twenty-six years old.

Elizabeth Gissing: Realist novelist introduced to Lear by Stephen Lushington, political reformer and anti-slavery campaigner, at his Sussex home.

Dante Gabriel Rossetti: Renowned Pre-Raphaelite painter, he was an English poet, illustrator and translator. The painter of *Lady Lilith*, Rossetti also wrote limericks that were inspired by Edward Lear's nonsense.

Christina Rossetti: Poet who composed 'Goblin Market' and sister of painter-poet Dante Gabriel Rossetti.

Gussie: Augusta, Lord Westbury's daughter. Lear long considered proposing to her, despite their 26 year age gap.

Turner: English painter of landscapes.

Maharajah Duleep Singh: Nicknamed the 'Black Prince of Perthshire'. In 1849, the ten-year-old maharajah of Punjab was exiled to England after his title and power had been devolved by the British. Despite his exile and the removal of sovereignty, he became famous as a friend of Queen Victoria and for his extravagant lifestyle, enjoying the countryside and game-shooting in particular.

Stephen Lushington: A friend of Lear and Franklin Lushington's cousin, he was a British judge, an MP and an abolitionist.

Mrs Campbell of Mashoobra: A resident of Simla who later moved to Mashoobra.

Lockwood Kipling: Father of the author Rudyard Kipling, John Lockwood Kipling CIE was an English art teacher, illustrator and museum curator who spent most of his career in India, including Bombay, where he founded a school of art. Later, he became the curator of the Lahore Museum.

'But is not life more or less a series of leaps in the dark?'

IT IS JANUARY 1874.

A large man, asleep on a small four-poster bed, finds himself unable to breathe under the weight of three enormous woollen blankets. Two loud gongs ring out in the darkness as the chill of January runs like a bolt of electric current through his arms and legs.

'I am *in* Kurseong,' the six-foot-tall man murmurs, drawing up his legs that are sticking out from under the pile. A long-drawn sigh breaks the stillness of the room as a faint shimmer of shadows appears on its walls.

It had taken nearly four weeks, mostly by train, to travel from Bombay to Calcutta. Traversing the belly of India, diagonally, so to speak, and stopping in quaint towns before arriving in Banaras, where he swore he saw bloated corpses floating down the Ganges. In Calcutta, he had stepped out of the train onto a smoke-filled and noisy station to be ferried by liveried servants across the river to the Government House. It was the very epitome of opulence, in fact, the stolid nerve centre of the Empire, where perfectly manicured lawns competed with the sheen of tightly stretched silk sheets across the immense four-poster bed. '*Mal de barquement*', was the phrase Lord Northbrook, his host, had used to explain why – even after four weeks – Lear still felt that he had not left the boat. Surprisingly, however, that feeling dissipated almost as soon as the horse cart departed from the gate of the *dak bungalow* in the foothills of Pankhabari and made its way up a steep, curving road, depositing him, his eleven items of luggage and manservant eight hours later outside a dimly lit cottage in Kurseong.

The stiffness around his ankles and thighs reminds him of the seemingly unending ride up the hills the day before. Trundling all day long through narrow, winding roads lined with pine and bamboo, the pony cart had left him under the crumbling porch of a thatched stone house. This was the *dak bungalow* on Kurseong's Weathercock Point. After clambering up the steps in the dark to the front gallery, he was cheered by the sight of two oil lamps sitting on top of a broken mantelpiece. The air was icy cold. The spluttering fire in the fireplace, visible at the far end of the room, presented a scene that he had only encountered in books read long, long ago. *The Castle of Otranto* – yes, that was it. The shadows swaying almost imperceptibly behind the heavy curtains that reeked of damp and decay were straight out of the pages of a gothic masterpiece. The perfect abode of unquiet spirits, geckos and bats, not to speak of strange housekeepers with wizened, pale faces and dressed in dark, flowing gowns. As he passed through the narrow corridor beyond the gallery door, he noticed the passing draught lifting the covers on the mantelpiece. The doors trembled intermittently. Giorgi, his manservant, went about his business unperturbed, lifting the bags and carrying them to the room before vanishing into the darkness.

After lying still for a few minutes, Lear strains his eyes at the small window to catch any sign of light, but the darkness outside hangs like an impenetrable black curtain. No one had warned him that his destination in the Himalayas – the *dak bungalow* for which he had travelled thousands of miles, all the way from the port of Genoa through the heart of India – would be a forbidding three-room thatched cottage with plaster crumbling from large portions of the lime-washed walls. There was not a shred of viceregality visible anywhere! The three-day journey from Calcutta to Kurseong reminded him of the time when his little fingers felt a loosely coiled and knotted skein that he had once found in an old attic chest. The exhaustion of being on slow Indian trains, clanking along, and on even slower pony carts could only be matched by the many sensations that surged through his heavy eyes and ears. The unexpected transitions from suffocating heat to numbing cold; the gaggle of early-morning workers on the streets outside train stations girding themselves for work; the long-drawn half-understood conversations with colonial officials and interminable verbal exchanges with native Indians about directions or monetary payments; the pungent odours rising from broths served on frail pale blue china.

Were his travels worth the pain and tedium that he now feels throbbing in his bones? Would Kurseong offer a view of the mighty Kanchenjunga that he can capture on just an ordinary sheet of paper by merely using a graphite pencil bought from an old shop in Genoa? Had he perhaps been too ambitious in hoping to turn a simple pencil sketch into an oil painting that was worthy of being hung on the walls of viceregal rooms? Would the painting ever be able to match the splendour of floors covered with the most expensive *sumac* rugs. Had the handsome commission promised by the Viceroy of India been the lure that had brought him, in the midst of winter, to these remote mountains? He knew that the offer had come after years of quiet anticipation as he saw the years slipping by and arthritis beginning to trouble his knees. All along, he had known that his decision had been driven by an unnameable need to escape. But escape from what? From a world where the shadows of his own life lingered as ghosts dancing on the shores, where the haze after sundown cast long shadows on the sea, bringing in an unexpected tide, where the words of Sophocles echoed, 'Whose tale more sad than thine, whose lot more dire' – words uttered in a sonorous, clipped Greek?

Lying on the bed, he inhales deeply. The chilly mountain air rushes up his nostrils into his skull, filling every cavity. His first trip outside English shores – to Italy nearly forty years back – had been possible solely because of Lord Derby's impulsive generosity. It had come with no obligations. 'The Italian sun will fire up your paintbrush, Edward,' the good man had said as the two sat in Derby's Knowsley garden, watching a single thrush perched on the bare apple tree, huddling against the driving autumn wind. Up and back, he had walked, in his mind, the night in Calcutta a few weeks before he left for the mountains, picturing the 'Old Person of Burton' fumbling, bumping into the opulent furniture in the dark, murmuring, 'My answers are uncertain.' Two good years he had spent in quiet expectancy after the Viceroy had suggested it in a letter that arrived on an unusually warm spring day in 1872. His heart had leapt at the words scribbled in brown ink: *The India trip will be arranged.* Even on the day of his voyage, the prospect of stepping on the shores of India had seemed utterly unreal. He had twice pulled out the tickets from the deep pockets of his large overcoat before walking onto the ship. Even then, the letters printed in blue and black seemed to float in and out of his vision, very much like the ocean waves he saw lapping around the hull.

From the adjoining room, the gentle snores of Giorgi reach him like the rush of a distant train chugging away through fields of mustard. Hard as he may try to keep his eyes closed, his thoughts move like a cluster of shiny garden geckos he had seen scurrying around in the garden in Calcutta, one second in the sun and the next in some dark, deep crevice.

After a few minutes of lying straight, he raises himself. A gentle rumble in his belly reaches his ears. If there's one thing he cannot stand, it is trying to fall back to sleep on an empty stomach, the other being looking for an excuse for deferring a task undertaken voluntarily, without any coercion. More than being just a loyal friend and benefactor, the Viceroy had been an admirer of his landscapes ever since they had been introduced in Rome. The Viceroy had hinted that he wanted Lear to try his hand at doing something large, something more ambitious, like an oil painting that could be hung on the walls of his home in Stratton Park.

Wiggling out from under his blankets, he now thinks about the prospect of a hot breakfast. The thought of eggs placed next to a pile of crispy toasted bread is enough to try on the pair of warm socks he had procured in Genoa and leave his warm bed. 'One *must* stop thinking about the *task* at hand,' he mutters to himself. After a few minutes, the warmth returns fitfully to his toes. Mornings had been generally much kinder to him than he feels right now, but he resolves to start the day without asking more questions. After fluffing up the pillow, he lowers himself from the edge of the bed. As he hobbles towards the door, he notices the pale and timid light of dawn beginning to steal in noiselessly from between the louvred window at the far end of the room.

In less than an hour, Edward Lear finds himself sitting in a room filled with the smell of burning pine needles. He tries to shake off the lingering sleepiness by drinking his third cup of tea. It is breakfast time at Weathercock Point's *dak bungalow*.

'*Jibro*! Tongue for you, sir!' the cook utters under his breath, placing the plate of boiled tongue and broccoli on the table. The *sahib*s will eat anything, the cook thinks, seeing Lear's look of delight at the piece of shrivelled, dark meat lying on the plate. 'I am beginning to get weary of curries,' he had told Giorgi the day they took their leave of the caretaker at Pankhabari *dak bungalow*, who had, very proudly, served up his spicy curries swirling in oily fried onions and cumin. The recurring indigestion that he had had to deal with, in the nearly five weeks of travel through India, made him think of returning to his old favourites, and so, that morning, as he took his seat at the table, he was delighted to see the word 'Tongue' scribbled in bold on the handwritten menu.

The overcooked broccoli, served next to the tongue, does not look too appetizing, but Lear is glad that a large bottle of sherry and a smaller bottle of what the manager calls 'local wine' stands next to the plate. Skins hang from the walls, and so do pelts of what appear suspiciously to be unknown hairy rodents.

'My back is much better this morning,' he tells Giorgi, who is sitting across from him, idly stirring his tea.

'I'm glad.'

Giorgi peers at an old newspaper, and as soon as the cook leaves a plate of baked beans and eggs, Lear straightens his cuffs and picks up the fork to scoop up a dollop of the runny mixture.

Breakfast over, Mr Fraser, the Eurasian manager of the *dak bungalow*, joins them in the long gallery. 'I hope the tongue was made to your satisfaction, Mr Lear. The cook is a new chap, a high-caste Nepali. Hard to train locals to serve pure English food. Almost like ordering the local tailor who you see working on a battered sewing machine to stitch an English coat!'

He laughs at his own sharp wit and continues. 'This chap came in a week ago after the old cook who had served for the past twelve years was found senseless and bleeding by the road. Totally unreliable, these Bhutiyas. Mountain people, you see. Habitual dipsos!'

Mr Fraser is in a mood to chatter. Lear is told that the 'mountain' people loved their brews prepared from maize and millet. 'Unlike these Bhutiyas, caste Nepalis do not eat anything that is even remotely related to the cow family. The mountain tribes will eat anything – beetles, crickets and every crawling creature you find on this blessed earth. Even that.' He points to a large green cricket sitting on a bush outside the open window.

Lear sips his tea noisily. Giorgi excuses himself and leaves the table. It is almost nine, an hour to go before they leave for the spot selected by Mr Fraser for Lear to begin his drawing. Stepping into the garden, Fraser points his long, narrow finger to a large plot of land lying between the hydrangea bushes, where rows of celery, rosemary, thyme, and what looks like English rhubarb, flourish in the reddish-brown soil.

'Our very own kitchen garden, one of its kind in all of Kurseong. First planted, I believe, by Mr Tyler, a friend of Sir Eden, who now plans to build a school for the English in these parts.' Plucking a sprig of rosemary, he offers a few crushed leaves to Lear, who sniffs it and murmurs, 'Does not have the same sweetness as the rosemary of Corfu!'

'Kurseong's English weather is *ideal* for growing everything that English people fancy.'

An uncommonly thin man with a receding hairline, Mr Fraser is very curious about Giorgi.

'Is he your manservant from England? Is he English? Does he serve as your footman? What cut of beef does he prefer?'

He pulls up the frayed cuffs of his pale blue shirt.

'I must tell you that the new cook only allowed the tongue to be brought into the kitchen after he was assured by me that it was not from a cow but an ox.'

Mr Fraser waits for the tall and large Englishman to say something, but the figure does not respond. All he does is stare at a bush, his large nose picking up the scent of an unknown flower.

Giorgi stands close to his master while he bends down slowly to straighten the bottom of his trousers. They are both ready to venture out to the spot on the ridge that the manager claimed offered the most *delicious* view of the Kanchenjunga range. 'Almost impossible to avoid the mists and clouds at this time of the year but well worth a try,' the manager says in hushed tones. 'You must be very patient. The locals believe that the Kanchenjunga only offers a glimpse of its divine body when its devotees sit in silent meditation.'

'Divine or not, all I want today is to get a view clear enough to begin my drawing.'

Giorgi hands Lear his large scarf and hat before picking up the three-legged sketching stool.

The uphill walk from the gate of the *bungalow* takes them northwards – away from Weathercock Point and towards the high ridge. 'We have to get used to our new upslant life here, Giorgi,' Lear remarks, 'tilting forward to move up, bracing backwards on our heels to slow down an unexpectedly swift descent.' Seeing his master pause, Giorgi stops and waits by the side of the path, under an old oak. A loud sneeze from him takes Giorgi by surprise. He offers his handkerchief, and to his great astonishment, the man simply snatches it from his hand and blows his nose noisily into it. He's never seen his master be so indelicate before! But they are in India, after all, far, far away from the world of drawing-room niceties.

'Must procure an air cushion,' Lear reminds Giorgi as they pass two heavily gowned ladies propped up in two straight-backed wooden chairs carried by four men. They are followed by a young, bearded Englishman sitting on horseback. What an unearthly sight. Lear thinks of the large cargo he had seen being brought ashore by half-naked men at the Bombay Harbour, all tied up, ready to be deposited next to large wooden crates marked STANLEY.

As the horse and chairs disappear behind the mist creeping up the path, Giorgi, in his characteristically bemused manner, says under his breath, 'Pale English ladies, they surely are. Sadly, *wrong* shoes for these mountains.'

Lear grins from ear to ear, noticing the four gaunt, pale-faced men straining under the weight of the large, gowned figures, who sit very still with pursed lips, their blank faces held up against the mist.

'I would fancy a ride on a chair like that, especially if four *sturdy* men – the kind you see sitting by the wayside near the cantonment – can be found to carry me.'

When Giorgi reminds Lear that the last time he had weighed himself he was close to fourteen stone, Lear responds with a smile, 'Not sure how accurate the scales were in Genoa. The springs were all rusty. I am surprised that you had not noticed.'

An expanse of empty blankness stretches beyond the edge of the ridge where Giorgi places the sketching stool. Under the raised patch of ground ferns and grass, Lear can feel the unevenness of the ground. The skies are beginning to clear, but very gradually. Sitting on the stool, Giorgi moves his body in several different directions.

'I think this will suit you quite well. No rabbit holes here.'

Lear places himself very gently on the three-legged stool. His eyes dart around and rest on the spotted, wrinkled skin over his left wrist. He is nearly sixty-two years of age. Old, quite old. Giorgi is fifty-seven – not young, but five years can make a difference, especially in the mountains, where one cannot walk more than fifteen feet before facing yet another climb uphill, not to speak of the number of times one has to rest and gasp for breath. But he has complete confidence in the abilities of his manservant. Is he not Giorgi Kokalis, the tall Suliot who calls Corfu his home, a reliable travel companion, a man who speaks four languages and shares his master's never-waning *wanderlust*, having accompanied him through the vast length of the Italian peninsula, to Corsica, Crete, Greece, Corfu, Malta, Egypt, Petra, Jerusalem, and also traversed the rough wilderness of Albania? Had he not, one autumn morning in Genoa, about six weeks back, joined him on a crowded ship that sailed to the shores of distant Bombay? And that was the *second* attempt! Just last year, at the end of October, they had set out on the same journey but got only as far as the Suez. To repeat the same feat with total equanimity was something he marvelled about Giorgi.

Lear smiles, remembering the letter he wrote to his dear friend in England, Chichester Fortescu, after that failed first attempt to reach India. '*Neither you nor Lady Waldergrave will have any Indy-ink or Indy-rubber brought by me from Indy as I promised, and a fit of*

Indy-gestion is all that remains to me of that Oriental bubble.' Frances Waldergrave's beautiful chin, the radiant, dark eyes, the flowery headdress she wore the last time they met, and Chichester's resolute nose, his thinning hair pressed down on his wide forehead, and his perfectly shaped teeth that were visible when he smiled, flash before his eyes. Through this long sojourn – from Bombay all the way up to the foothills of the Himalayas via Jubbulpore, Cawnpore, Lucknow, Allahabad and Calcutta – Giorgi had served as his sentinel, carefully examining every dish that was placed on his table and scrutinizing the label of each bottle of medicine that he offered to his master from the small brown leather bag. Had he also not procured – from the dark recesses of innumerable *dak bungalows* they stopped at – the beers and sherries that he had craved for quietening his nerves after a long ride on a creaky pony cart? Did he not step unfailingly into the room at night to adjust the lamp as he sat sketching, only to return ever-so-noiselessly to his own bed in the adjoining room? Through foot injuries and fatigue, colds and calluses, the Albanian soldiered on without complaining. Such steadfastness, such dedication and fortitude, he must surely be part of a vanishing species of trustworthy servants.

The mist lingers as the two wait. Giorgi stands erect at a distance, behind Lear. As soon as the first light touches the very tops of the pines, two peaks reveal themselves in the distance. The diffused light cast by the barely visible sun makes them look almost spectral. Sitting very still on his sketching stool – his second since he arrived in India – the portly Lear picks up a pencil and strains his body forward to get a better view. All he sees in front is an abyss, a boundless, floating world filled with unknown eddies. His fingers are ready to trace the first line on the sheet of paper placed on the wooden stand easel in front. It is a decisive moment:

as the shimmering slopes, the multiple points and precipices of the mighty Kanchenjunga take shape before his eyes, the tip of his pencil begins to move, and very soon, the lines begin to branch out steadily across the page.

As his finger moves, images of a crumbling house, blind alleys and crooked streets begin to crowd his mind quite unexpectedly. But almost instantly, they give way to something that makes him hold back. Out of the mists that sweep down from above, he sees the long, graceful form of Etna set against a few masses of rock and rough swirls of a river, the brown ink awash in the midst of clearly drawn strokes of pencil. Then the vision dissolves almost instantly, and in its place, Mount Athos appears, standing like a vigilant sentry, guarding the remote distances of Elerigova. Standing against a pale pink and blue sky, the snowy peak of Athos looms above the surrounding hills of blue, amber and brown. That was in 1856, nearly two decades ago. A *pile of awful form* is how he remembers the white monastery that stood in the middle.

A djinn's carpet has carried him over distant landscapes, and as if by magic, he has stepped through a little, invisible door into the distant past!

Feeling the tip of the pencil with his forefinger, Lear casts a quick glance at the paper. The broken-up lines in front are slowly changing as the mountain range transforms into a ribbon of crumpled satin. Lear steadies himself and adjusts the horn-steel-rimmed eyeglasses that sit awkwardly on his bulbous nose. All around, the stillness is almost palpable, and even the sound of cowbells that reach him from the forests below is quickly carried away by the cold gust of wind.

An air of the unforeseen sweeps through the surrounding pine forests. He senses a slight tremor in his fingers. Oh to be released from time and memory and not be burdened with the question of angles, shadows and depths! To free the ears of the fearful tremors of approaching footsteps and replace them with those heard softly on the sand amidst the crashing of waves. Franklin Lushington, a man of law, strides ahead confidently. His beautifully curved mouth spouted words from ancient Greek that seemed to curl around the room in Corfu. It all began with walks. Years before, they had walked together around the ruins of Malta. When they met again in Corfu, the first thing they did was explore the coast, stepping over rocks, flotsam and broken glass. After their excursions, Lushington would sit very still on a large armchair, expecting his glass of sherry. Every so often he would bring up the subject of the history of ancient Greeks, the philosophy of Gorgias, and the conjugation of Greek verbs. Frank Lushington, the descendant of the eminent Sir Stephen Lushington of India, who had held several high and confidential situations in the Company's service, was more than a judge at the Supreme Court of Justice in the Ionian Islands; his fervour for ancient Greek was only exceeded by a deep passion for hunting. The whiskered face of Franklin Lushington continued to hover in Lear's mind, but over time, it had taken the form of a quivering, contorted shadow that would flap noiselessly before slipping away into the gathering darkness.

Unseen cowbells tinkle somewhere under the trees.

Screwing up his eyes, Lear makes a conscious effort to clear his mind. Absent-mindedly, he goes through his pockets, looking for the flask of brandy, but all he can find is a crumpled handkerchief.

It is nearly midday, with less than two hours remaining before the dull winter light begins to fade, and the cold, heavy air settles on the ground. He can almost hear the metallic crunch under his heels as the early frost begins to settle on the ground and coat the grass with a thin, almost invisible, layer of ice. He can feel every little bump of the pony cart he rode in, on the unpaved road from Kurseong to Pankhabari.

That morning, however, before he had helped himself to his second cup of tea, he had been cheered by the sight of a bottle of claret he spied lying on top of the mantelpiece in the breakfast gallery. And next to it lay a book with yellowing pages, which he soon discovered was the *dak bungalow*'s 'guest book'. Leafing through its pages, he had read: *'One mile up the road take a sharp left. A most excellent, dream-like view of K – our first – and undoubtedly the best.'*

But there were more words scribbled on the next page, in faint blue ink, signed by one Miss Julia Davenport (York).

'Ghosts Everywhere. Spectropia! Saw the world turn into wisps of nothingness.'

Ghosts everywhere? Had Miss Davenport encountered ghostly presences? Had she witnessed shadows trailing on the lawns outside her window? Or, were they simply the words of a young woman with an overactive imagination, someone just bewildered and confused after a sip or two of the local wine? Julia Davenport's eyes must certainly have witnessed the same waves of green and grey receding into the distant horizon, the same shadows stretched across the darkening sky, creeping towards her, then dissipating like apparitions, and then moving noiselessly under the bed before entering her head like the mists seen curling through the pines.

Must shake off this strange reverie. Lear looks for another pencil.

The skies are now returning to a perfect blue, and under the command of his eye and mind, Lear can feel the pencil tip as it moves noiselessly across the blank sheet in front. Casting a sideward glance, he sees the gigantic ferns cascading down the hillside like green torrents whose delicate, deep green leaves begin to finger out and fly through the emptiness in front. He moves his body abruptly to the right. The sketching stool creaks.

'I am not like a runner bean that can run only when tied to a stick,' he remembers telling Giorgi once after the latter had told him that, perhaps, he should think about curbing his restless urge to keep moving and instead settle down in one place and let his imagination do all of the travelling.

'You do not live in a shoebox where you have to put up with having to turn a corner every minute of your waking hour. Your Italian home offers the most splendid and clear views.' Behind this exchange of witticism between master and servant lay a deeper question that Lear had fretted over for years without resolving anything: What was, in reality, *his* home? For someone who had, as an adult, moved like a restless spirit between the warm sun of the Mediterranean and the smog of London, and much earlier, as a child, between the confusion of different draughty attics and shelters, the word *home* was little more than four letters of the English alphabet strung together somewhat arbitrarily. No one waited at the table, there were no familiar smells – of soapsuds in the bath or of stews brewing in a pot on the stove, not even of an arthritic cat sitting on the edge of the windowsill. Only sheets of unfinished sketches and gouaches, all piled under a table, ready to be packed into a creaky wooden box.

As the cold wind sweeps down from above, Lear pulls down his frayed bowler hat, buttons up his oversized overcoat and wipes his nose. His mind returns to another question – one that has been nagging him ever since he first saw the Himalayan range appear through the thick bamboo forests as they approached Kurseong:

How does any artist get the middle ground on paper through all the blurriness? The middle ground – such a key concept for understanding perspective – does it even exist here, among the blank distances and indefinable depths? All he can sense now is the insistent pawing of an unknown creature grazing against his half-frozen legs. In a low whisper, he asks himself: Is it possible to leave a faint trace of a line on paper where the middle ground should be? Or, perhaps, it can be simply left blank, empty? After all, the background – the panoramic snowy range gradually emerging in the sunlight – can be readily captured on paper. In fact, the Kanchenjunga's fierce outline that one also saw in photographs was *very* drawable. He can also glimpse the foreground, quickly running his eyes over the maze of intertwined shapes of ferns that lie close to his feet. The intricacy of hoops and loops and indeterminable depths of light and dark will be a challenge to pencil, no doubt, but not impossible. But the *middle* ground? What *does* one do with so much emptiness right in the middle of a scene?

A steady chirping of crickets breaks the stillness, which calms him down momentarily. Lear allows his fingers to continue working the tip of the pencil, using as little pressure as possible. But the dark tip leaves a barely visible mark across the middle. And as he does, almost immediately, his ears catch an odd, scurrying sound, as if an unseen stream was running through a craggy ravine below. *With such a pencil, such a pen, You shadow forth to distant men, I read and felt that I was there.* His dear friend Tennyson's words, composed for him nearly two decades ago, echo from the mountains.

'*To distant men?*' He had been amused by Tennyson's strange phrasing. He always prided himself on the fact that the *most* eminent poet of the present age was an ardent admirer of his playful verses, especially for the way, as Tennyson once said, he 'matched the language of nonsense with the sweeping vistas of foreign landscapes painted in washes of brown, green, blue'. A topographical artist *par excellence*, the poet had called him, in the presence of the esteemed painter Holman Hunt while they sat in the latter's house in London.

To be able to capture the imagination of a man of Tennyson's reputation was a matter of great pride, no doubt, but Lear was never quite sure if he just amused his friend with his personal absurdities or if he truly comprehended what he wrote. But how does one *comprehend* nonsense, he asks himself, holding the pencil still. Smiling, he looks intently at the peaks in front. They seem to be moving, almost imperceptibly.

Aha, a shape-shifting mountain! A mountain that eludes the will of the pencil tip! A mountain that, at one instant, looks like a shard of broken glass sticking out of a snowy ground, and at another, the top of a feather stuck in a haystack.

In that strange stillness, his ears catch the same scurrying sound he had heard moments ago. Symmetries of sound and shadows – and the unknown life that is coiled inside them! He clears his throat and shifts his weight to his left. The sketching stool creaks again.

Shadow and Light on a see-saw, Flinging their hands high up in the air. When not doing their classroom sums, they roamed the forests, soundlessly and without a care.

The easy elegance of these lines that come to him that instant appears to imitate the rhythm of the young mummer's song he had once heard in the park near Highgate as a young boy holding his sister Ann's hands.

Dressed in scraps of brightly coloured fabric, the mummers fling themselves up in the air, their rhymes ringing out like church bells on a Sunday morning in June. Children with bright faces recite lines from poems in the tiny room in Tavistock Square. They have just learnt to draw simple figures of owls and pelicans. Turner hums a song in Hullmandel's lithograph workshop.

'Sun and shadow, sun and shadow,' he repeats as he chuckles under his breath.

Eleanor and a dark-haired boy sit on the old see-saw. Sitting on the plank that moves up and down, little Eleanor is screaming with excitement. Blackbirds, taken aback by her shouts, flutter noisily out of the blackberry bushes nearby and fly away. Mother sits by the window, looking out at the nervous squirrels, with their furry, twitching tails. Her face is marked by great perturbation. And sister Harriet – as always – frowns and looks at him suspiciously.

Father has gone. No one knows when he will return.

But before he can get his mind back to the drawing, a strange, other-worldly ringing descending from the dark canopy of trees reaches his ears. Without warning, the sound begins to move with the gentle rhythm of the thin, liquid gold light that he saw moments ago pouring down silently through the gaps in the foliage.

At that very moment, his ears catch the call of a bird from above. A whistling thrush? A wren-warbler? Or, perhaps, a laughing thrush or even a mountain starling? He isn't sure. Straining his left ear to catch the notes once again, he turns sharply on his stool.

A drawn-out ringing that fills his ears is followed by a lull.

The stool creaks. Eyes throb. His body sways.

In what seems like more than a lifetime, Lear opens his eyes, feeling a tingling sensation on his left cheek. He moves his right finger over it and realizes that it is bruised and a bit raw and also that he is lying flat on the damp ground. His head is resting on

Giorgi's left arm, and his upper body is propped up against Giorgi's bent knees. 'Mister Lear, Mister Lear. You fell.'

'Let me lie on the ground, Giorgi. Do not raise me up.' Lear's words are scarcely audible, even to himself. Lying on the ground on his back, he gazes at a hawk hovering above. An impenetrable, towering depth swirls on the tops of trees, descending gradually to his naked, hatless head. No *middle* ground, just the blankness of infinite space. The irregular beating of his heart is followed by a lull – a calm, descending on his entire body, right down to his toes.

2

'MR MULLER IS VERY ILL and will no longer receive guests.'

The postmaster's words take Lear by surprise. Five minutes ago, as he had stepped into the large, cramped post office in Darjeeling, Lear noticed that the badly lit room where the postmaster sat was full of men going about their business, some handling the mail, others selling stamps at the counter. The important-looking officials with stern faces were ordering the workmen around, cursing the *coolies* who were bringing in the large boxes through the side door.

In the midst of all the bustle, a long row of broken chairs stacked up against the walls is visible. Parts of the ceiling have crumbled. The large windows facing the street offer a clear view of the grey stone building outside. 'The town hall,' he was told by a tall Catholic priest walking into the post office, a burly, red-faced Irishman carrying a bag full of letters to post.

Lear soon discovers that the four inhabitants of Darjeeling for whom he was carrying letters from his friend in England, Joseph Hooker, were either dead, untraceable or had left the town years ago. The postmaster – a nervous-looking man with a slight limp – also tells Lear that Mr Muller's illness had been quite sudden. 'Mrs Skinner, his housekeeper, is too gouty to take care of old Muller, and he has no living relations left.'

Leaving the post office, Lear takes slow, deliberate steps, reaching the flat ground on top of the hill from where the Kanchenjunga shines like an ethereal, towering deity, hovering over the roofs of the houses below and over the vast expanse of tea gardens dotting the slopes towards the east. Visible beyond and towards the north is just a blur of blue and green. Taking off his hat, he sits on a wooden bench next to an old, shaggy dog curled up on a tattered gunnysack. A flock of pigeons suddenly alight on the ground and begin feeding on the grains thrown by a passer-by.

'Perhaps I can do another sketch,' he mutters to himself, pulling out a sheet of paper from his bag, but he hesitates and decides to put it away. An hour to go before he meets Giorgi on the road outside the church.

Three days back, he had lain on his bed, thinking. Was it the sound of the invisible bird that made him startle so, or was it one of his *morbids*?

He runs his finger over the bruise, now healing, but he can still feel the dry, cracked skin.

Morbids. An odd grittiness to the sound.

Lushington, Fortescu, and even Emily Tennyson had laughed at the strange word he had coined to describe his 'falling malady'. He told them that as a child, his family thought he suffered from poor nerves, a belief affirmed by his awkwardness and tendency to drop books, pencil cases and school bags while leaving the house. And when it struck, Mother would look helplessly at his face as he lay on the ground and wonder if the child had to be taken to the doctor down the street or just be left on the bed until he fell asleep. Most often, she would tuck him into his bed, draw the curtain and leave. Later, she would hand him a bitter brew and say, 'Drink it up.' When he recovered, Ann would put his shoes on his small feet and take him to the park.

'It's all because of your wicked body.' Harriet has a squeaky voice. They are sitting in the dimly lit room for supper. She leaves the room abruptly as soon as Ann enters. What's so wicked about falling down?

The sheer weight of falling bodies … how helpless you feel when you open your eyes and find no one around, the rattling, drilling sound gone from the ears! *Why* had it happened at the moment he sat down, pencil in hand, ready to draw? Was the rickety stool not firm enough to bear his weight? Was it the dreadful cold air that froze his ears? Or did he find himself being sucked into another dark, windy vortex?

The thought that his *morbids* has pursued him on his travels fills him with dread.

As he sits still on that cold bench in Darjeeling, it appears to him that the very thing against which he had struggled all his life in order to be able to draw, write, colour, paint, entertain children – and also to traverse the vast globe through the uprisings in Italy and turmoil in Greece and through the lands where dervishes whirled – was beginning to get the better of him. He feels quite helpless thinking about his future plans of travelling through the vast continent, uncertain whether Giorgi will be able to bear the burden.

He smiles, thinking about the sound of the word that he had coined so cleverly. 'MORBIDS, *MORBIDS*. MORE-*BIDS*,' he repeats to himself. 'Linguistic perversity,' Fortescu had told him once. An uncontrollable force emanating from a dark, wild world that had inspired him to draw pictures of a large grasshopper sitting on the neck of a man, or that of the 'Old Man of the West', who was set up to spin on his nose and his chin!

There's Harriet and Mother and Ann slicing bread. Father is still away. Dinner over, he climbs the stairs to his dark attic room. A figure shows up among the flickering shadows on the wall. A sweeping red tide, visible in the swell of the ocean, leaves the shores bloody red. Breaking into a thousand sparkling pieces, the tide leaves tiny fragments gleaming on the wet sand. A darkness descends, sucking the light out of these gleaming things. He is with Ann on the shores of Margate, in the house that stinks of rotting seaweed.

Over the years, he had learned to accept the familiar world filled with shadowy faces, the sound of the chatter of siblings and the strange crashing and splintering of things all around. He was as reconciled to this world as he was to his own inability to keep the eyeglasses on his nose while putting on his overcoat! But the *morbids*, the slow torque in his guts that reached up to the tongue and slithered down to the toes like a serpent uncoiling, left him teetering, unable to hold himself up even when holding on to the edge of the table!

The clock strikes ten. He walks up the steep hill. Standing under the spire of St. Andrew's Church is the lone figure of Giorgi, his gaunt face half concealed by the shadow of a large tree, waiting for his master to join him. It was on Giorgi's urging that very morning that Lear had agreed to go looking for the famous Darjeeling sanatorium. 'A historical institution built by none other than the legendary Dr Archibald Campbell, a friend of your botanizing friend, Joseph Hooker,' Giorgi had told him the evening before at supper.

But just before he saw Giorgi waiting under the tree, Lear

ran into a young English surgeon, the tall, blond, middle-aged
Dr Nelson, who told him that Archibald Campbell had recently
died at his English home in Slough. At first surprised that the
postmaster had not communicated this bit of news, he then
realized that he had not actually shown the postmaster the letter
intended for Campbell. It had remained in the wooden box where
he kept his journals.

Giorgi is unflustered by the news of the doctor's death in
Slough. 'The doctor must have been quite old when he passed. It
appears that your friend, Joseph Hooker, is the only living person
you know who lived in Darjeeling when the doctor set up his
sanatorium! Hard to believe that he returned to England to die
in Slough!'

Lear nods. There was no doubt that along with Dr Campbell,
Joseph Hooker was a living legend of old Darjeeling, the botanist
known for wandering through forests for days in search of rare
orchids. Even the young owner of the hotel in Darjeeling claimed
that his father would often have the charming botanist as his
dinner guest to discuss why some Himalayan ferns preferred the
sun while others thrived in the shade.

Although Giorgi was not present when Lear visited the
botanist during his last visit to England, all he heard from him after
they reached Kurseong was about the 'famous' Joseph Hooker of
Darjeeling, presently the director of the Royal Botanic Gardens. A
rare distinction, no doubt.

During his first and only meeting with Hooker in London,
Lear had been struck by the botanist's unfathomable *gravitas*. The
venerable promoter of science and a close friend of Darwin had
returned from India more than two decades before with over forty
kinds of exotic plants, some of which still survived at the Kew. Five

years his junior, the bushy-eyebrowed Hooker's long, frizzy beard seemed to grow not out of his prominent chin – as one would expect – but oddly, from his throat and neck, which made him look older.

But during that meeting, Lear was unaware of the story that made him famous until Evelyn Baring, at breakfast in Calcutta, related what had happened to the eminent botanist during his Darjeeling sojourns. Slicing a piece of pineapple, Evelyn said, in his inimitable style, 'Darjeeling is spectacular, but dear Lear, do forebear the thought of wandering *off* like Hooker did.' The sensational 'Hooker' story – about the daredevil botanist stealing away to Sikkim from Darjeeling in search of a rare orchid – had, in fact, been featured in an essay in *Himalayan Journal* that Evelyn had gifted Lear. From it, Lear learnt that Hooker had been captured and imprisoned by the Royal Sikkim Police after he was found wandering around the kingdom without an official permit. The incident also precipitated a military crisis, and it was only through the Governor General's timely intervention that a conflict was averted, and Hooker's release secured.

It was Tennyson who had first arranged for him to visit the intrepid Hooker. That October afternoon, after he had spent the day with him in his large stone house, the three – he, Hooker and his quiet wife, Frances – walked out into the garden when the botanist pointed to a rhododendron bush growing beside an ash tree. 'The seeds were procured from Darjeeling,' he said as Frances bent down to pick up a stray pebble from the ground. Lear wondered how the eminent botanist, whose face reminded him more of a contemplative and high-minded theologian rather than of a botanist-adventurer, had borne the rough travel on ponyback up the foothills of the Himalayas in 1848. The roads must have been little more than mountain-gravel paths, if they existed at all. But Hooker had been young then, brimming with strength, energy and the spirit to explore the unknown, including rare varieties of rhododendron and orchid. Not an individual like him who, though he appreciated nature and was willing to travel, could scarcely balance himself while sitting on a stool!

Over lunch, when Lear announced to Hooker that he would not only visit Bombay and Calcutta but also travel up to sketch the Kanchenjunga, the man's face lit up. The oil painting of the Kanchenjunga commissioned by the Viceroy would take him to Darjeeling from Calcutta. 'Of course, you would have to make many sketches of the scenery for Northbrook's large picture. And there is so much to see in that part of the world besides the Kanchenjunga!' Hooker's voice was suffused with the excitement of an explorer getting ready for the first time to set sail for foreign shores. Bringing out a scroll from a tattered silk bag, Hooker laid it out on a large table. With the rays of the autumn sun streaming in through the open window, Hooker opened the scroll very slowly, patting it gently with the tips of his fingers as if it were a sleeping child. It was an old atlas of the Himalayas over which Hooker's long and delicate index finger moved, slowly outlining the eastern boundaries of India and Tibet, tracing the long, sinewy white line all the way up to Bhutan. His low voice could be heard uttering the strange, foreign names of the five peaks of the mighty Kanchenjunga range. 'Kabru, Rathong, Kokhtang...' The words sounded like an incantation.

Lear's thoughts about Hooker and his fascination for the Himalayas take him back again to the conversations he had in Calcutta with Evelyn about Darjeeling. In Northbrook's absence that day, Evelyn had taken it upon himself to brief Lear. Darjeeling was a new town when Hooker had visited and met the eminent doctor. The sanatorium had been the army's first great initiative, and Dr Campbell had been its first superintendent. Soon after the region had been ceded to Britain through a deed of grant, it had prospered, turning into a popular summer resort for the English residents of Calcutta, and in less than a decade, became a prized centre for producing tea.

'The empire and tea.' Evelyn's voice was charged with the same passion that Lear had sensed when the former talked about the glories of England's great mission in India.

But there had been changes that were palpable in the very air of Darjeeling. Even the shop, Doyle's, where he had picked up the Bourne and Shepherd photos of old Darjeeling, had brand new plate-glass windows that gleamed in the fleeting sun. The old photos he had purchased, however, showed a different picture – of grey wooden storefronts with broken metal gutters and stores around the Mall fitted with old wooden doors and windows, with hardly any human beings around, except for a stray Himalayan terrier or a lone Tibetan man leading his donkey.

'The old times are long gone.' When Lear heard the words of the hotel doorman the evening before, he realized that Evelyn Baring's story about this glittering new town nestled in the Himalayan foothills grazed against what he discerned all around him. The doorman was eager to share the story of the hill town – that in less than a decade, a tiny Lepcha village was transformed into a bustling European town, complete with spires and stone houses with steeply pitched roofs. Hansom carriages carried pink-cheeked ladies in their fine hats. Men in top hats thronged the hotel rooms. But in less than three decades, that sheen began to wear off. Silvern Cottage had been pulled down. Miss Daisy Ostrove had sailed back to England, or was it South Africa? The magnificent oaks were being cut down to make way for new roads, new markets. There were new people everywhere. And there was talk about the new train that would make its way up the steep mountain ridges from the plains below.

Giorgi taps Lear gently on the shoulder. 'Are you ready for the long walk? The road is quite steep.' Lear is startled by the sound of *long*. 'How *long*?' he asks Giorgi, but all he hears back is, 'Master, look, a giant fern. As tall as a palm tree!' Giorgi is pointing to a giant *Cyathea brunoniana* standing right in front of the gate. The Latin name rings in his mind with the sharpness of a metal spoon striking the rim of a china cup. He was so impressed the first time he had laid eyes on the delicate and intricate illustrations of a tree fern in William Francis's *British Ferns* that he had quietly noted down its botanical name in his notebook. It happened on one of those early summer afternoons in 1846.

The Queen has retired to her chambers for her afternoon slumber. It is the second week of teaching Her Majesty the rudiments of pencil drawing. She began by drawing an oak tree, getting only as far as the trunk. The crickets are singing outside, and the water in the large fountain gurgles like a happy infant.

It had taken him a few days to convince the Queen that not everything in a scene *could* or *should* be represented, a matter that she confessed she could not quite comprehend.

'What is a picture for if it failed to provide a mirror to nature?'

But she was often quite exhausted by the sheer energy it took to make up her mind about the exact proportions of an oak tree standing tall in the garden outside.

It is suddenly very still. The gurgling has stopped. Sitting alone in the large chair, looking at her half-finished sketch. He picks up British

Ferns from the table. He has been staring all day at the intricate designs on the oriental carpets that are spread out on the floor as the Queen struggles with her drawing. Outside, the owl leaves its perch. She is not likely to reappear, and it is beginning to get dark.

Until that day, he had not known that ferns could come in so many shapes and sizes! Next to the copiously illustrated book was his very own *Illustrated Excursion in Italy*, whose dramatic treatments of 'foreign subjects' had so delighted the Queen that she had bought some of the watercolours he had shown her. That was nearly thirty years ago! Three full decades since his eyes had first fallen on the illustration of the giant fern in a book. It was that very year that the Queen had become a mother for the third time, but her German blood allowed her to move around with the energy and verve of a sprightly twenty-year-old!

Her face reappears even now with the clarity of one of Winterhalter's portraits of the young Queen, leaning against a red cushion with her hair unravelled and falling over the left shoulder. Widowed for twelve years, she was *now* nearly fifty-four! The statue of the monarch, placed under a beautifully carved and stately marble canopy on a busy crossroad, had caught their attention as they drove past it on their second day in Bombay. What an amazing spectacle, he had thought, to see men pushing handcarts on a busy morning, stopping to gaze at their Queen's eternal youth that had been carved to perfection. No one would ever guess that the Queen was now a portly, maternal figure who always dressed in black and whose second chin was prominently visible in all her photographs.

Lear smiles, looking down at his own figure reflected momentarily in a long mirror being carried by two men.

Giorgi lights his tobacco, signalling that it will take a minute to finish smoking before making the ascent on the road to the sanatorium. Lear decides that he will return before leaving the town to do a quick sketch of the fern tree. 'Not sure if England has any giant fern trees left any more, Giorgi.'

Although it is the height of winter in the Himalayas, Lear has not been let down. Granted he has not seen *all* of the fabled Himalayan flora, but the perplexing verdure all around has captivated him no end. When he sat down to write one evening in his small room in Kurseong, he noticed how his words began to come out on the page of his notebook: *The inconceivable expanses of woody distance and the fern-like creepers all over the tree trunks, with their deeply polished green colour.* To 'go botanizing' – for that is what he called the activities of simple folk in England who went moss hunting in the countryside – seemed so tame compared to what his eyes have caught all around – the vast drapery of ferns of all hues and shapes and of startlingly green grottos that seemed to heave up into the sky.

'April is the best time to see the flowering of the tree orchids, Mr Lear,' Edgar Ware, the assistant commissioner in Kurseong, had told him while walking through the garden outside the *dak bungalow*. He had come to meet Lear the day before they left Kurseong.

'The word *Kur-seong* means the land of the white orchid. Just imagine thousands of species of flowering plants, nearly three hundred varieties of ferns, countless types of mosses, algae, fungi.' The commissioner's voice had trailed off as they walked down to inspect the garden below. Lear's ears only picked up bits of his companion's discourse, '…of course, in addition to the orchids… in the alpine zone, there are magnolias, *Bucklandias, Pyrus*, conifers, weeping *Tsuga brunoniana*, junipers, a dizzying variety of oak.' All he can recall now are Edgar's words flowing like a stream through the delicate veil of mist that once swept through the low shrubs and trees of London Zoo so many years ago. There, as a young man, he found himself drawn to the dark trunks of trees and to the bright flowers that grew in the deep shades all around, spending hours in the late afternoon filling his notebook with sketches of odd-looking pistils and curious calyxes.

'An artist of botanicals! What an admirable profession!' Aunt Lily is leafing through the drawings, her eyes lighting up. 'Admirable work, Edward,' she says, placing a cup of tea on the small wooden table by the window.

But as much as he found the Latin names of Himalayan flora coming from the mouth of Edgar curiously fascinating – chiefly because of the manner in which Edgar's lips moved – he wished he could be left alone to wander on his own. All he wanted to do that day was to take in as much of the scenes around, run his fingers over the petals of flowers, feel the shapes of leaves that came in so many sizes, colours and shapes. To go botanizing in the middle of winter – Edgar would most certainly have found such behaviour puzzling. But a few azaleas were still visible concealed under the leaves and so were the dried-up hydrangeas that encircled a bed of rose plants bearing a few striking pink and red blooms.

So, after Edgar had departed, Lear began walking through the mist that was beginning to sweep through the garden. Quite unexpectedly, out of the thick gusts of wispiness appeared the whiskered and the eye-browed *Rollulus*. The purplish guan crept behind while the *jungle-bukr* slid between the bodies of several *aequitoon* and *ging-e-jonga*. All of his favourite nonsense creatures had quietly stepped out of the pages into the Himalayan garden to feast noiselessly on the red berries in the bushes. And behind them, a happy-faced cockatoo peered out of the calyx of a *Cockatooca superba*; tiny little piglets attached to the long stalk of *Piggiawiggia pyramidalia* let out soft squeals; a row of narrow boots swung on the tall stalks of *Shoebootia utililis*. A host of odd botanicals reared their heads all around. *Minsysia deliciosa, Sophtsluggia glutinso, Stunnia dinnerbelia.* A fat bird that had his bearded face was flying up in the air, its beak holding a bunch of odd-looking grapes. Among them, his dear sister, Ann, stood among the flowers, dressed in a white frock, waving. The poor, miserable, unnamed wanderer appeared in the midst of all the verdure, lurking among the shadows while leaves trembled as that elusive figure disappeared into a clump of trees. That very instant, Edgar appeared and waved to him. In less than a minute, Lear found himself back in the gallery that was all ablaze, the fire crackling in the fireplace.

Lear hears Giorgi say something about losing the sun and not dallying any more. He is waiting at the curve of the road. No more tarrying. They begin walking together, but soon, Giorgi is ahead by more than twenty feet. Lear certainly has very little breath left! The road narrows into a dark, muddy lane, but in a few minutes, it curves sharply to the right and leads into an unevenly cobbled road. Magically illuminated by a sharp ray of sunlight streaming down from above, the road seems to have been paved in pure gold. They are both glad to leave this stretch of impenetrable, dark dampness behind them. The few rundown wooden houses give way to a stone wall that runs for half a mile along the left side of the shining road.

From behind the wooden gate in the wall, a tall Tibetan man appears quite suddenly. He is holding a prayer wheel – a cylindrical metal object with tiny seashells attached to the rim and mounted on a metal shaft. Lear chuckles at the man's brightly coloured boots that are stitched out of layers of bright silk, fur and hay. The gentle tinkling of the prayer wheel has echoes of another world.

The *Prince Phantasmion of Palmland*!

'Phantasmion dared tarry no longer; he used his wings vigorously... Potentilla, the fairy god of insects, is Phantasmion's protector... Ulander, Penselimar... Valhorga, Feyeldeen, Oloola...' Ann's voice fills the air as she reads slowly from Sara Coleridge's tale and then trails into a soft whisper.

Placing his prayer wheel on top of the wall, the man bends down to pat the head of a shaggy dog that lies curled beside the road. Standing on the other side, a little boy in a red and blue cap stares at Lear. On his arms hang strips of flowery fabric that he holds up as soon as he realizes that he has caught the corpulent man's attention. He is selling brightly coloured aprons with lace frills attached to the ends.

The fingers slowly press down the white and grey chalk. An autumn excursion to the Lake District – to Crummock, Buttermere and Loweswater. The fat woman in a frilled yellow and blue apron sits very still under the white light filtering through the trees, stippling the quiet surface of Crummock. Next to her is a brown terrier wearing a red and blue collar.

Despite being interrupted by these scenes from the past that descend on him quite unexpectedly, Lear pays two *annas* for an apron, places it in his satchel and continues his slow walk up the road, thinking about the many sunsets that he saw firing the silent sky in the Lake District.

Up that lonely road, they soon pass official-looking houses with gardens opening out to the south, with well-weathered rickety fences, and stone lodges with names like Periwinkle House and Carnation Corner. It is much nicer here – plenty of light and a line of men walking their pooches dressed in hats and mittens. A handful of young native men are hanging outside a modest stone building with the sign 'Gorkha Regiment' placed over the broken metal gate. A broken postbox is draped in vines of bright purple morning glory.

Seeing him staring at the sign, Giorgi intuitively grasps that his sixty-odd-year-old master is in quest of something deeper than the perfect view of the Kanchenjunga. But he cannot quite put his finger on it. His master excelled at what he did – sketch, paint and write the occasional funny verse about non-existent creatures with odd names – and was a person willing to endure the unfamiliar cuisine of the country's *dak bungalows* and travel for days on rickety trains and bone-rattling pony carts. But that quest for *something more* was a different story. Lodged deep within his strangely concentrated look lay a craving akin to what possessed the Hungarians he had heard about – wild men from Europe reported to be wandering around in the Himalayas. His master was, however, neither an audacious botanist nor a daredevil adventurer, and he never explained why he had agreed to make this arduous way up the Himalayas to sketch a mountain peak, a task he could have easily accomplished by copying from lithographs and photographs. One had to acknowledge that the commission from the Viceroy *did* come with a handsome monetary offer, a lure complemented by the promise of travelling through India!

Up beyond the sign, the road winds through a clump of pines. Lear thinks about doing a quick sketch of the sanatorium, if the light permitted, or perhaps even taking a quick stroll through its famous orchid garden. Would they run into a nurse by chance, someone who as a child had seen Campbell and Hooker strolling among the orchids? Or have a quick exchange with one of the present inmates recovering from consumption?

More than an hour passes, but they see no sign of the famed sanatorium. Just a few derelict houses with abandoned gardens and a stationary pony cart lying on the side of the road, with just one wheel. Giorgi stops to ask an old English lady dressed in a frayed pink frock sitting on a wicker chair in a garden filled with winter geraniums. 'Oh lord! The surgeon major's sanatorium! Is that what you are looking for? Well, if my memory serves me right, it was moved more than a decade back!' She sets down her knitting on her lap. 'The new one, I believe, is somewhere down below. Not sure if I know where.'

Giorgi is more dismayed than Lear. The lady tells them that not only had the famed doctor's sanatorium been pulled down, but also its stones, wood and iron had been carted away to build cottages for the new English planters.

'Them planters,' the old lady says contemptuously, picking up her knitting, 'are the evil kings of Darjeeling!'

Lear looks ahead at the steep incline of the road and suggests to Giorgi that there is not much point in continuing their walk.

'Nothing to see, not even an old crumbling wall.'

So, they slowly make their way down.

Two women wait near a shop, selling little cabbages. A curious-looking headdress sits on the tiny head of one woman with a diadem on top and a row of turquoise sewn all along the border. A long necklace with two intertwined serpents, in turquoise and red coral, gleams on the neck of the other woman. A basket full of red berries, and purple and yellow flowers lies near her feet.

Lear bends down to have a closer look at the flowers. Standing very close to the basket, he lifts a flower delicately and feels its papery weightlessness with his right forefinger. Lines on the pale yellow tinged with mauve run along the rim of the bright orange petals and dip down to disappear into an unknown centre. The shiny red berries, probably of an exotic variety, are plump with juice. 'They are almost like jewels.' He smiles as he holds up a bunch for Giorgi to see.

'They hardly look like fruits.' Giorgi places the bunch back in the basket.

'The fantastic fruits sold by the goblin merchants!' Lear exclaims under his breath, picking up the bunch again and running his fingers slowly over the taut skin. 'Goblin Market. That startlingly odd poem about the pretty sweet-toothed Laura who traded her golden curls for these ripe cherries.

'The goblins…the goblins… Come buy. Come buy. What did Miss Rossetti have in mind?' Lear continues to mutter under his breath while the woman with the diadem smiles at him.

'Fruit not for eating. Medicine. Poison.' The woman takes the bunch of berries from Lear's fingers and puts them away in another basket.

Lear is startled, and the silence swells between them. He senses her slow exhalation as the breeze lifts the ends of the shawl draped over her shoulder. An old man stoops down to pick a few of the remaining berries from the basket.

'A cat's face, a whisk'd a tail, One tramp'd at a rat's pace, One crawl'd like a snail.

There is no going back…once she gorges on them, she craves for more and eventually wastes away.'

Giorgi is not surprised by his master's mutterings, having caught him uttering, on more than one occasion, poetic lines interspersed with words drawn from some magic formula found in old scrolls.

As Lear continues to walk, his large shadow drifts, as if undulating on the surface of the rough, stony road. He has to slow down, he tells Giorgi, who is striding down the road quite rapidly. 'Medicine and poison, medicine and poison.' The trees appear to echo the woman's words like an incantation. Giorgi appears, waiting at the turn ahead, pointing to a narrow lane leading down to the main road. Visible between the gaps through the long, dark row of wooden houses are shops with slabs of meat hanging on metal hooks.

As soon as they enter the lane, Lear feels the wind pick up from the north. Bracing himself against the strong, chilly gusts, he looks up to find the sky darkening ominously, with patches of brightness appearing only to dissipate in an instant.

A noisy rattle suddenly invades Lear's ears, as if an invisible artillery is firing at him.

'Not snow, Master. It is hail!' Giorgio exclaims, picking up a hailstone and biting into it. Appalled at Giorgi's thoughtless action, Lear looks away and hastens towards an open veranda with a low, rusted tin roof. Giorgi follows, seeking cover. The bushes and the surrounding treetops are rapidly turning white. Lear glances around, rubbing his hands for warmth.

A sideward glance reveals a beautifully carved door to the left. Looking up, he sees a large, wooden house with brightly coloured flags fluttering on a long string tied to the branches of a large tree. He walks rapidly towards the door but stops as soon as his eyes fall on the carvings on it. Two fierce creatures, their fiery orange tongues protruding from open jaws, stare at him. Encircling these dragon-like creatures is a circle adorned with images of a conch shell, a multi-petalled flower and assorted semi-geometric forms, all painted in white, bright blue, pink, yellow and gold. Flanking them are brightly painted figures of two women with long, flowing hair – one carrying a basket of vivid red berries and the other holding a garland of purple and yellow flowers.

'It is the door to a Buddhist pagoda!' Lear mutters in hushed tones. 'Medicine and poison.'

Stopping to run his fingers very gently over the painted flowers, he breathes in the cold air. A strange buzzing reaches his ears. He looks behind and above, and almost instantly, the carved dragons on the door begin to move, nearly imperceptibly, their sinuous bodies uncurling in the way the clouds were seen moving around the peaks of the Kanchenjunga. They bare their fangs to reveal brightly painted tongues. But oddly, the creatures do not seem menacing.

A gentle push makes the door swing open wide, and as Lear walks into the inner sanctum, a dark and damp space, his nose picks up the odour of burning camphor and the unmistakable reek of old, wet wool. On all sides, he senses invisible bodies and elbows pressing in. The footfall of a young woman coming through the door is followed by someone taking his right hand and leading him in.

The dark room in the narrow attic at Margate that the young boy has stumbled upon by accident. The house is empty. Not a single soul is in sight. Ann has stepped out to buy bread. Crawling up the rickety ladder to the attic door, he sees, among the cobwebs, boxes, a pile of rotting fabric and paper, and on the decaying wooden floor, a small pool of rainwater. An almost overpowering stench. He clambers down the ladder in sheer panic and rushes outdoors to look for Ann, who appears almost magically that very instant through the gate, dressed in a long, grey skirt and a blue shawl draped around her shoulders. A faint whiff of lavender hangs in the air around her.

He only sees the cowl placed over the head of the person standing in front, and almost immediately, the door creaks shut. Dark, except for long shadows cast by a row of smoky oil lamps placed on a low wooden platform, the chamber is lit by the intermittent flickering of the flames. Painted on a panel on the wall behind the platform in front is a long line of figures – of celestial animals with human heads and human torsos attached to animal heads. A truly grisly scene! A tiger is flanked by a fox and a boar and painted in blue, red, yellow and pink. A smiling fish with petals growing out of its forked tail is visible below them. Poison and medicine! The bodies pulsate in the half-light.

'The distant cousins of my own nonsense animals!' Lear exclaims so loudly that he is startled by the sound of his own voice. All the creatures that he had once drawn appear to have stepped out from his sketchbooks that moment, moving with the motion of shadow puppets and letting out low growls.

Almost immediately, a gentle cough breaks the stillness. There is not a soul around, so Lear continues to stare, in semi-darkness, at the painted wall, his eyes moving slowly from the left to the right.

Someone is reciting a prayer. It's little more than a slow drone. Lear's eyes fall back on the wall. Just above the fantastic animals are a row of tiny human figures, all fleeing in terror from a monstrous blue foot with long, curling toes and sharp claws. With their mouths wide open and arms raised above their heads. Above them is another row of little Norse Loki-like figures with open jaws, triumphantly gorging on parts of the human torso, their arms and faces stained with blood.

Lear's eyeglasses begin to mist up, so he takes them off and bends down to take a closer look.

In the murky light is a blurred mass of details, a set of irregular lines and hoops made out of half-defined shapes.

A blue, clawed foot of a gigantic, pot-bellied figure. Multiple feet with innumerable toes and countless arms, big and small, attached to a blue torso, evoke petals pushing out of and encircling the calyx of a giant flower. Flaming out of the core of the figure are large tongues of red and orange flames that extend outwards. Even more startling is the tableaux placed just below this figure. The innumerable feet of the demonic figure trample on a small, crumpled-up human figure laid on its back and resting on the petals of a delicately painted white lotus. Like the multiple arms, the feet resemble the trunks of fantastical trees growing out of a dark, impenetrable centre.

Lear stands in silence, his eyes taking in all the details, one by one. A window somewhere shudders in its frame. Suddenly, he finds himself chuckling with uncontrollable glee, as if filled with a child's pleasure at discovering jewels hidden in a dark, unknown cave. The pot-bellied demon is most certainly a comical figure of horror blended with hilarity. Medicine and poison. Lear feels a little drop of water dripping onto his forehead. Then, the touch of human fingers, the barely perceptible feel of someone caressing him, makes him sit down on a stool, almost breathless.

His eyes move back up again to the nearly six-foot-tall demon. A corpulent belly, painted in vibrant blue and gold. Flaring dark eyes stare out, and an open mouth displays sharp, pointed teeth.

The Krampus devil in the park during the mummer's play! The trees around stand still, and the other children around him scream in terror as the devil leaps and runs after another player. But the young boy is not scared.

Here, in the heart of a sacred shrine is an *oriental* Krampus devil, crowned with human skulls instead of horns. Below the white lotus are the delicately curling waves of a cosmic ocean that fuse the sublimity of the painted scene with the expansive nothingness of the skies around.

A dancing pose! Like the statue of Shiva he had seen years ago at the museum in Fife House with his dear friend, Fortescu.

Now, sitting on a low stool, Lear finds himself half mesmerized by the gold pulsating in slow motion and flashing around like a beam of light. The brocade of a royal princess shimmers as she descends from the podium to meet the courtiers. The perfumed air blows through sheer silk curtains. From a distance, the trumpets blow, heralding the arrival of her royal consort.

Then, a door somewhere creaks open, and a narrow beam of light falls on the wall.

'Are you in there, Mister Lear?'

It is Giorgi.

In an instant, the curtains fall.

That night, as the cold wind howls outside the room in the hotel, all he can put down in his notebook is: *Near sunset, we were at the little Buddhist shrine.* The details are too numerous and perplexing to put down on paper. As he writes down the date, he remembers what his eyes fell on just before he stepped out of the door of the pagoda. A tiny gilt figure of the Buddha placed right above the head of the pot-bellied creature of claws and flames, with one finger of the right hand touching the ground, the other placed over his folded legs, and the half-closed eyes gazing down. Medicine and poison. The words leave a trail in his mind like a long-forgotten path winding through the marshes of Corfu. *Pharmakon.* Lushington had once spent an entire evening talking about the word that Plato had used. As he spoke about the powerful but puzzling concept relating to the great oppositions through which our thought is marked and authorized, the book resting on his thighs had suddenly fallen to the floor. 'Matter and spirit, reason and unreason,' he repeated. 'Just think about the system of British justice we follow on this small Ionian island.' His words belied the expression of wry amusement that passed over his face as he picked up the book.

Lear pauses and looks out of the window of the hotel at the moon rising above in the western sky and shuts his notebook. The three finished sketches of the Kanchenjunga are placed before him, and in each of these drawings, the peak of the Kanchenjunga sticks out into the sky like a piece of an opaque icicle gleaming in the sun.

The broken window through which the freezing air sweeps in has at its centre a shard of sharp glass that looks so menacing that a single jab can enter effortlessly deep into his belly when he is asleep. The pane was shattered in the autumn, and all Mother had done to keep away the cold was to place a tattered shawl over it. 'It will be replaced after Father returns,' she said.

The chill descends.

Must get to bed early. We begin another journey tomorrow.

3.

'A FAMINE?' LEAR PEERS AT the note from Edgar that Giorgi hands him at breakfast. He has just finished slicing a large piece of boiled mutton.

Must proceed directly to Agra. Avoid Bihar.

'Famine?' Lear looks at Giorgi, who is happily brushing his shoes.

'Edgar mentions a famine in Bihar. A *famine*,' he repeats. 'You must not have read the note.'

Placing the lid back on the blacking bottle, Giorgi nods. 'I know, Master. I read it. I was born a few months after the *year without a summer* ravaged my village in Albania. No harvest meant little food. People abandoned their homes and fields and fled, never to return. I *know* famines.'

The year without a summer! How remarkable! Just last year, Lear had heard Lady Derby complaining about the morning frost in the middle of May, which ravaged her garden. He had shivered in his boots during his trip to Scotland in early September of 1841, when, a week before in England, he had sipped cool lemonade with his friends! But after hearing Giorgi's description of starving babies and the old and sick being carried in the arms of men who still had the strength to make their way through the mountains, he pauses.

A garden in full bloom at the Red House in Ardee, Ireland. Among the roses, four men are discussing the Great Famine. Dressed in a white suit and vest, Fortescu is standing near the broken fountain and looking at a squirrel sitting on top of a dry spout. A gentleman in a large hat is talking very animatedly about English indignities in Ireland. Fortescu's impassioned indictment of the English for their unconcern for the Irish makes the dark-haired young woman in a white frock whisper under her breath, 'There you have a liberal in flesh and blood.' She turns her eyes away from Lear, realizing that he had heard what she has muttered.

That was in 1857, nearly sixteen years ago, when he had sensed that the topic of famines had not gone down well with Fortescu's guests at the garden party. But to think about these grim events now seems quite uninviting just as one is preparing for a new journey. So he looks at the words he has just scribbled in his notebook: *Drawing my last inspiration from soon never-to-be-seen-any-more woods of the eastern Himalayas.* In the midst of all this greenery, he reflects as he looks outside the open window, are dying crops, parched lands and emaciated bodies. Human and animal carcasses strewn on the dry earth. Rivers that have gone completely dry.

Pulling out a badly folded map from his pocket, he places it on his knees, and running his finger on it, exclaims, 'Bihar is not very far from here. In the plains, but not very far at all.' Giorgi is sitting out in the sun staring at the sky.

Nearly a month before, on a cold, crisp morning in Calcutta, while walking in Evelyn's sprawling garden, Lear had noticed a tall native man watering the rose bushes. His lean face glistened in the sun as he moved around, digging and deadheading the wilted blooms. Evelyn joined him. 'This man is the youngest in my team of five. An exceptionally talented chap. Knows virtually everything there is to know about the local flora. Not bad at roses either.' They both looked at the man, who was walking up to the well at the far end of the garden to fill his watering can. Bending down to retie his laces, Evelyn continued, 'I was told that when he came to work here about seven years back, he weighed little more than three stone. Lost his entire family to the Orissa famine.'

The sunburnt arms reached down as he gently worked the soil, the firm hands breaking down the lumps. That was the first time Lear had heard about famines in India. Then he heard Evelyn, who was about five paces behind him, say, 'What happened in Orissa was regrettable, but it was destiny that no government could prevent or alleviate.' Walking down the beautifully manicured lawn, Evelyn pointed to another young man. 'Do you see the lad with the limp over there? His entire village, just outside Calcutta, was wiped out in the hurricane of 1867. Nothing remained of the town of Canning or the villages nearby when the storm was over.'

The man with the limp was raking leaves. Evelyn's long arms stuck out of the sleeves of his dark grey coat.

'The tropics! Nature in this country is so utterly unpredictable! But the government has been compassionate, providing work to the many affected so adversely by nature's fury.' Walking up to the veranda, he picked up a glass of lemonade and smiled. 'The lemon tree in the garden gives lemons by the dozen every day without fail this time of the year. The Viceroy loves his lemonade, so he has ordered more trees to be planted.'

I have known Evelyn to be a faithful man of the Empire, but

never before have I heard him express these sentiments – and without a tad bit of hesitation, Lear thought. The great *benevolence* of the English government in India! Evelyn Baring had certainly turned himself into a valiant defender of the Empire, which was not surprising in the least. After all, he was the Viceroy's cousin, appointed to oversee the everyday running of a country that stretched from one ocean to the other. Perhaps, the young man knew more about these matters than the Viceroy or even I did. Far be it for me to speculate about the difficulties of running an empire!

Looking at the gardener's face, he had paused for a moment, seeing the soft shadows cast by the winter sun. However, he could not help himself from holding back the questions that raced through his mind. How many of the disasters Evelyn had named were instances of nature gone awry? Did the misery of Indians signify that the English had been unable to serve the world they claimed to rule so ably? Perhaps the benevolence of English rule was a mere façade that concealed something that no one could speak about. Lord Northbrook was different, he knew from his friends in England. Hand-picked by Gladstone to run India, he was a good, well-meaning man. But Evelyn's tone suggested that he preferred to ride the old horse and use his whip to move it along, as many before him had done. After all, the Empire was a *business*, and someone had to take hard decisions!

Although new questions had bubbled up in his mind, he had chosen to remain silent that morning. Perhaps it was not appropriate to bring up such matters. After all, he was the Viceroy's guest, and his dear friend, Evelyn, was the Viceroy's favoured cousin. As he sat sipping lemonade, the gardener came up and announced in a low voice that the carriage had arrived to take them to Tollygunge.

That was the end of his ruminations about disasters and famines. He was in India and had been entrusted with a very special task, one that had absolutely nothing to do with assessing the Empire's achievements in India.

Hearing a large, white cat calling from behind the bushes, Lear now turns to Giorgi, who is counting the items of luggage placed on the floor. The pony cart should arrive any minute. Giorgi looks thoughtfully at the broken stool that has just been repaired.

Suddenly, a thick band of clouds sweeps through the front lawn, and through the haze, Lear sees a vision approach him. A tall, cleft-chinned, blond man attired in a red, fitting jacket, white bottoms, very white gloves, a handsome cross-belt, buckle and claps, and shiny black boots. He was not expecting a visitor, especially at this hour, just when he was getting ready to step back into his room to have a quick rest. But before Lear can steal away, the man strides up to him, holding a feather-crested white cap in his left hand while extending the other for a quick greeting.

'The Viceroy's eminent guest. Truly honoured by your visit to our beloved Darjeeling. Peter Hornsford at your service.'

Lear takes off his gloves.

Not just any visitor, the man with the feather-crested cap who walks up to greet him is *singularly buccaneerous*. No doubt, it is George Wickham, *in the flesh*. Another figure stepping out of a novel, but this time, it's from none other than Jane Austen. So very amusing! Lear shakes hands with the apparition and offers him the straight-backed chair.

Captain Peter Hornsford informs Lear that he belongs to the famous Bengal Sappers and had served in the seventy-year-old corps for nearly ten years before fate brought him to this lovely Himalayan town.

Giorgi leaves the luggage on the floor and returns with two steaming cups of tea.

'Three sugars, please,' the man says, sitting upright. Lear scrutinizes the cap, whose white feathers are beginning to fray. The biscuits arrive, and the man helps himself to one, apologizing for the crumbs that fall on the floor. Lear wishes he could just wrap himself in a large woollen blanket and get a quick shut-eye before starting his journey to Edgar's home in Kurseong. It would take at least nine hours, the manager at the Darjeeling hotel had told him the night before, to travel from Kurseong to the plains of Siliguri. A long, exhausting ride down to the plains.

Hornsford's voice reaches Lear as he straightens the cushion on his back.

'The Treaty of Sinchula. You must have heard about that famous treaty, Mr Lear. We fought on the front, against the Bhutanese, nearly eight years back. What a triumph for Her Majesty's forces that was!'

Hornsford sounds vaguely north country. As he continues to speak, Lear cannot take his eyes off the well-weathered face, the touch of grey on the temples and the sturdy thighs that strain against tight-fitting trousers. Two squirrels are playing around the flowerpots, scurrying across the grass, while a single woodpecker sits on the bough of a magnolia tree, looking for something to peck. Lear stirs his tea, his attention riveted by Hornsford's sinewy thighs. Somewhere, he can hear the steady bleating of a goat.

Sinchula? A treaty? Her Majesty's wars? Although perplexed, Lear chooses to remain silent, fearing being dragged into a lengthy chronicle of matters military. Battles did not interest him in the least. In fact, none of his funny verses had any scenes of battle, much less swashbuckling soldiers. But perhaps he could compose a song about Peter Hornsford and his feathered hat and impressive thighs! But he needs to change, without further delay, the direction of the conversation without appearing to be ill-mannered. But how? Suddenly, he has a brainwave. *Distraction*. That is the best strategy, he thinks, to get his interlocutor to turn away from the tedious discourse on military matters.

'I am a painter of landscapes and botanicals.'

Hornsford looks amused as he reaches for the plate of biscuits. Lear prepares himself for the task at hand.

'*Ophioglossacea, Marattiaceae, Gleicheniaceae, Brassavola, Dendrobium.*' The names of Darjeeling's flora flow from his mouth like a venerable priest's recitation of the Lord's prayer in Latin. The military man can do little but stare at Lear's strange beard.

'*Curiosiovera, Stupedendiumrossa,*' and after a brief pause, he continues, '*Magicallicium grandiflora.*' The force of an African lion chasing a wildebeest appears to animate Lear. Under his tight trousers, the muscles of Hornsford's legs appear to twitch occasionally.

However, the counterattack only partially succeeds as Hornsford resumes his discourse soon after he has finished his second biscuit.

'Doubtlessly, a painter's task *is* to capture Nature's bounty, but the soldier's duty is to remind the world that the bounty you describe *belongs* to Her Majesty. All settled and sealed on paper – the majestic Himalayas, the lovely valleys, all of the orchids – secure and safe from the warlike neighbours to the north and east. May I remind you, Mr Lear, that the loftiest measured mountain in the world now belongs to England!'

Like all wars fought in the colonies this century, Lear soon learns from the captain that Her Majesty's forces had prevailed and that the victory had conferred immeasurable advantages to the region.

'The biggest challenge in this century was the Mutiny but look what came of it.' There is a triumphant look in Hornsford's eyes as a tiny squirrel comes up close to the feathered cap sitting on a cushion and studies it as if it were an exotic bird.

Over the next few minutes, the gallant captain's expressions alternate between the bravado of a soldier returning victorious after putting down an insurrection of natives – reminding Lear of a young man he had once met in Cannes, who had fought in the military expeditions in Crimea – and that of the youthful excitement he had seen on the face of a seventeen-year-old he had run into at London's Covent Garden who, fresh from winning his first rugby match, was biting enthusiastically into a fresh peach bought from the fruit seller.

Striding up and down the veranda, he stops, quite abruptly, next to the old hatstand as thick bands of mist sweep through the garden.

A cramped theatre. People's low voices, someone coughing at the back. The curtains rise, and the twitter dies down.

The young captain enters the stage. Tall and attired in green, he paces up and down frantically, apple in hand, uttering, 'We have to rescue poor Mercy from the flames! We are Britons. Will never be slaves.' Miss Baring sits next to him, looking nervously at her pocket watch. That cold evening in Calcutta, the two sit silently in the darkened hall. Evelyn's sister, the petite Miss Baring, whispers, 'The famous Sans Souci, led by Miss Leach, opened its doors years ago at a spot not too far from here.' Her words are barely audible. 'Everyone in Calcutta has heard about Mrs Leach. She left the city for three years and returned to meet an awful fate. Fatally burnt after her gown caught fire from the oil lamps kept in the wings to illuminate the backstage.' A shudder runs down Miss Baring's body as she speaks.

On the poorly lit stage, the handsome Peter Slocombe recounts his military exploits in a voice that reminds one of the rumblings of a hansom cab trundling along. An unspecified war in an unspecified region of India had taken him away for five months. He is wooing a pretty widow, Letitia, whose entry onto the stage is marked by the sudden strumming of an unknown musical instrument. She stands silently in the corner, sighing occasionally.

Scene two is no better. Peter's singular ravings about the misadventure of his battalion continue while Letitia stares vacantly at the audience, readjusting her large hat and straightening her long, green skirt.

The curtains drop, and the two steal out of the theatre noiselessly.

'Not sure if it is a five-act play, but we cannot take the risk of remaining in our seats any longer.' Miss Baring's words are barely audible as they step into the carriage waiting on the street.

The vision of the heroic Peter Slocombe pacing up and down on the stage is interrupted by Peter Hornsford's drone relating his military adventures. Lear rises and walks towards the squirrel. Staring at the little animal playing with Peter's feathered hat, Lear thinks of another strategy to deflect him.

'As a military man, you must have travelled the length and breadth of India and seen things that defy the imagination. During my stay in Genoa last year, I heard reports about a French explorer encountering creatures of eleven different species living together in a tiny cave on an island in the South Seas.'

Hornsford's whiskered face twitches. He is quite unable to grasp the sudden shift in the conversation.

Lear continues. 'Then, a close friend who spent many years in

South America has reported the oddest case of cross-pollination in the Amazon forests that has resulted in the creation of a species of flowers known to devour live rats. Even my dear friend, Darwin, has not been able to explain this rare phenomenon.'

Spinning tales about these strange phenomena in nature, Lear finds himself transported to newer heights of fancy. Nonsense botany, nonsense natural history are all part of his new arsenal of stories. Unstoppable, he becomes a soaring eagle that uses its powerful wings to navigate the high winds of his imagination, way up in the sky.

The look of utter perplexity on Hornsford's face adds more power to the wings.

'Wish I had the time to tell you about the curious behaviour of green-tailed fish in the seas of Papua New Guinea that hatch their eggs in the mouths of little octopi! Or about the roosters of Rhodes that imitate the voices of the boys' choir at Cambridge. Or about the silver salamanders of Samoa that spoon slime from the salty waters of the sea. You must surely know the *Photographic Journal*, Captain. It is full of exciting details about the explorer's world. Absolutely fascinating.' Lear is on fire.

Hard as he tries, Hornsford cannot picture salamanders spooning slime from the sea.

He rises, stretches himself and pats his thighs.

'Dinner will be ready at my home in Kurseong. Hope you are hungry, Mr Lear.' The assistant commissioner has just appeared, walking through the door. Lear is delighted at the prospect of baked chicken and potato with gravy. 'Exceptional lunch today, dear Edgar. Goose, pork, tongue, onions, tart, cheese, sherry and soda.' Lear turns towards the door at the far end of the veranda. His nose has detected the whiff of roast beef.

Meanwhile, Peter Hornsford has already picked up his feathered hat.

'It is past nine and well past breakfast time. My mastiffs must be hungry.'

Giorgi hears Lear heaving a sigh of relief as Peter heads towards the gate. In less than a minute, the metal garden gate clicks shut.

The mail arrives from Calcutta just as Lear is opening the letter from the Viceroy. An old pony cart laden with bamboo baskets and filled with burning wood waits outside the gate. The single grey pony seems restless. The clock in the main room ticks away. No *coolie* in sight. When Giorgi approaches the local policeman standing on the road for help, the latter simply stands and stares at him.

Finally, after an hour, the luggage is piled on top of the cart and the three – Lear, Giorgi and Edgar – take their leave of Darjeeling.

Two chairs have been placed in the sun outside Edgar's *bungalow* in Kurseong. But Lear is restless and walks to his room to lie down. A wave of exhaustion sweeps over him. He misses dinner that night, but just before he goes to bed – soon after Giorgi has handed him his hot cocoa – he asks Edgar about the fiery demon-like figure he saw in the shrine in Darjeeling.

'No demon, Mr Lear. That man with flames coming out of his sides is a divine fellow – a jolly scary deity. Mahakaal. A wisdom protector in his wrathful appearance.' Edgar's face breaks into a smile. 'Buddhists here pray to more gods and goddesses than one can care to count, each one stranger than the other.' Lear stares out of the window at the moonless night and hears a dog bark outside. *Divine and wrathful?* 'Medicine and poison,' he repeats under his breath, 'the folding together of unfathomable opposites.'

The next morning starts out hazy, but soon, the fog clears and the pine forests come into view, sweeping down the valleys and ebbing like waves into the far distance. Lear wipes the moisture from his eyeglasses with his large handkerchief. The sun drapes the valleys in a golden silk sheet, and Lear's eyes are transfixed by the movement of little things all around it – a blue and yellow butterfly startles him as it flutters around and sits on his hat; a bee-eater stares at the cat sitting by the gate; golden-green jewel beetles cluster around a damp clod of earth under the bushes.

The skin on the back of the pony quivers as the cart moves along the road down to Siliguri. Mudstone, sandstone and shale interspersed with granite line the edges. The gaunt trunks of pines stand like the pillars he once saw in Petra. However, in less than fifteen minutes after they have begun their journey, Lear signals to Giorgi to request the driver to stop. Climbing down with some difficulty with Edgar's help, fingers fumbling, he sits on a boulder by the side of the road. He senses a twitch in his arm. Through the mist, he can see the tea gardens cascading like green waterfalls through the vast blue foothills.

'Hard to avoid that churning feeling in the stomach when you descend on any of the roads from here to the plains.' Edgar's voice seems to come out of another large boulder against which he is resting his back.

Along with the pine, bamboo of all sizes and colours shoot up into the half-visible sky, some curled on the top and some drooping and some, like the pines, straight and tall, unmoving, their sloughed-off skins lying on the ground. After they get back to the cart, the driver points north. Out of the canopy of pines, the Kanchenjunga rears its head as if an invisible hand had unfurled an enormous *trompe l'oeil*. A flashing last vision of the enormous mountain peak partly shrouded by the gathering clouds.

Northbrook kindly suo moto wishes me to carry out the picture of Kanchenjunga for himself, for which I told Evelyn Baring what I intended to ask, viz., five hundred pounds.

Words that he had scribbled in his notebook come back to him as the peak vanishes from sight as swiftly as it had appeared. Lear had surprised himself with his own decisiveness when he agreed to take on the Viceroy's commission. But new doubts crowd his mind. Are the half-defined contours of the Kanchenjunga drawn on mere sheets of paper adequate to begin and complete a painting in oil – one that is nine feet in length and four feet high? How will he be able to fill in the depths in such a large painting? How true will it be to the original? Will it satisfy the Viceroy's desire to have the Kanchenjunga show its true majesty in its painted image?

The sounds of the wheels soon combine with the wind whistling through the pines.

A child on a rickety carriage sees his sister gazing out. The ocean is only an hour away, she tells him. A field of cowslips is spread out on the flat meadows. They are yellow and grow in delicate clumps, like bells, but not quite like regular bells. The tea that is made from cowslips is especially for the boy lying in bed, Ann tells him. He can feel the ocean in the air but cannot hear it, yet. The flat horizon is empty and almost without any colour. A seagull sits on a stone, tearing into a fish. 'Father will be there when we get to Margate.' Ann's voice is carried away by the wind.

That was more than half a century ago. There are no cowslips here, anywhere, nor can he hear the roar of the ocean or the harsh cawing of seagulls.

But the stillness that Lear senses all around him lasts for a long time, until it is abruptly broken by the sound of creaking wheels. A curious scene unfolds before his eyes: laden with wooden cases, a line of ox carts appears through the mist, resembling a line of battle-weary soldiers returning home, and in front is a man riding bareback on a grey pony. Dusky, his hair grown full and long over the jaw and chin and meeting with the sideburns but lacking a moustache, the rider gets off his pony as soon as he sees Edgar.

Christopher Perry offers his hand to Lear, shaking it with unusual vigour. Lear finds himself transfixed by the man's flourishing sideburns.

'About forty years ago, Johann and Sophie Wernicke arrived in Darjeeling. Moravian missionaries who set up the Wernicke Estate. Mr Perry now manages the Wernicke tea business.' Edgar smiles as he gently pats the man's broad shoulders.

Moravians! Astonishing! How on earth did they get to Darjeeling from Moravia? His first-ever meeting with a missionary in India happened during a dinner held at the Government House in Calcutta on a cold December evening. Seated next to a nice Miss Dampier was mouse-like Mr Clarke, a fellow he later described in his notebook as *a browny, clerical-missionary, dummy and queery.* An odd lot, these missionaries. The interminable talk about salvation, grace and mercy that evening had left him in desperate need of fresh air, and although it was cold, he stepped out onto the balcony and looked up at the cloudless sky, only to realize that the missionary man had followed him. Mr Clarke spoke interminably about the mission's work in the mountains. 'Even before we arrived, the Belgian Catholics went up the Himalayas and placed a giant crucifix facing Tibet. A gritty lot, you have to admit! Of course, *we* never believed in such shows,' he said, taking out his pocket watch. 'Christian piety *through* deed – that is our motto. The unbelievers need us, but our noble mission's success depends, of course, on the actions of the present government.' His hesitant tone suggested that he expected the Viceroy to do a lot more for English missionary work. That evening had ended with his host, the Viceroy, failing to show up for dinner, which disappointed Mr Clarke so much that he departed soon after the pudding was served and he had hastily gulped down his seventh glass of water.

'I assume Mr Perry is interested in missionary matters,' Lear asks Edgar, seeing the man offering a carrot to his pony. But Lear finds Mr Perry eager to describe his *real* vocation – to warn people about the lurking dangers of 'disease and distemper' in India.

'You have heard of *Simla trots*, have you not, Mr Lear?'

Mr Lear has not, so Mr Perry explains, 'It is the worst kind of diarrhoea, almost diabolic, that lasts for days. An inescapable reality here that threatens the life and soul of all Europeans who have made India their home So, be very, very careful when you eat anything offered in India.'

Lear winces and takes off his glasses. 'I think I never felt physically more fit than when I wandered through the banks of Banaras.'

'Banaras!' Extreme consternation sweeps over Mr Perry's face.

Lear stops himself from going into the details of what he had actually witnessed in the waters of the Ganges in Banaras. Any mention of bloated corpses floating down with crocodiles splashing around would most certainly make the poor man wince.

Lear's placid tone takes Mr Perry by surprise.

'I now intend to travel through the mighty plains of India, and if all goes as planned, visit Ceylon by the year end.'

'Splendid!' Mr Perry gives his pony another pat. 'But, *Banaras*! Certainly, it is little more than a festering wound on the chest of India!'

'Mr Lear spent a great deal of time walking around and drawing on the *ghats* during his visit to the holy city.' Edgar's comment elicits a look of horror combined with disbelief.

'Thank the merciful Lord it is winter when much of the contagion is under control. In any case, extra caution should be exercised at all costs and in any season.'

Lear takes off his eyeglasses and puts them back on after giving them a vigorous wipe.

This fellow was not a conventional missionary like his forebearers, but, in fact, worse – a medical missionary, an evolved species! No word about the indigestion he had suffered during his travel comes out of his lips. Any more of Mr Perry's sermonizing about health, contamination or sanitation now will undoubtedly aggravate his trembling affliction!

'My family built a fortune on tea and timber trade after the military pact with Bhutan had been sealed. My uncle – the last in a line of daring people who had made Darjeeling their home – was the true pioneer.'

Lear's ears are filled with the sounds of crickets and unknown birds that come from the woods.

The pony lets out a snort.

'I trust you have had the opportunity to taste our tea brewed from the finest leaves collected from Kurseong's finest estates.'

Lear tries to signal to Edgar that he is ready to resume the journey, but he is nowhere to be seen.

'The real pleasures of Darjeeling are the bridge games by the fireside and the tennis matches, and of course, the forests are full of game.'

Delighted to see Edgar appear from behind the bushes after a few minutes, he proceeds to make his way slowly back towards the pony cart waiting by the side of the road.

Does the Empire breed such species? This endless staging and posturing, the mouthing of words prepared by a master dramaturge. Where else could he have actually encountered a flesh-and-blood Prospero casting his magic spell but on a desolate road somewhere in the foothills of the Himalayas! To his utter surprise, Lear realizes that the slight dizziness that had descended on him earlier has been completely cured! Undeniably gone. Cleansed. The contagion has vaporized.

As Mr Perry engages Edgar in a discussion about the poor state of the roads, Lear's eyes begin to wander restlessly, his attention falling on a large canopy of juniper growing along the wayside. The needle-like leaves and blue-black flat cones are quite extraordinary. He is eager to leave, but Mr Perry appears to have some serious business to discuss with the assistant commissioner. Giorgi has just stamped out his cigarette and smiles at him. Unexpectedly, a strange buzzing sound pierces the air. It appears to come from the juniper bush. Fearing a repeat of the experience a week back in Kurseong, he takes off his glasses and shuts his eyes tight. When he opens them a minute or so later, his eyes fall on a small, shiny creature sitting among the clump of dark green moss that spreads out on the flaky barks of the juniper. Humped and rounded, its body is folded within a glittering glass shell.

'A golden tortoise beetle,' says Edgar, who notices Lear gazing at the strange creature.

'What a perfectly designed clockwork creature this is. The innards look like cogs in a machine waiting to be fired into motion. But it is so still and gleaming, like the most beautiful archangel guarding the gates of heaven.'

The word 'archangel' works like magic. A look of alarm passes like a shadow over Mr Perry's eyes. Fearing that he may be in the company of a Popish sympathizer from England, he immediately beats a hasty retreat. After saying a quick goodbye and wishing them a 'safe onward journey', the man with the impressive sideburns leaps onto his pony. In less than a minute, the creature trots away into the mist. The carts bearing tea boxes begin to rattle up the road.

The triumphant look on his master's face assures Giorgi that his master is ready for the downward journey. This, decidedly, was his master's very own *Popish Plot!* How adept he was getting at warding off the fiercest combatant without firing a single gun!

They are ready to depart, but the coachman is nowhere in sight. Edgar walks with Giorgi towards a small hut on the side of the road, looking for him. Soon, the creaks and squeaks and chirpings of little insects that fill the air make Lear look around at the light gradually retreating into the hollow of the foliage. He misses something, but he is not sure what. It is only nearly late in the afternoon, but he can sense the advent of dusk.

The darkness descends without warning. The Greek coast to Viewpoint Kouramilia. Franklin Lushington has just announced his decision to leave his post as magistrate and return to England. He stares at the sea as the tide draws out, leaving little white, sheep-like waves to scurry along the long shore. Suddenly, there is a sound that begins with a singular chirp but rises to a deafening crescendo. Alone at his desk, that evening, he dips his pen into the inkstand and thinks about dear Gussie in her white gown, smiling sideways as she walks down the gravel path. Lord Westbury's youngest daughter certainly does not have any special airs.

Gussie's neat handwriting – marked by a series of giant loops – floats before his eyes as Lear glimpses the sun turning into a pale yellow blob and sinking into the distant horizon.

London. He sits inside his room by the fireplace with Gussie reading her fairy tales. She tells him that fairy tales fascinate her no end, and one day, she intends to publish her own collection that she had been writing during her spare time. 'Fairies come in all shapes and sizes, not unlike my stories,' she says, taking the sheaves of paper from his hands and placing them in her large satchel. Sitting very close, he can feel her breath. She is curious about his drawing of the trees in Hackwood Park and loves the way his pencil has drawn the elms. So lifelike. A perfect April day. Irises and bluebells pop out magically from every corner of the greens. Chattering starlings drive him to get up to shoo them off. But proposing to Gussie, the daughter of Westbury? She is twenty-six years younger than I, old enough to be my grown-up daughter! And I possess just about as much charm as the English garden statuary sold in Windlesham.

He had, from time to time, thought about a matrimonial possibility with Gussie, but it increasingly felt like dealing with the locked gate that refused to open. The two were on a boat on the London canal that day, and the much-awaited canal excursion they had planned ended with the two of them climbing out to sit under an elm tree, only to be driven by the pouring rain into a tiny wooden shelter draped in blue wisteria. There was little sign that the lock-keeper would return anytime soon, so Gussie brought out sandwiches and lemonade from the straw hamper.

'Augusta! Augusta!' A young man in a blue jumper shouts out her name from a boat that goes past them. The lock gate has just been opened. Would she like to join them? Gussie just waves back.

Age difference notwithstanding, Lear wished he could overcome that nagging sense that Gussie would certainly refuse him if he proposed. Apart from the difference in age, it was his unmentionable malady. How could he bring it up? But it did not seem right to conceal it, knowing how much Lord Westbury trusted him.

Those questions often came up, but that was years ago – when the world still seemed young and full of possibility. That world crumbled – bit by bit – as the years passed, much like the wooden garden shed in his garden in Corfu that had pretty flowering vines growing on it until the rot made it turn into a heap of ruins. Making a home with Gussie was fraught with peril. For one, he had guessed from the look on her melancholic elder sister's face one evening as they sat for dinner that she would never approve of a man more than twenty years older to be her sister's suitor. Lear could only second-guess how her father, Lord Westbury, would respond. The balding man with an unusually ruddy face was, after all, Lord Chancellor, a peer and member of the Privy Council and a man with a reputation for aiming his sarcastic humour with remorseless fury at members with whom he disagreed. Granted that *he*, personally, had never been a target of his derision for as long as they had known each other, but that possibility always lurked in the background. More than violating the fine line of intimacy between him and the Westbury family, he feared that any formal proposal for matrimony would provoke Westbury's ire.

They are back on the broken road, the pony cart moving very slowly over crevices and rocks that jut out in places where the surface has crumbled away. Gussie's gleaming face begins to flicker, and in its place, Franklin Lushington's gaunt and whiskered demeanour drifts in front of his eyes.

The Scroobious Pip sat under a tree
By the silent shores of the Jellybolee;
All the insects in all the world

About the Scroobious Pip entwirled.
Cicadas and beetles with purple eyes
Gnats and buzztilential flies
Grasshoppers, butterflies, spiders too,
Wasps and bees and dragonflies blue,
And when the gnats began to hum
Bounced like a dismal drum,
And every insect curled the tip
Of his snout and looked at the Scroobious Pip.

He was not sure what had prompted him to dash out the lines about Scroobious Pip with such haste that evening after he returned home after his walk with Lushington. All he can recall is an agitated Lushington leaving the dinner table midway and rushing out of the door. No word came from him for the next few weeks. Before picking up his pencil that evening, he had stared for a long time at a dead moth lying next to the lamp, still wondering if Lushington was upset about something he had said during dinner. Was it about him not answering his letters or mispronouncing an ancient Greek name from Plato? Hardly ever did Gussie throw a tantrum in his company. She seemed as even-tempered as his tiny kitten, smiling softly at the summer flowers that he pointed to as they walked through the park. Even his wild drawings elicited a soft, gracious response. When he showed her the sketch of the ostrich wearing boots, she had exclaimed in her timorous voice, 'How original!'

Gussie and Lushington! Two ends of a boat leaving behind a wake that would only dissipate under the force of other, fiercer waves. Had Frank Lushington only seen him as just another expatriate in an alien land with whom he could spend evenings talking about the complexities and beauty of ancient Greek? Fate had brought them together in Corfu after their first meeting in Malta. A frequent visitor who finished an entire bottle of claret while discussing Aristotle, Lushington was also prone to periodic bouts of inexplicable gloom when the intense face, the eyes that flashed with honest fire, turned the man into a dark soul in mourning. Sitting silently across from him while Lear sharpened his pencils, the man would leave the room abruptly, uttering a half-audible 'good night'. Being with him was like inhabiting an abode of dust and air, in which the buzzing life had been unexpectedly smothered by unseen hands. Just two days before Lushington's birthday, he had received a note declining an invitation to dine together. His excuse: he would be up in Albania to hunt. *Hunting in Albania*? As he tossed the note into the fireplace, he had wished – perhaps for the first time – that their paths had never crossed.

Did his mind just conjure the lure that he imagined seeing in Lushington's eyes? Although they had known each other for years, Lear could never be sure if Lushington's ears ever caught the sweet cry of insects or the joyous buzzing of flies while they walked on the shores of Corfu. Was his yearning to have Lushington by his side a sign of his own hope that one day that firefly spark would turn into a flaming fire?

The streaks of red among the darkness descending around him make him think of the bright embers flying out of the fireplace where he had once cast all the crumpled, unfinished letters written to Lushington. The black, trembling tongues in the midst of the dying fire, the sound of an occasional sharp crackle, ashes from a dying star: Lushington had remained a stranger; his own head had been resting all along on a pillow fluffed up with empty longing. Delusion that struck him with the comfort of an invisible, loving hand.

The road ahead has been recently repaved, so the pony cart moves at a steadier pace. The sky looks like an arabesque, the dark and light patterns of its canopy moving with the drift of the wind itself. The sudden creaking of the wheels signals that the cart is slowing down, until it comes to a stop. As the driver climbs down from his seat to disappear behind the bushes, a band of clouds sweeps down. Among the tall grass, Lear spies a tiny golden beetle darting out and perching on top of a flowering bush. The setting sun sends out its last flash of light. How remarkably visible the little creature is. Like the beetle he had just seen, the wondrous toy-like being appears to be animated by unseen mechanical springs that tick away silently within its sparkling shell. The rhythm is unbroken. There are no sudden pauses, no sudden breaks, no stopping. The clockwork precision, the two antennae dwarfed by the long pistil of a wildflower. But how complete, how free-standing the creature was, its shell enclosing its sparkling being so completely. As it disappears into the folds of the petals, he hears Giorgi's light cough.

Gussie's handwritten fairy tales, pages of lines written in giant loops and wavy curls, had remained locked in a tight wooden box. Granted, that while her runaway imagination did not quite match her long frocks and wide bonnets, Gussie's realm of fairies, gnomes, hobgoblins, pixies and leprechauns touched the edges of his world of *Gramble Bramble*. Perhaps this was the invisible thread that had brought them together, that made possible the laughter they shared walking under the plane trees of London and imagining the breeze caressing the tips of red summer tulips.

'Excellent for nervous disorders.' Fortescu is telling him all about tea made from cowslips.

The excursions with Ann in Margate, and she is excitedly pointing to a field of cowslips, the bright yellow spreading out like fire. The world opens up like a summer peony uncurling. Little things come into sharp relief – the sound of crickets, the gentle rustle of the grass, and even the comforting clickety-click of Ann's old sandals and the smell of her tattered woollen shawl.

Cowslips and his awful *morbids*. Cowslips and Ann's long, pale fingers. The fairy tale-obsessed Gussie's green and grey mackintosh. All disappear into the folds of the yellow flowers that lie beyond the ruby-red tulips.

Lear takes off his eyeglasses. Even Giorgi, who stands barely three feet from him, dissolves into a blur of green and grey. He remembers that as a young boy, his eyes altered the way he saw the world. He always felt a strange power in his own ability to control how much of the world he would allow into his range of vision. By pressing the top portion of the eyelid, he could bring the fuzzy world into sharp focus. Releasing the pressure made it sink back into an undefined blurriness when all he was aware of were sounds and the vision of blurry lines – the motion of wheels, the crack of the whip and the occasional cry of the seagull. This was the source of great power, giving the young boy the ability to grasp the incomprehensible world with just the tiny pressure of a fingertip. He is sure that Ann knew about his little trick but had never said anything about it. Years later, when the first eyeglasses were placed on the bridge of his nose, he realized that the only way he could repeat that magic was by taking them off, which enabled him to return the too-sharply focused world to magical fuzziness.

Had he glimpsed that magical world, sitting on his sketching stool that cold day in Kurseong? Did it propel him towards the strange sense of delight that he experienced as a nine-year-old, sitting without his glasses, in the house in Margate and drawing his strange, incongruous creatures? Ann had kept all those drawings in a box under the bed. After Father left, she bought a copy of the copiously illustrated *Botanical Magazine*, and they spent many an afternoon leafing through its pages. The near-sighted young boy, sitting on the floor, would often take off his eyeglasses while concentrating on the fine lines of the flowers he saw by holding up the book barely inches from his nose. Taking up his pencil, he would then focus on getting his drawings just right but never letting go of the asymmetries that emerged in them. Over the years, along with stick drawings of funny people and strange birds, he sketched pictures of real birds, butterflies and shells with the help of Ann. They all went into the bright green album that Ann had bought from the shop on High Street.

The sisters breeze in and out of the house in such a tizzy that the little boy takes little notice of them. Father leaves, and the large family moves away. Harriet, Eleanor and Ann find a tiny house on the edge of New Street, so tiny that they have to share one bed.

Hornsey Fields, Gravesend…

In this alien and noiseless world, Ann's voice suddenly falls silent. Only the sound of the restless pencil tip scratching on paper. Then – as the two come close to the sea – the fury of tempest-tossed waves throws up the entrails of an unknown dead sea monster.

A strange shudder runs down Lear's arms. Giorgi is struck by Lear pulling down the hat to cover his eyes.

Out from the bushes emerges his very own *Bountiful Beetle* with purple eyes, carrying a green umbrella. He always did carry an umbrella when there was no rain but left it at home when it poured. The *Runcible Raven*, the *Vicious Vulture*, the *Melodious*

Meritorious Mouse, the *Abstemious Ass* and the *Fizzgiggious Fish* follow and sit very quietly under the junipers, waiting to be discovered by a wayfarer. Without warning, the air is filled with the sound of unknown insects, rising and ebbing.

The foothills below are suddenly illuminated by the strange light of the setting sun. Lear strains his eyes to see what is visible below. Somewhere in that gloomy land of shadows must be the lonely rambler, wandering among the sand dunes. The happy days with the girl he pined for are long past. The fireflies always lit up bulrushes when he went looking for her. But at this hour, there is no music, only silence, and the wanderer is nowhere in sight.

The sound of the moving wheels merges with other sounds. Lear pulls up his hat and puts on another pair of gloves. Noticing him tapping his fingers to the silent beat of a half-familiar song and bending over sideways as if to catch the drift of a silent conversation, Giorgi knows that his master is back in the company of nonsense creatures that have clambered miraculously out of the pages of his drawing book. Creatures with feet dangling from the edge of a precipice or sitting on a red Morocco chair or walking around on stilts, they could be always trusted to bring back the ruddiness to his wan cheeks. Giorgi rests his head back in the comfort of knowing that Lear will no longer pull the hat over his face.

The pony cart creaks along.

When they arrive in Siliguri, it is just past six in the evening. In the darkness of that twilight hour, Lear recognizes the house as soon as he steps down from the pony cart – its large lime-washed walls, the well-kept garden in front, and a long veranda encircling a row of small windows, with smoking oil lanterns hanging from the rafters. It is the same *dak bungalow* they had stopped in on their way to Pankhabari nearly two weeks ago. Looking around, he notices that some of the branches of the mango trees by the gate have been cut down.

After lying on his bed for a few minutes, Lear raises himself, puts on an extra layer of woollens and makes his way to the desk. Under the flickering light of the lamp, his pen moves rapidly, and the words appear on the blank pages of his journal:

The immense plains are clearer than yesterday, but still, a wide, dim expanse of cloudy veil. How tiny all other landscapes seem compared with these. Last evening and this morning, a very melodious bird cried or crew or crowed… Quiet and the immensity of the scenery; the silence of forest… Hollows and basins, ravines and depths.

It is January 30th. More than two months have passed since he set foot on Indian shores. The faces, vistas and sounds of his journey ebb in and out, but the last thing he remembers before falling asleep is the grim face of Christopher Perry floating in front of his eyes and a distant voice echoing in his brain:

If I were a cassowary
On the plains of Timbuctoo,
I would eat a missionary,
Prayer Book, Bible, and hymn book too.

4.

IT IS AROUND EIGHT IN the evening, and with dinner over, Lear takes a look at the notes that he has just penned. The lamp on his table casts a feeble glow, making the words appear like dancing shadow puppets. He smiles, thinking about the donkeys he had seen earlier, sniffing around the bony remains lodged in a tangle of thorny bramble, and a tail-wagging, body-swaying king crow sitting on the branch of a dead tree. A blotch of ink left by his clogged pen resembles the shape of a swollen river. It has been a long day. The sun is dying, and slowly, the red western sky dwindles into a haze of pale yellow and grey.

From the corner of his eye, Lear notices a Eurasian-looking man peering at him through the open window. His face is barely visible, but he can hear him speaking to the gatekeeper in an unmistakable mishmash of English and Hindoostani. 'The staff here is not really up to the mark,' he mutters to himself, thinking about the all-but-nude servant who had appeared in his room to hand him a towel. Hair tussled, chest bare, only clad in what looked like a loincloth, he was certainly not fit to serve in a hotel.

However, dinner had been most satisfactory. He can still taste the tender roast mutton that came with cabbage and peas. While he spooned the peas from his plate, the fat brown lady sitting on a couch on the veranda smoked a hookah, the smoke filling the air and gliding through the row of pillars. It turned out that Mr Morris, the hotel keeper, was from Fortescu's Ardee, in his beloved County Louth. The fat brown lady, he was told, was his wife's *ayah*, now pensioned off but a permanent resident at the property.

Lear asks Giorgi to shut his window.

That man is his usual self – utterly unflappable. Even when, upon arrival at the hotel, they were told that the two had to share a single room, Giorgi strode in with the confidence of a land surveyor, examined the furniture, and without a moment of hesitation, began moving the large chair that would supplement the too-short bedstead, placing it at its foot. 'That's enough room for me. I hope this arrangement will allow you adequate space to move around, Master.'

They had reached Mr Morris's hotel in the late morning the day before after suffering a series of exhausting dusty train rides from Sahibgunge, Colgong, Jamalpur and Arrah, before reaching Monghyr, from where they had boarded a slow-moving train to Chunar. Before Sahibgunge, they had made their way from Siliguri via Kishengunge and Purnea on bone-rattling pony carts, only stopping at wayside stations to allow the animals to rest and feed. At one point, only a brake van was available to take them to the next station as there were no signs of a train arriving any time soon. The stationmaster could be seen sitting out in the sun, dozing, while two porters sat on their haunches chewing tobacco.

In the nearly one week of travel since they had departed Kurseong, Giorgi's moods had alternated between extreme fussiness and indifference, which made Lear wonder if it would be best to send him back after they reached their next stop. Back home in Greece, he usually sulked when he suffered bouts of sleeplessness, but lately, his disposition had become quite unpredictable. Perhaps, the lodging arrangements at the train stops were not satisfactory. Perhaps, he was beginning to miss home or was just worn out from the compulsion to speak in English or pretend to be an Englishman in the service of another Englishman.

True, Giorgi rarely dawdles, but his recent frightful sick glum drives me cold-dead-mad, Lear thinks, shutting the notebook.

The moon rises outside the window just then, throwing long shadows of unknown trees on the ground below. Perhaps one way of drawing him out of his enervation would be to engage him once again in another lesson on irregular English verbs. But will that work *now*? The lessons, conducted over a decade ago when Giorgi could hardly utter a single complete sentence, would hardly work now. Lear had marvelled at the pace at which Giorgi cottoned on, offering his philosophical ruminations in Italian interspersed with English phrases as he turned discarded curtains into dusters and aprons. Admittedly, it had been little more than a fumbling through. He would pause mid-sentence and then stare at the ceiling for minutes before resuming. But it had worked. By the end of the second year, the Suliot had mastered the language, thoroughly impressing Lear's English visitors with his generous use of words such as 'decidedly' and 'doubtless' or when he described a night owl's call as being 'matchlessly sinister'.

But the image that sticks out in his mind now as he sees the listless Giorgi is the unmistakable vigour of his carpet beating in Corfu, an activity that often sent street dogs barking and howling all across the street! Puffs of sparkling dust swirled around the tall figure as the sun streamed through the trees. Giorgi had once told him that he had learned the techniques from his wife, who was at that time living with his mother in Parguinote. He suspected that the wife's carpet-beating skills helped her vent her pent-up emotions towards a mother-in-law who always complained that 'she was *not* a true Suliot' and did not deserve a husband like her dear son.

Strangely, he had never heard of the word before Giorgi entered his service. Suliots were descended from a long line of military commanders of the Tsar, Giorgi had claimed. Lushington once called Suliots a 'mixed-up race', people who had fled to the mountains of Suli to escape the Turks. Giorgi's high cheekbones, deep-set eyes, prominent ears and unkempt hair, including the frayed cuffs of his white shirt bunched up above his wrists, seemed to confirm that ancestry. He certainly has the air of a people who had to flee for safety. The hairy arms of a pack of wild Albanians sitting on the gnarled branches of a tree that he had sketched years ago suddenly flash before his eyes. Of course, he could simply be imagining the residual traces of that wildness that he now sees in Giorgi's face. He had always been struck by the strangeness of that world but never had he seen Giorgi wear the purple frock, scarlet vest and black waist of *Ghegheria* or the many fluted *fustianelles* and white caps of *Berat*. It was apparent that Giorgi's Balkan core was wrapped up in uncountable layers and contours of Parga, the Ionian Islands and beyond.

At this moment, however, Giorgi stands before him, stirring a cup of hot cocoa, confident about his place in the world, listening for any sign from his master to fetch something important. How swiftly the man had recovered from his sullenness!

A soft thud startles Lear. An ominous-looking gecko crawls

slowly on the floor and then darts towards the wall facing the window. How astonishing that such creatures can take such a fall from the ceiling and still be agile enough to dart towards their next meal with such alacrity. In an instant, a whole flock of tongue-flicking creatures appears, scurrying in all directions. Their shadows flicker on the wall.

> *... the Old Man who supposed,*
> *That the street door was partially closed:*
> *But some very large rats, ate his coats and his hats,*
> *While that futile old gentleman dozed.*

He worries that the vile reptiles had their homes inside *his* room, behind the two doors, in the crevices of the ceilings, and who knows, may still be lying in their comfortable nests under *his* bed! The last time, at the Kishengunge *dak bungalow*, when he had pointed to a brood lying in wait for the next insect to come crawling out, Giorgi had smiled.

'Quite harmless, I hear, although I believe it can kill a man if one accidentally falls into a pot of boiling soup.' Lear had not found Giorgi's words the least bit comforting but had remained silent.

From where he is standing, Giorgi can see his master sitting on the chair and staring at the wall. 'Now, does not that one little thing have the face of a rat?' He points to one that is beginning to creep closer to the window.

My Suliot is clairvoyant, or else, how could he have known that it was a limerick about an old man and rats that had run through my mind at just that very moment? It is, most assuredly, one of the traits he has inherited from his exotic ancestry.

Lear's large folio and two saddlebags are placed precariously on top of the table. They sit too close to the oil lamp, so Giorgi moves them to the floor. One improvises as one travels. The pillow smells of camphor, but he does not mind. He only hopes that the little beasts on the walls find their dinner and tuck themselves back into their nests, away from his bed.

Minutes after, Giorgi lies on the bed placed at the far end of the room. Lear can hear him snoring lightly. He lowers the wick of the oil lamp till he can only see a dull glow on the walls. The narrow and dusty roads in a *garry* drawn by two skeletal ponies, the metallic, rhythmic sounds of the wheels of the train that seemed to stop at every station along the way, and his recurring backache begin to dim. The last thing he notices before falling asleep are the dark shadows of the distant ramparts of the Chunar Fort looming outside the glass-paned window.

The next day, the light of dawn wakes him just as he hears Giorgi stirring in the room. After an early breakfast, Lear and Giorgi return to the room and peer out of the window. The shadowy ramparts from last night are now clearly visible, a scene waiting to be captured in brown ink and wash. Placed against a vaguely defined low bridge of hills, it reminds him of the landscape he had drawn nearly thirty years ago in brown ink and wash – of Sant'Eusebio in the distance. That picture had quite enchanted Lushington. A handsome amount of ten pounds for a painting that had taken him a day to complete. Lear now wonders if his friend had handed that drawing to James Edwards after his departure from Corfu. Perhaps, it had simply perished in Lushington's airless attic in London, turning into the papery fragments of an Egyptian mummy.

Stepping out of the metal gate, Lear casts his eye at the scattered cluster of lime-washed houses and the large canopied trees lining the road just outside. This queer place is so tenantable, except, of course, the staff. He is thinking about the half-naked native man who had brought towels into his room the day before. Waiting outside the metal gate is a thirteen-year-old European-looking Nolan, a cheery-faced fellow with an unwashed face and dark brown hair. They had first met him outside the railway station just after the train they had taken had puffed out of the station teeming with monkeys perched on the benches. Young Henry had taken the two to meet his uncle, Mr Morris, the owner of the hotel.

'Can take you in, but you must rough it!' Mr Morris had said, offering them a single room at the far end of the long veranda, flanked by lovely flowering bushes. Despite the arrangement, Lear was happy to spy a number of *tin-potty* birds – and in the distance, the trees and the lovely fort, the red sandstone gleaming in the afternoon sun. And the single room they were offered was surprisingly spacious and airy.

Just as Giorgi picked up one of the larger cases, Mr Morris had said in a loud sing-song voice, 'Mr Lear, your guide to the fort will be young Henry, my nephew who lives around the corner.'

So, here he was – Henry Nolan – greeting them with a joyful wave. The boy is only too eager to lead. He skips as he walks in his long, baggy trousers, leading the two through a scraggly forest path. Looking up, Lear notices that, unlike the trees in Kurseong, the ones here have much wider canopies, and the long, serrated leaves move and swish in the breeze, emitting a low hum. 'Neem,' he is told by Henry as Giorgi steps on an old anthill and watches it crumble to dust. Large green barbets with startlingly red beaks move among the dark brown branches. One, sitting on a low branch, holds a long, fat worm in its beak while the others on the top branches make strange rasping sounds.

'*Basanta*,' says Henry. 'The bird is called *basanta*.' He is playing his part perfectly, thinks Giorgi.

Lear signals that he intends to stop to do a sketch but quickly realizes that getting the full details of the bird sitting up so high is futile.

The path widens as they keep walking, till they find themselves near two small, exquisitely carved temples. Thoroughly Indian, Lear thinks as his eyes skim over the half-disintegrating sculptured pillars. But they do not stop. They have got to get to the fort first. Walking in a single file, Lear and Giorgi follow the boy past an ancient tree with its gnarled branches reaching up to the sky. All he can hear is a gentle rustling sound punctuated by the rush of the westerly bluster making way noisily through the giant branches.

Quite unexpectedly, an unfamiliar rasping sound from the distance reaches their ears, followed by a mild tremor that seems to run under their feet. They look up ahead. A battalion of the Indian infantry is marching down a narrow path towards them, about five hundred feet away, kicking up enough dust for Lear to pull out his large handkerchief very swiftly to cover his nose. The three stop walking to give way to the battalion as it approaches them. The dry, wintry air brushes their cheeks.

A large band of soldiers are striding down the village road in Bologna. March 1860. Garibaldi has just landed at Marsala. Revolution is at hand. Off the Italian soldiers go, their faces lit up by the spring sun. The crowds in faraway Covent Garden chant, 'Garibaldi forever!'

The season of revolutions and mutinies that had raised so much dust then is now little more than the whiff of the breeze that skims the surface of the fields of mustard. Lear takes off his eyeglasses and squints. A pie dog stands wagging its thin tail.

A line of men appears, derelict figures with missing arms and legs, many hobbling on crutches that make rasping sounds. Some have misshapen faces. Others, dressed in tatters, stop to recover their breath and gaze vacantly at the fields ahead. Their leader, a healthy young European sergeant, waves to Henry.

As the battalion goes past them, Lear's eyes fall on a man hobbling on a mere stump of a leg. Lear turns away in horror as his eyes meet those of the man's gouged-out face.

'They are mutiny prisoners, sir.'

Henry's hushed voice is almost inaudible.

The mutiny? That happened nearly sixteen years ago!

Henry has resumed his commentary on the sights of Chunar. 'You may not know, but Chunar is a very old fort, sir. Two thousand, no, eight hundred ...' But his words just trail away. Lear cannot tear his eyes away from the stump wrapped in soiled rags. The middle-aged soldiers must have been so young in 1857.

'Chunar Fort is now a military garrison. After 1857, it was turned into the home of the Company of the 107th.'

The old man they had met at the station sitting on a broken bench had mentioned that the English had a garrison stationed in the ancient city.

Were they native soldiers who had disobeyed their superiors during the conflict? Or were they European soldiers who had fallen on the battlefield but could not return home, their faces darkened by the harsh sun and no longer recognizable? Could the Crown be credited with their welfare, or had they been forgotten and left nameless, taken out for their daily marches dressed in rags?

Before he can ask these questions, an official-looking man approaches, waving to Henry, who has started climbing the steps of the rampart in front. A note in his hand, he indicates is for Henry. The young boy immediately runs down the steps to receive it.

Henry's face falls as soon as his eyes go over the note. He returns, looking despondent, wiping the perspiration on his face with a bright green handkerchief. 'Sorry, sir, I have to return to the station. My liberty day ticket has been refused.'

'*Liberty* day? I am not sure if I know what kind of ticket *that* is.' Giorgi is curious about this new phrase: *liberty day*.

'A bit of a chit from a skipper to the lieutenant to let you hoist your trotters over the gangway.' Seeing the look of puzzlement on his manservant's face, Lear clarifies, 'Military language, Giorgi. He has been asked to report back for duty at the officers' quarters. You do remember that Mr Morris, his uncle, is also a sergeant. I am sure he has military duties to attend to.'

Disappointed to see the young boy go, Lear follows Giorgi as he ascends the steps of the fort very cautiously, one foot at a time. Sitting on the parapet holding his pencil, Lear screws up his eyes and looks out at the river and beyond. On most days, the Kanchenjunga was little more than a phantom presence. Even when they were on the pony cart making their way towards Purnea, the rosy, snowy pale lines of the Himalayas, set against the expanding horizon of the plains, had seemed as unsubstantial as they had first appeared to him sitting on the three-legged sketching stool. In contrast, the fort ahead looks so real that he has to adjust his eyes to the rising solidity of its ramparts – the heaving and gleaming bulk of the sandstone blocks piled one on top of the other.

A single eagle swirling above alights on the branches of a dead tree. In the distance, the braying of donkeys reaches his ears. Under the glorious sky lit up by the early February sun, the waters of the mighty Ganges glide as if there are two rivers instead of one, moving into each other like two fluid sheets, expanding and contracting with each passing moment. Lear sits down on the edge of a block of sandstone. Giorgi places a sheet in front of him. Sun-bleached bones of animals, possibly goats, are arranged in stacks around the shrubs growing on the banks.

Lear begins to sketch vigorously, his pencil moving with machine-like precision. Bold lines appear even where the rapidly moving waters touch the solid, stationary walls. Standing erect, the walls offer bold, vertical lines. Horizontal strokes, with a few swirls and turns, just where the sandstone plunges into the water. He changes his mind twice about positioning the sun above.

A watercolour – that is the ideal medium to catch the splendour of the sky and the intensity of the reflected light on the waters. He wants to get as much detail as possible using his pencil, and so, he begins outlining the architectural features of the fort and the ramparts. The middle ground is so firmly in place here that it appears to dominate the entire scene. Its uncompromising solidity takes him back to the conversation he had with Holman Hunt a week after they had returned from the coast in Hastings. When he saw the completed painting that Hunt had titled *Sunlight on the Sea*, Lear noticed how magnificently his friend had captured the light of the sky and the reflected light on the two flanking hills, fusing the middle ground and the background while retaining their distinctive shapes and positions. Light merely served as a kind of space between moving objects.

'The distinction between the middle ground and background is false, my friend,' Hunt had said in his endearing voice. 'When you are drawing with just a pencil in hand, you are responding to that moment. The spaces you are able to capture on paper are really about the silences that you *hear* at that moment. A lull, space is an interlude between moments. One always draws a line *in* time, but time and space are inseparable.'

He can almost hear Hunt's voice. Was the lull Hunt referred to all about making absence speak? Is absence not about a new – perhaps a more spiritual – meaning of what one called different *grounds*, depending on how you saw, heard and felt between moments? He looks behind at the fields through which he had seen the maimed men enter the fields of mustard. But all that is left is swirling dust that appears to hover over the vast expanse. Not a single figure can be discerned in that haze. The air is still but also filled with muffled sounds.

Gazing at the waters of the Ganges, he suddenly remembers the outlines of the Kanchenjunga he had sketched. In his first attempts, they were little more than scribbly drawings, with some slanting lines in the middle and a few fern-like shapes in the foreground. Preoccupied with the middle ground, he had not remembered Hunt's words.

'Absence! Absence!' He repeats the words to himself, almost mechanically.

He has a view of the river from the two-gun battery and the broken stairs above which the sun moves across the sky on its late winter arc. The sound of the scratching of the pencil follows the rhythm of the distant call of a bird and the uncertain flap on the water. Ah, the porpoises on the river Hoogly as he walked on the *ghat*s on Christmas morning. Giorgi was certain that the sound came from the tide moving in, but Lear *knew* that there were porpoises cavorting in the waters. What he hears now is perhaps the river currents moving in, or perhaps there was *something* coming up for air from the depths below.

The outlines of the ramparts are slowly beginning to take shape as Lear moves his pencil vertically. The sky in front and above his head are two expanses of varying shades of yellow, gold, pink and blue that look like they are reflections of the two rivers below, meeting in indeterminable lines of contact. Lines for the sky are slowly making themselves visible on paper, undulating with each horizontal movement of the pencil. Silence. No real horizon to speak of, no colour still, and yet there is a sense of a limit – somewhere – a space that, when later transferred by colour or even sepia ink, could come close to what he had experienced during his long walks along the shores of Corfu. The scraggy horizon of cliffs that he had drawn and then painted with such delight; the uneven and unbroken lines created by the movement of the sandstone walls and reflected in the moving river now *is* a painting, finished without a sense of finality. Certainly, no distinction can be made or *felt* between beginning and end or between movement and stillness.

Rock and water, water and rock. As his glance moves vertically and then horizontally, he begins to see where the boundaries of light and space embrace each other and become one.

Was this the ideal that Turner had aspired to? All he can think of is Turner's handling of light *through* the medium of paint, his remarkable ability to delineate space that appears somewhere in the distances concealed by light. Even Tennyson had sensed that interval, that in-betweenness.

Break, break, break,
On thy cold gray stones, O Sea
And I would that my tongue could utter
The thoughts that arise in me.

Lear hears himself repeating the lines. The poet's handsome face floats in front of him. But in an instant, his thoughts return to his art. If, after mastering watercolours, he chose to paint in oil, would he not have to find a wealthy patron willing to commission his work? Seeking patrons was always so fatiguing. Perhaps he would ask Northbrook to commission a painting of the fort at Chunar as part of his 'India' collection? Perhaps Lady Waldergrave would show an interest?

He is amused by how quickly an ageing artist like himself, with limited financial resources and aching knees, moves from reflections about art to thoughts about money. The truth of the matter is that working on oil costs money, quite a lot of it. The house in San Remo had already taken out most of his savings. And soon, he would have to settle down, cultivate his own beans, grow old with Cat Foss and Giorgi – that is, if he stayed. Tennyson was fortunate not to have to ever fret over money. But he did not grudge him his fame and fortune. His poetic achievements were unsurpassed, and he deserved the very best from life, including the splendour of Farringford House.

Dismissing his thoughts about money and big houses, Lear picks up his pencil and the folio and walks towards the end of the rampart leading down to the stairs. Giorgi is ahead of him carrying his bag. No alligators or porpoises are to be seen, as they did while crossing the same river in Sahibgunge. The Gangetic scenery there was a pleasure to draw in the full light of the February sun, but it was uncomplicated. He remembers sketching at the *dak bungalow* before catching the train, straining to visualize the movement of the river's currents.

That evening at the *dak bungalow*, he had been woken up in the middle of the night by the sweep of the shadows and the steady sound of the man pulling the cord of the swinging fan. He sat so very still in the far corner of the room. Lear slept fitfully, his mind buzzing with the same questions: Was the man who sat stoically pulling the cord in control of his *own* breath? Were his arms being impelled by a force greater than what his thin arms could exert? Why was his face as empty as the walls around him? The swish of the air, the slight movement of the leaves of the vine that had crept into the inner walls of the veranda, the occasional pause when the punkah slowed down – the scene returns in delirium as Lear sees the light fade and the path ahead appear as a grey tunnel.

Nightfall is imminent. Two shadows – the punkah *and the other, its shadow. Two angels swaying.*

The words he had penned that evening return as the two walk away from the fort. The silhouettes of the citadel's huge multi-tiered ramparts overlooking the river loom in the distance, the steady movement of the arms of the *punkahwallah* and the shadows swinging from one end to the other across the walls return to him.

The two begin to make their way home through the grove of neem trees.

Lear looks around to see if he can still spot the barbets. But they are not visible. Looking back, the red sandstone walls of the fort stand out in the fading light.

Jerusalem from the Mount of Olives, painted in 1859. The pink sandstone, the serrated skies of pink, orange and yellow, the dome of the mosque, a shepherd in the middle foreground, leading his sheep, and in the foreground, the branch of the olive tree in striking green. Then the sense of the dry desert air sending his hat scurrying on the road. The painted scene and the image in his mind's eye swing in unison.

Lying down in bed that evening, Lear sees the flame of the lamp spluttering fitfully. Giorgi fell asleep as soon as his head had touched the pillow. The night before, he heard his gentle cough from the little bed he had arranged at the far end of the room.

The angular contours, the valleys under his eyes and the ravines around his prominent Albanian cheekbones reappear with the same vividness as when the man first showed up at his door in Corfu wearing a black and white scarf. But was Giorgi beginning to show signs of wear and tear? Or had the portrait of the man who always stood silently in the shadows lodged itself in his feverish brain? What kind of heroic resilience had armed the man to suffer in silence and accept his master's plans without raising a single question? How did Lear appear in Giorgi's eyes? Did the man notice the deep hollow that often startled him as he saw his own reflection? Could he accept that the energies of the 'diligent vagabond' – as Tennyson called him – a man intent on travelling, even at the age of sixty-one, for the sake of art, laughter and poetry, were now slowly ebbing? It felt as if he were sitting down in the darkened theatre in Calcutta waiting for the curtains to fall.

Lear turns on his side and pulls the blanket up to his cold chin.

Ann's long fingers hold a little boy's shoulder at the theatre. The thick curtains descend on the stage at the sound of a bell. The ten-year-old has turned his face away from the stage. The claps follow as the lights come back on.

Sleep eludes him. Restless, he turns towards the window. Emerging from the darkness is the face of the maimed soldier turning back to look. Through his entire journey, he had put up with insolent servants, officious babus, noisy porters, industrious gardeners, lazy drivers and silent *punkahwallahs*, exchanging with them half-uttered words and glances. But this was the first time that the gaze of that gouged-out face had emptied his innards, flinging him across continents and years.

Paris, 1859. Maharajah Duleep Singh, hawks and all, dressed in silks and jewels, with a beautiful golden turban wrapped in strings of pearls, the folds of gold, silver, red and pink swishing around him, is stepping out of a plush Paris hotel. Kidnapped from India and exiled when he was only fifteen, the eyes of the tall, handsome, bearded man's eyes strike Lear almost immediately. He is told by a passer-by that the Maharajah owns a collection of jewelled parrots. He is the Black Prince of Perthshire, a favourite of the Prince of Wales, who often goes shooting with the handsome young man.

The magical aura of an exiled Indian prince and the broken face of an Indian soldier…as he shuts his eyes, Lear sees, once again, the battalion moving down the bend and fading into the haze of the yellow mustard fields. The broken ramparts lose their golden light. The soldier's face has merged into the shapes that appear in the late mist gathering from the fields. Could his own *syllablubbery* ever capture the stories that lay behind that face, the disfigured body? He knows that as hard as he tries, he will never be able to animate them on paper, in ink or in portraits and words.

Lear now feels as if his own bones have been broken to pieces and all he is left with are limbs that sway like those of a puppet hanging from a string placed out in one of the shops in Calcutta.

> There was an Old Person of Chester,
> Whom several small children did pester;
> They threw some large stones, which broke most of his bones
> And displeased that Old Person of Chester.

He tosses around and then sits up. No point lying in bed when sleep seems impossible. His old bones ache. His body refuses to obey his will no matter how hard he tries to keep up.

Lushington moves with a confident gait. Long and sturdy. 'Hurry up, Edward. Your bones are surely strong enough to withstand the force of a speedier walk.' The voice comes from a corner of the darkening skies. 'It is getting very late.'

The half-darkness of the room, where they sit drinking claret, is only lit by the curtains catching the moonlight. They sway imperceptibly in the breeze that is wafting through the open window.

Lying down once again, Lear shuts his eyes. Nothing stirs outside the window.

His longing for Lushington was the worm writhing under the wet sand, the truth that he could never share with any of his friends. From the tone of Giorgi's repeated phrase, 'Your friend, the juror,' he guessed that Giorgi perhaps knew more than he ever conveyed.

What made it all so very baffling was the fact that Lushington had *never* ever hinted that he was fully conscious of his feelings towards him. When, on occasions, Lushington went away on his tours, Lear would write how much he missed his company. But never ever dared to use the word *love.* The words he preferred were 'fond, devoted, kind' – words that were as empty as balloons. When Lushington wrote back – which he did very promptly – he sent details about either his family in England or the sights, smells and sounds of his travels. Worse, he detailed the maladies of persons or dying friends with whom Lear was barely acquainted. 'Mrs Cortazzi died peacefully in Paris' were the words with which he began his letter from Paris in 1859. After reading, Lear threw the letter in the fireplace and stepped out for a long walk around the marshes through Potamo. A week after being away for over a month, Lushington returned to join him at dinner. That evening, the conversation centred around the fragments of an obscure Greek poet, pieces recovered in a medieval monastery on an Ionian island. After dinner, he left, but not before complimenting the cook.

From outside, the cricket's chirp combines with the insistent hoots of a night owl.

For you, Edwardus, I shall say no more
Than that your griefs are fudge, yourself a bore:
Return at once cold, stewed, minced, hashed mutton–
To wristbands ever guiltless of a button–
To raging winds and sea, (where don't you wish
Your luck may ever let you catch a fish?)
To make large drawings that nobody will ever buy–
To paint oil pictures which will never dry–
To write new books which nobody will read–
To drink weak tea, on tough old pigs to feed–
Till spring-time brings the birds and leaves and flowers,
And time restores a world of happier hours.

Drifting into sleep, he thinks of travel in the days ahead – another journey by train, first to Allahabad, and then on to Agra to see the Taj. He places his head on the cold pillow and looks at the glass panes of the window – a solid black rectangle against which a large, thick-shelled insect taps constantly as it attempts to escape into the darkness outside.

It is 10 February 1874. He has just enough energy left to pen:

From the two-gun battery so-called, the view of the Ganges is indescribably beautiful, and I wish I could have drawn it; I tried twice but had to give up since the enormous amount of detail in it would have required a far longer time than I could give... Certainly, I never saw a more magnificent river scene than this of the Ganges from Chunar Fort. The richness of the vegetation is unspeakably beautiful, and the immense semicircle of the broad placid Ganges, gorgeous. Came down and walked around the fort to the west side, but the length of the whole is too great for a drawing.

'Will you please shut your window, Giorgi? The night moths might enter the room.'

In the room, Giorgi snores, his body wrapped snuggly in his favourite Witney blanket.

5

CURTIS ELLSWORTH'S LITTLE GIRL, ANNE, observes Lear drawing an owl and pulls her stool very close to his chair. 'Oh, please also draw a pussycat! You know how they went to sea in a boat one day with plenty of honey and money wrapped up in a five-pound note.' Shaking her blonde curls that fall unevenly over her shoulders, she opens a clean, new copy of *A Book of Nonsense,* and turning its pages hastily, points her finger to the 'The Owl and the Pussycat'.

'This is my *favouritest* poem, and my best friend here, Manjoo, loves it too and has learnt it by heart, although she does not go to *my* school.'

Manjoo stands very close to Anne. Petite, with quick eyes, her long hair is tied up in a ponytail that she flicks with every turn of her head. Anne is dressed in a crisp green frock with a white frill. Manjoo wears a faded yellow cotton frock with a white muslin scarf tied diagonally across her chest and over her hips. The sunlight dances on both their faces.

Lear and Giorgi had arrived at the little hotel in Allahabad the day before. Situated close to the banks of the Ganges, Kelner's

Hotel, run by Mr Curtis Ellsworth and his wife, Lizzy, is a modest brick *bungalow* with a rusted tin roof. Mr Ellsworth's residence, a larger house, in brick, with freshly painted walls, is encircled by a small garden lined with rows of peas and carrots. The brightly painted gate to the hotel leads to an inner yard, where roses and hollyhocks grow in clusters.

Standing on the long, covered veranda, Lear had glanced at the picture-perfect garden and immediately spotted a giant grandiflora rising above the bushes of Chinese tea roses. 'Such unusual beauty. Must get it down on paper,' he muttered. However, his first impressions of Allahabad had not been favourable. *The ever-odious succession of right-angled roads with fearful* bungalows, *barracks and buildings of all sorts, each one uglier than the former, here and there one of tolerable form and proportion,* he wrote in his notebook. But the view of the junction of the two rivers, the Ganges and Jumna, had not disappointed. A grand sight, the view of the river here was similar to that of the rivers coming up close to the walls of the fort at Chunar.

Dinner was full of new delights: cabbage soup, roast mutton, peas and carrots and a lovely plum pudding.

Now, with breakfast – of toast, eggs, jam, tea and slices of freshly cut guava – over, Lear feels refreshed and happy to be surrounded by two active girls who run around and chatter.

'*What* kind of name is Derry Down Derry?' asks Anne when he tells her that it was *one* of his many names. 'You have more than one name? Manjoo calls me Titli, and that means a butterfly.' She peers intently at his eyeglasses.

'Will I dance? Will I dance?' Manjoo joins in, her eyes sparkling with joy. 'I sing "Owl and Pussycat" in Hindoostani. You understand?'

A short musical recitation follows, in a language that appears to Lear to be little more than a steady flow of sibilants strung together by the rhythm awakened by the steady tapping of the girl's left foot. Swinging her hips, raising her arms and periodically pointing her right finger to her nose, she repeats, 'his nose', the only words he can make sense of, the hissing getting more marked as she raises her voice.

Not to be outdone, Anne raises her voice.

'Enough singing. I will *now* teach you how to cook.' In the midst of Manjoo's intermittent 'You are! You are!' is Anne, listing – in an insistent manner – the ingredients for what she announces to be her 'grandmother's *English* soup'. 'Cabbage, pig feet, pepper, carrot.' Then she pauses, looks at Lear's eager face and continues, 'Eyes of frog, skin of gecko,' and here, she stops, her lips quivering, then continues, 'Tongue of evil Queen, tail of *Jiggywiggyrooten*. You'll find them growing in my garden, under the hibiscus tree.'

Not to be outdone, Manjoo rattles off a list of ingredients with rhyming nonsensical names. '*Cabbazelligwig, parsnipperilia, celeriwishwash…*' While she speaks, Anne moves around busily, handing out imaginary plates, napkins, knives and forks. 'The knife on the right side only, Manjoo, and the fork on the left, and do learn to fold the napkins properly!' She repeats, 'If you drop any of the soup on the table, you will need another big napkin to wipe the mess.'

'Gutter soup. Gutter soup! Die if I eat!' Manjoo makes a face at Anne before raising an imaginary spoon to her mouth, out of which flows a torrent of words in Hindoostani. They sound like rifle shots fired by the Volunteer Corps!

Lear thinks of the last evening they had spent in Chunar, when, after dinner, the constant tapping of the beetle on the windowpane had kept him awake most of the night. As he lay on his hard bed, it felt as if someone in a distant land was attempting to communicate using a telegraph code. Now, the children's babble takes him back to that tapping, to that flapdoodle world from whose core the creatures had appeared among the bushes a week before and were now summoning him back to their world.

'Do you know about flowers that grow in old shoes? They smell like hot chilli. Hot, hot, hot. Have you ever seen a snail that carries a bottle of jam on its back? It goes pat, pat, rat a tat.'

Anne's earnest face beckons Lear.

'Can you please help me draw the snail?'

Manjoo speaks very softly as she hands him an empty jar. 'Bottle like this. I draw bottle. You draw snail.'

The snail takes shape in a minute. A face with a wide smile appears on its tiny head, and two enormous eyes with eyeglasses protrude from the top.

Manjoo struggles with the jar, drawing what looks like a teapot with a giant spout. Anne picks up Manjoo's half-finished drawing and holds it close to her nose.

'It looks more like a pumpkin with a nose!'

Snatching the drawing from Anne, Manjoo runs to the far end of the veranda and then walks stealthily as if she were a cat, speaking in low tones in Hindoostani. Anne begins to translate Manjoo's words.

'From the yellow jar comes the yellow snail, from the yellow snail comes…'

The shadows stretch on the long veranda, and the mynahs begin to sing from the tops of the trees. Giorgi and Lear find themselves in peals of laughter as Anne tries to pirouette, and after a minute, sits on the floor, dizzy, laughing uncontrollably. Giorgi, who hovers over the two girls, smiles, and picking up *A Book of Nonsense*, looks at its cover. 'You are quite a celebrity in these parts, Master. A beautiful edition this is. I can smell its freshly cut pages.'

A flock of birds lands on the branches of the grandiflora, and a giant lizard stretches out its long body on the grass.

The afternoon at Knowsley with Lord Derby's children flashes across Lear's mind, seeing Anne stretched on the floor looking quite dazed.

Walking around the menagerie, they gaze excitedly at the crowned pigeons, pintails and a medley of curious-looking birds. The shiny green turtle, climbing out of the little pond to lie next to the crowned pigeon. All around, shrieks of delight. The little boy pretends to be like a pigeon strutting around. He loses his balance and falls to the ground. Peals of laughter.

It was very much a day like this one – the sound of children laughing and running around, the hydrangea bushes bursting with colour and the tall plane trees casting deep shadows on the rockery. Soon after, he received an invitation to a special tea ceremony at Lord Derby's. *A Book of Nonsense* lay on the grass next to a patch of daffodils, and the children surprised him by putting up a short enactment of 'There Was a Young Lady'.

As he waits for the performance to commence, his ears catch the strains of strange music, perhaps coming from a stringed instrument. The Derby children are ready for action. The ten-year-old sharpens her chin with her little fingers and strums on an imaginary harp. She then proceeds to sit on a stool while the others begin dancing around her. The ground is strewn with bits of dry grass and petals of daisies. The garden boy is sitting on a low stool strumming a Moorish guitar. The Young Lady of Dorking walks in, wearing a very large straw bonnet and large shoes. The children rush after her. 'Back to Dorking! Back to Dorking'

they scream. Off she runs towards the arboretum, pursued by the rest.
The grandfather laughs till tears roll out of his eyes. The next day, Lear
receives a hundred pounds for his drawings of the birds.

Lear finds the two girls staring at him, waiting for his next move.

'Wait, I have a poem for you.' Taking off his hat, he begins to
recite, in slow, measured tones:

There was an Old Person whose habits,
Induced him to feed upon Rabbits;
When he'd eaten eighteen, he turned perfectly green,
Upon which he relinquished those habits.

Anne looks up at Lear.

'*Re-lin-quished*? All squished up! We have a few rabbits in our
garden. Shall I tell you how I cook squished-up rabbit? You need
ten fat rabbits!'

'Ten! I am not sure if you need *that* many. I am an old man now,
and we will be just three at the table for dinner tonight.'

Anne taps her fingers on the table.

'In that case, I will make pumpkin soup.'

Then, turning back to Lear, she says, with a quizzical look on
her face, 'Why did the Old Person turn *green*?'

'Because he put too much spinach in his soup.'

He picks up the copy of *Nonsense* lying on the floor.

'Here is a poem about you, Anne.'

There was an Old Lady of Chertsey,
Who made a remarkable curtsey;
She twirled round and round, till she sunk underground,
Which distressed all the people of Chertsey.

The two girls look at each other, and after a pause, break into wild laughter, slapping each other's faces with their small fingers.

'Curtsey? My daddy is *called* Curtis!' Anne is so excited that she is beginning to sound like a screaming budgie.

'Did the Old Lady come out on the other side of the earth? Were her clothes filthy?'

'Wait, here is *another* limerick.'

Lear feels the sensation of being on a moving train as he recites, one after another, his limericks, as if invisibly propelled by the force of moving wheels and by the voices of people around, chattering, hollering and singing. Travelling from Jubbulpore to Cawnpore, he began scribbling the first lines, one fragment after another, finishing them while waiting on the platform. But when the two went looking for a post office, they lost their way and found themselves standing next to a large gunnery. Eventually, Giorgi slipped them into the postbox placed outside the gate of Kelner's Hotel.

Human chatter and machine talk: the clickity-click of voices, the whistle, the wind swishing outside the moving train. As Lear prepares himself to recite another limerick, the vision of the Moorish tower in Vauxhall Garden flashes before his eyes.

A clear and chilly October evening. Ann and he stand in astonishment seeing the undaunted Mr Blackmore make his terrific ascent up the tower, surrounded by flames of fire. Drums beat along with trumpets and bells. An outing he had been looking forward to for many months. All summer, his fits came one after the other. There he is, after remaining in bed for weeks, surrounded by peals of artillery. The fireworks – in red, blue and green – flash in the pitch-black sky. Ann's face is full of wonder and amazement. She pulls him up close and kisses him on his cheeks. He is filled with unmeasurable joy.

The faces of the two young girls sitting in rapt attention, conjuring up a world that had vanished for him years ago. He is on one of Brunel's fantastic steamships, embarking on a voyage back in time and seeing children waving from strange shores.

The lines flow while the two girls sit absorbed. 'There was an Old Man who said, "Hush!"' Lear's voice begins to sound portentous. The girls raise their fingers to their lips. 'There was an Old Man of Vesuvius,' he continues, sniffing the air. The girls bring out their handkerchiefs. 'There was a Young Lady of Bute who plays a silver-gilt flute.' Taking up the book, he rapidly turns the pages. The two girls break into a caper.

Anne flutters her eyes listening to 'There Was a Young Lady Whose Eyes'.

After he has recited the first two lines of 'There was an Old Person of Sparta', Ann stops him.

'Can I tell you my own story now? My daddy has one daughter – it's me, it's I! The girl who loves to read poems and do puzzles. There was one son of the man of Sparta who disappeared behind a bush and did not come out for ten years!'

Pausing, she settles down on her haunches and begins:

The other five sons play cricket
But no one can even take a wicket!
One is very tall,
The other very small.

She is unstoppable.

The daughter loves to eat croquets.
Carries two in her pockets.

One daughter and five sons
Share a basket of hot cross buns.

There is a long pause before Anne declares, 'Well, that is the end of *my* poem. Think I like it better than yours.'

Meanwhile, inspired by Anne's rhymes, Manjoo straightens her pleats and begins singing in Hindoostani. Anne translates, explaining that Manjoo's song is about sweet baby Krishna stealing butter from his mother's kitchen and hiding in the cowshed.

After Manjoo has finished, she takes Anne by the hand, and the two rush into the orchard and run around the large mango tree.

When they return, Lear asks, 'Have you heard about the Old Man of Calcutta?'

Anne is quick to respond. 'Calcutta! Calcutta! I know Calcutta. My grandmother lives there, you know, Mr Lear, in a house with sixteen cats. She loves to make my English soup. But she is an old, old lady!'

The limerick about the old man choking on a great bit of muffin elicits a long-drawn scream from Anne followed by, 'Never eat a muffin, never eat a muffin.'

Meanwhile, Manjoo repeats, '*Kalkatta! Kalkatta*,' prompting Lear to say, 'Ask Manjoo if she can teach me a bit of Hindoostani spoken in Kalkatta.'

'I am English and Manjoo is Indian. Manjoo will teach you Hindoostani, and then I will teach you *proper* English, the kind that my mother teaches me from *Rhymes and Roses*.' Anne wipes her face vigorously with the hem of her skirt.

Not wishing to miss a single moment of the time allotted to her, Manjoo begins, 'A is for *anaar*, B for *bakri*, C for *koel*, D for darling, E for elephant, F for fool, H for *haathi*…'

Their laughter echoes as the two dart about like two squirrels, chasing each other around the pomegranate tree. Breathless, they sit silently on the ground, their faces turned up to the sky as if silently taking in the scents of the garden air. The light of the fading sun throws long shadows on the gravelled ground.

Ockham Park. Mrs Gaskell's two daughters sit in Stephen Lushington's large drawing room. The curtains sway ever so lightly in the breeze. The voices of the two young women rise as they sing while their mother, sitting across in a straight-backed chair, looks at them in rapt attention. They talk animatedly about Manchester, about the virtues of Latitudinarian Christianity. Mrs Gaskell's gentle but steadfast voice describing the working poor of the north flows through the room. The grave Stephen Lushington directs his gaze at Mrs Gaskell's wide forehead and her kindly face. A strange calm descends as soon as the two girls pause.

The voices of the two young girls echo in his ears although he cannot recall the song they were singing. Holding Anne and Manjoo by their slender waists, Lear draws them close to his knees. 'Wait, I will tell you a story about Ann. Ann – not Anne with an "e". It's a lovely story about my older sister, Ann, a pretty creature as ever the sun shone on.'

The two girls listen with open-mouthed wonder as he tells them about a sister who drew beautiful pictures but was strong enough to ward off a raging bull with a spade, who loved to dress in her favourite red frock, who danced like an angel, played on the harp and gazed at the open ocean when she was not working in the garden.

There was a young lady of Portugal,
Whose ideas were excessively nautical,

She climbed up a tree,
To examine the sea,
But declared she would never leave Portugal.

'Is *Portoo* a country?' Anne plays with Lear's laces. 'Why did she never want to leave *Portoo-girl?*'

'A narrow and long country Portugal is, and the young lady did not wish to leave it because she hated the idea of going away from her brother, who lived all alone at home in that country. He was very small and could not sleep at night without her.'

Ann. Ann. Although she had soothed him as a young girl with her gentle voice, as the years went by, the tremors in her voice began to grate in his ears. As much as he adored Ann, he could never have been like his beloved sister. A mental traveller of great talent and imagination, she had never allowed herself to leave known shores, never felt the thrill of resting after walking uphill in fog and mist, nor ever savoured the silence after the echoes had ceased while walking on the mountain paths of Albania. No, Ann loved being at home in England and never wished to go anywhere else. During her last visit to London to meet him, she had tried her hand at colouring a sketch he had made of Jerusalem. They were sitting in the little room that overlooked the narrow garden filled with peonies. Her eyes had lit up when he had complimented her. She was past sixty. Her vision was not as good as it had been before, and she often woke up at night, coughing. Secretly, he wished that she would go and live with Sarah, who was still single and a few years away from becoming Sarah Street and moving to New Zealand with her new husband.

But Ann could never leave, go away...

Lear feels a gentle tug. Manjoo is pulling at his cuffs very gently and is pointing at the page showing a young person in red wearing a large bonnet.

'The young lady of *Portoo's* best friend was a young person in red. Her bonnet was made of leather and ribbons.' Lear's finger is gently tracing the rim of the bonnet.

'Did the lady of *Portoo* also wear bonnet?'

'Sadly, she did not have the money to buy bonnets, so she covered her head with an old and tattered woollen scarf. Her mother was poor, very, very poor.'

Lear turns to Giorgi, who is sitting on a stool, mending his shirt. Giorgi smiles.

'We were twenty-one, in all, I was told.' Lear rises from the stool and faces Giorgi. 'To be honest, twenty or twenty-one. Never really counted. Ann, Sarah, Eleanor, Jane, Harriet, Henry, Olivier and many others. My brother Charles, four years older than I, went to Africa as a missionary when he was just eighteen and married a very hot-headed native girl. Ann, a lot older than I, called me Biffin. She helped Charles with his spellings when he was about six or seven. Ann was like a mother to us.'

Giorgi remembers the room in Corfu overlooking the cape, where letters from Ann lay on the table for weeks before his master opened them to read.

Lear gazes at the faces of Anne and Manjoo.

The slender Ann holds the young boy in her arms and walks around the house. When he cries, she wipes his tears with the ends of her long, grey frock. When she smiles at him, her broad nose wrinkles up. 'The park has a new cage with two monkeys. Would you like to see them?'

Ann sits by the fireside in a near-empty room, Lear imagines, reading his letters written during his travels abroad. The dying embers in the small fireplaces next to her give off a strange odour.

Twelve years back, on a chilly spring day, he had opened the letter that was placed on the old, creaky desk.

At ten past seven in the evening, she joined her maker. Funeral arrangements were made by the vicar and the baker's wife.

Regret and desolation. How often he would pick up his pen to write to her – and then stop.

The shadows of the trees are beginning to lengthen.

Father has not returned even once after he walked out of the broken door that spring morning. A stray dog waits at the door for his scraps. Mother remains as silent as ever. Days are turning into months. Gone to help Aunt Stella pick strawberries from her fields, Mother says. Then, one day, while walking in the park, Eleanor bends down to whisper into his ears, 'Debtors' prison. That is where he now lives.' The befuddled, awkward four-year-old who always dropped his books and pencils while getting ready to leave for school simply stares at Eleanor's face. She does not explain. Just hurries him back to the house with the broken door.

Anne and Manjoo are silent. It is beautiful outside, the spring sun slipping behind the mango and tamarind trees while butterflies flutter from one bush to the next. Manjoo chatters away in Hindoostani, frequently slipping into English. The birds in the bushes join Manjoo's chatter, and before long, the air is filled with songs and squeaks.

Lear's mind is swerving back to the muddle of new sounds around him and to the churning sounds of many alien tongues that stirred his imagination as he had walked through the *bazaars* of Calcutta.

It's odd that Lushington, who loved the ancient language, was always fazed by the sounds of modern Greek.

'The sounds never quite match the sense,' he had remarked to him, hastily retreating into his chambers after a brief meeting with a well-dressed native Greek who had spent ten minutes going over the fine points of his legal case.

Giorgi, who preferred to keep himself busy – as he was a few minutes back, darning and thinking about the beaches of Corfu – plays with Manjoo's pigtails. The new sounds do not bother him much. Quite the contrary, he enjoys following the movement of lips of folks who speak alien tongues.

The two girls are sitting under a towering bush of red bougainvillea, from where Lear can hear Anne sing, '*They daaanced by the light of the moon, The moon, The moon, They daaanced by the light of the moon.*'

The pages of *A Book of Nonsense* flap in the breeze.

Breakfast time at the fashionable hotel on the Italian Riviera. The seven-year-old Daisy, Terry and the tiny Alfred listen in rapt attention to funny rhymes. 'Derry Down Derry: what kind of name is that?' The little girl's blond pigtail swings as she bends to have a closer look at the picture of the fat man. Daisy sings a song about four frogs dancing in the moonlight.

Lear picks up his pencil and feels the tip. The thought of seeing a line appear on a blank sheet and watching it turn into a remembered landscape or a funny-looking cat makes his fingers throb.

'Now let us get back to my drawing. I have just finished the owl, and now, I will draw the pussycat. Why don't we draw together? Here is a poem I wrote when I was a young man. It is called "An Old Man with a Beard".'

Clearing his voice, he begins:

There was an Old Man with a beard,
Who said, It is just as I feared!—
Two Owls and a Hen, four Larks and a Wren,
Have all built their nests in my beard.

'Look at me, I have a big beard. Can you draw it?'

The girls do not move. The outline of the Old Man begins to take shape as he runs the tip of the pencil over a sheet of paper. When he is finished, he hands the pencil to Manjoo and nudges her to draw the beard.

A confused swirl appears around the face of the Old Man.

'Now you can draw a little hen sitting on his beard.'

Manjoo hesitates, so Lear guides her fingers.

After a few minutes, Anne joins them.

Two little circles and a triangle appear on the beard.

'The owl and the wren. They are good friends. But let us not forget the larks.' Noticing the expressions on the faces of the two girls, Lear adds, 'Larks are little English birds.'

Out of the nest of squiggly lines appears just a beak.

'Maybe we should put a peacock here instead of the larks.'

Seeing a proud peacock appear perched on the beard next to the two circles, the two girls clap with glee.

'You made a *real* peacock. A peacock with such a long tail!' Anne's eyes flash with delight. 'You are the *real* Old Man, are you not? Can I touch your beard? It's like a big bush? Does your mummy like your beard?'

Manjoo, who has been sitting quietly in the corner, bursts out, 'Beautiful peacock. *More, more, more*. Peacock dance when rain falls. Pit, pat. Dance, dance, dance.'

This time, she remains sitting as she repeats, 'Dance, dance, dance,' rummaging through her bag, out of which come her drawings, done in pencil. A crocodile-like creature with long arms, a fish riding the back of what looks like a camel, and a butterfly with the face of a little girl in stick-like pigtails.

'Did you draw these? They are much better than any of my drawings.'

Manjoo blushes and hesitates before handing them to Lear.

'They all live in the forest. I can take you there. Lots of funny animals in the forest.'

Dinner at John's Gould. Someone at the table remarks that his drawings are all about the world of oddities – and of quirky creatures that appear in dreams. A young gentleman with a small chin says, 'Charles Darwin.' He is assisting Mrs John Gould with her drawings for her husband's A Century of Birds from the Himalaya Mountains. *Mrs Gould lists the ingredients for making bean soup. Someone chatters about the virtues of terrace gardening.*

Forty years ago.

When Lear's attention turns to Anne, he finds her still gazing intently at his beard. Undoubtedly, his beard had been the source of great curiosity for the many Indians he had encountered. In Colgong, while they were making their way to the Ganges, a young bare-bodied man dressed in a short *dhoti* was intrigued by the sight of two European men strolling on a deserted road. Lear's beard caught his eyes. A holy man in breeches and a hat, he must have thought.

'*Rusta kai Gunga?*' Hearing Lear speak Hindoostani, the man had smiled and asked them to follow him. The young man could not take his eyes off the beard. They walked down a narrow side road, and before long, the thin blue line of the river had appeared between the trees.

That was the first time Lear had used what Evelyn once called 'rough-and-ready' Hindoostani.

'Just three words, strung together, not very laboriously, I must add, made sense to a simple country bumpkin,' he recalls telling Giorgi that evening after they had returned to their rooms. Giorgi's wry smile had indicated that he was not fully convinced of his master's skills.

'They must have thought they were doing a pious act by helping an English *sadhu* find the right spot by the river where he could beg for alms. Never before have I seen two Indians look so bewildered when you used the identical words to ask for directions to the market in Jubbulpore. Do you remember?'

Manjoo holds her English primer very close to her face, her sharp voice, repeating, 'What is *this*? What is *that*? Is it a cat? Is *she* Pat?' while Anne, posing as her teacher, waves her raised right forefinger from side to side: 'Wrong, wrong *and* wrong! *You* native. Stupid, you are. A donkey, *gadhaa*. I am *English*.'

Manjoo's eyes flash with anger. '*You* drank tea with Queen of England? Eat minced pie? You do sums? Plus and minus? Count with fingers?'

Early summer. Sunday, after church. A pot of tea sits on the table, but there is nothing to eat. Charles's tutor has just left, complaining that the little boy was not keeping up with his arithmetic. Florence and Harriet immediately pounce on the nine-year-old and reprimand him for not learning his tables. Harriet's voice looms, 'You will be no good when you grow up. We will teach you the tables – from three into three to nine into nine. Listen very carefully. We know everything.' Charles ignores the sisters, and picking up the scissors lying on the table, starts cutting strips of paper and arranging them on the floor.

The clanging from the far end of the garden mixes with the voices of the two girls. In the trees, parrots gurgle, whistle and squawk. At the far end, a young man saws the branches of a tree. From the well comes the clank of the pail being raised by a pulley. The splash of water spilling out of the pail, more clanging, the cracking of a branch falling, the scrunch of boots. And in the midst of it, someone shouts, 'Curtis! Curtis!'

Early in the morning, the train has pulled into the Cawnpore station. He stands amidst the clanking of the wheels, the hissing of steam and the shouting of coolies. *Immense confusion; no luggage. Supposed all right and booked and labelled in Jubbulpore, but here, there is not a bag in sight found among the crates and boxes lying on the platform. The hunched young ADC appears and takes him to a room where a large Indian man is seated behind a large desk. A large cap in black with braiding on the peak, gold piping around and embroidered 'Station Master' lettering sits on his head.*

'Mr Edward Lear? Lear? Leer? Lear with an "a" or "e"? "E" and then "a"? What luggage? Receipt? Tin cases or leather? With or without inscription? Two bedrolls? Please also mention in complaint form: Morning train from Jubbulpore. Two signatures and dates, please. And full address.' *The stationmaster's closely cropped whiskers twitch as he shuts his ledger book. A young railway official comes up from behind and whispers something into the stationmaster's ear. He immediately straightens his coat and tie.*

'The Most Excellent Viceroy's special guest? I see. I see.' *His smile widens till the whiskers stop twitching and the eyes beam from his deeply tanned face.* 'The East Indian Railway Company is a company of great reputation and impeccable service. Been with the Company for exactly seventeen years.'

Another train clanks out of the station. Hands waving goodbye. The fruit seller picks up his basket.

'Chitta Biswas, our humble servant. Calcutta, my home. My BA, sir, from the most exceptional university – Calcutta University. William Wordsworth's poetry fills me with wonder – and Carlyle's prose – who can match his brilliance?'

On the platform, a turbaned man leads a red-capped monkey dressed up as a young boy. Through a hole in his tattered green trousers pokes out a thin tail. The crowd gathers around as the man sings. Screeches. Acrobatics. Dance. Monkey falls on its back. 'Punchinello... Panch-i-nello... nello... Blind, blind, blind.' The man pats the head of his monkey. Queer, queer, indeed. Punch and Judy on an Indian railway platform?

The Indian stationmaster drones on, 'Lord Northbrook, the most eminent Viceroy of India, the best that India has had in recent years. Bridge ironwork brought from England stolen by the evil mutineers... the chief engineer, a good friend of his uncle in Allahabad... Winter, without doubt, best time to travel.'

A young Indian man, a very self-conscious junior, comes up and asks the stationmaster something about taking the Viceroy's guests to a hotel. Both immediately switch to Hindoostani. Then the senior raises his voice and gesticulates wildly. 'Germany's Hotel! Germany's Hotel. How many times I have told you. Bay-wa-koof. Good-for-nothing fellow. Most inefficient. Cannot follow basic English, but what to do? Indians!' His face is half contorted with rage. Through all of this, Giorgi sits on one of the tin cases, looking at the monkey performing tricks on the railway platform. Unusually cold morning in Cawnpore.

The two girls have settled down with their pet squirrel, which had earlier been scurrying all around the covered veranda. The shadows deepen, and the garden in the inner yard comes alive with the chirping of small, quivering chipmunks. Then, quite unexpectedly, silence descends on the garden just before the clock inside strikes four. A young woman wearing a long, pink skirt and pale blue blouse, and carrying a pink parasol, strides up the garden pathway and hands a large cloth bag to Anne.

'Missy *baba*, this is for your mummy. Looks like your daddy is not at home. I have been calling out to him. Have to hurry now. No time for a chat. Dick, the bloody bugger has gone to Agra without telling me, and now I do not know what to do about the key.' She looks harried. Tall and fair-skinned, dark eyes, her pale yellow scarf tied over her head, she looks up at Giorgi, smiles and says, 'Miss Plummer. I am Anne's singing teacher.' After Lear has introduced himself and Giorgi, she picks up one of the drawings, exclaiming, 'Hilarious! Did you do them? The girls love to draw.'

She draws a chair and sits at the far end of the veranda.

'Please tell Mummy quick, quick.' Anne rushes in with the bag.

'An East Indian, you can tell,' Lear whispers to Giorgi. 'Did you not catch the lovely musical tones in her voice? A touch of Welsh, I presume. And what a striking face. Those dark eyes and rosy cheeks. Hunt would have paid for his own passage to come to India just to paint a portrait of Miss Plummer sitting by the bougainvillea, with her hands folded on her lap and with Anne's pet squirrel squatting by her side.' He hears someone shouting from the kitchen, and soon after, sees Miss Plummer leaving from the back door of the kitchen, walking down the path and closing the garden gate very gently. Giorgi sits at the far end of the garden and picks up Lear's boots, ready to give them a quick polish.

'Miss Plummer lives near the church and makes scones and *bhaji* for me on Saturdays.' Anne bounds out of the kitchen door like a little buck.

'Scones and *what*?' Lear's words are within hearing distance of Giorgi.

'A savoury,' Giorgi comments, giving Lear's boots a last-minute vigorous polishing. 'I remember asking the man selling fried fritters near the big flower market in Bombay, and he said *bhaji*.'

The beautiful lilt in Miss Plummer's words seems to linger in the air that is now full of the dying calls of birds returning to their nests. The children are colouring pictures. Picking up his notebook, Lear turns the pages absent-mindedly, stopping to read something that he wrote weeks ago, before they reached Calcutta.

'Of course, Dahlia Drayton. That's who Miss Plummer reminds me of – the lady accompanying Mr Drayton of Somerset in Ranigunge,' he whispers.

In an instant, out went the tall figure of Miss Plummer and in walked the petite Dahlia Drayton. It was as if the two were seated on a carousel going round and round with a gentle swing and he was a mere lad standing by, staring. Miss Plummer and Dahlia Drayton. Miss Plummer and Dahlia Drayton.

Rose by 5 a.m. in a fuss about being in time for the train. Got some tea and came to Ranigunge station, where the stationmaster handed two tickets. Much picturesque scenery and increasing variety of foliage, very luxurious vegetation. Arrived there 4.40 p.m., no trouble in getting luggage, to my surprise. Williams Hotel is close by, and to all outward appearance, a tolerably nice and comfortable one. (Anticipations since fully confirmed by fact.) Two good rooms were got and put in order. Giorgi dined solo. Party, at dinner, possibly wife, with the half-English speech and queer ways of East Indians. The gent was intelligent and agreeable, and we talked no end.

Lear had picked up his notebook and was turning the pages rapidly. The ink must have leaked from his pen. Several large blotches appear on the page that he had penned these words on.

How could one forget Dahlia Drayton, her quivering lips, the pearls that winked and gleamed on her neck?

The shadow of the lampshade fell on the wall, and there is a faint smell of lavender in the air. A pale, lean, athletic man in his mid-forties, outpost Indian Anglo, Mr John Drayton is dressed for dinner in a dark blue suit and shoes that sparkle. He speaks in clipped tones about his career in India working for the East Indian Rail Company. 'I am here to visit the mines. Our company has a contract with the coalfield.' As soon as they settle on the sofa, a young brunette enters, dressed in a floral, long, flowing pink skirt, with big lapels and ruffles at the waist. The pale cream blouse also has ruffles at the neck. A string of pearls intertwined with silver drops sits tightly on her neck. She rubs the ring on her finger. Smiling at Lear, she takes a seat at the far end of the room. The vision in pink is Dahlia Drayton.

'Tiring business, travelling to these parts. We were delayed this morning arriving at the hotel from our dak bungalow. The carriage man lost his way, and it took him more than an hour to find his way back into Ranigunge.'

Mr Drayton looks nervously at the kitchen door. The aroma of freshly baked meat pies seeps into the room. The lady in ruffles bends down to pull the straps of her white kitten-heel shoes. 'A pleasure to meet you, Mr Lear. Sorry, my posterior hurts excessively today. The blessed thing – the coach sent by Yule to drive us to Ranigunge! What junk. No cushions. Did you also take a coach to get here?' Before Lear can respond, her eyes flash, and out comes a volley of English, sprinkled very generously with words that are assembled like pieces of a jigsaw puzzle. 'The coach driver, a gawk, no sense of direction. 'Member, John'. 'Member?' I tell the bloody man, "Are you playing marbles with me, behaving like that?" And my, he did have a grog shop gob. Would have given him a slipperwack, if I was in Calcutta.' The words are like eddies in a stream, slipping and sliding, slithering, and occasionally tumbling out of unknown pits.

Mr Drayton sips his beer without a care in the world. Dahlia rises from her chair, walks to the dining table, draws the chair, sits down very gently, picks up her napkin and cries out, 'Boy, what's for dinner?'

Someone is hammering just outside the window, drowning Drayton's west country voice. Owen's College, and then India. An apprentice in the

city of Cawnpore. The Mutiny. He flees to Calcutta. Dahlia Drayton,
his first love, walks on the banks of the Hoogly. Mother in Somerset
has a fit reading the son's letter. Dahlia Drayton, the daughter of a
Eurasian, a ticket collector. Mother, a seamstress – not a very desirable
family. Drayton has the look of a young Englishman who had done
quite well for himself.

Dahlia's voice rises above the hammering. 'Have you seen the
blessed kitchen here? Had a peep in. Glad I did. The dekchis are all
black! Uff, man, the masala *stored in broken jars. The meat safe full of*
boochies. The runaway, Jack, is just outside the kitchen. Just imagine!
A'bli the manager is on leave, leaving the place in charge of a dirty
chokra boy who just sits and stares when you ask him anything. When
the cat is away, the mouse can play.'

Lear suddenly hears his stomach grumble. He wouldn't mind
a bite to eat but decides to wait. Anne and Manjoo are reading a
story from *A Pretty Little Pocket-Book.* Anne is explaining the moral
of the poem, 'Hoop and Hide'. Manjoo's confusion shows in her
eyes and the tone of her questions. 'Carefulness? Very long word.
Flies? Many fly? Like bird?'

Like this afternoon, that evening with Dahlia Drayton,
Lear had found himself riveted to the onslaught of new sounds
and words that came out of her pretty tinted lips. He had felt
as if tiny cannonballs were bouncing off the walls, setting off
an ungovernable chain of sensory associations in his brain. The
young woman's arched eyebrows, her gestures, the tone of her
voice and the half-recognizable words had made him feel as if he
was listening to two voices simultaneously, an adult's and a child's,
both intertwined to evoke an unheard-of melody. Strains of opera,
ballad, comic song – the song of the wanderer's lost girl. A full-
breasted woman crooning with her eyes closed, a cat looking for

her lost kittens, a jester entertaining the Queen. Very queer. Very happily queer indeed.

Anne pats Lear on the shoulder. 'Mr Lear, are you falling asleep? Dinner is ready. Today we are having,' she stops and giggles. '*Dawl* rice and stewed pipkins and *momlette*,' adding, 'I will tell you all about stewed pipkins later.'

Lear looks at her face, smiles and says with a wink, 'Do I have to crawl for my *dawl*?'

Slowly, Lear makes his way into the dining room. 'Babies crawl. You are too old to crawl, but you draw very well,' he hears Anne saying as she picks up a plate from the table and looks at her face reflected in its polished surface.

It was a foolish thought, but there within my brain it wrought, that I had studied the lingo before I came to India. That night, sitting at his desk, pen in hand, he gazes at the words before him. Snatches of Anne's singing reach his ears from the open window. *Oh, I do like to be beside the seaside...* But soon, the buzzing, tumultuous world – of unfamiliar words and the steady hum of even stranger creatures – drowns Anne's voice.

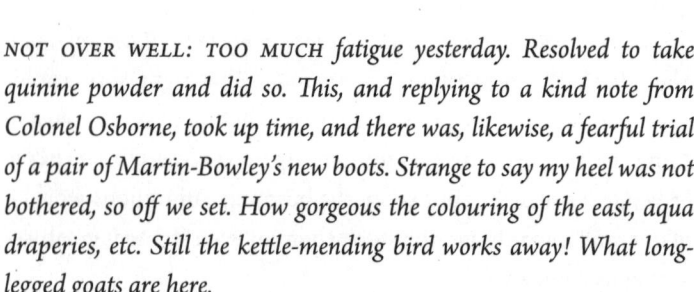

6

NOT OVER WELL: TOO MUCH *fatigue yesterday. Resolved to take quinine powder and did so. This, and replying to a kind note from Colonel Osborne, took up time, and there was, likewise, a fearful trial of a pair of Martin-Bowley's new boots. Strange to say my heel was not bothered, so off we set. How gorgeous the colouring of the east, aqua draperies, etc. Still the kettle-mending bird works away! What long-legged goats are here.*

Sitting in a large room at the Gwalior Residency, elegantly done up in swathes of silk, damask and velvet, Lear turns the pages of his notebook before looking at the sketches he had made of Agra and of the fort at Gwalior. A giant bed and a large table with several inkstands sit at the other end. The searing heat that day had made him want to seek shelter indoors, where he could just put his feet up and sip cold lemonade. The long-legged goats can wait to be sketched!

Somewhere in the garden are children, laughing, their voices wafting in through the open door, reminding him of the two girls who sat on the veranda chattering away, singing and drawing pictures. The journey from the Residency in Dholepur to Gwalior had taken an entire day. Glittering in blue velvet, the eleven-year-old Rajah of Dholepur had greeted them in English. Crossing the Chambal, a fine, broad stream on a broad bridge of boats, they had made their way through ravines and volcanic-looking clay peaks. A group of pilgrims carrying baskets on poles had, without warning, stopped in the middle of the road.

Meanwhile, the quinine powder had made his stomach turn. But he had been alert enough to notice that the men in this region were, without exception, finer and more manly looking than those he saw in Bengal.

Entering the room, they see Mrs Willoughby, the tall, gaunt wife of the Resident at Gwalior, leafing through a book about English gardens. Striking, well proportioned and stately but stone-faced, the cummerbund stands behind the lady.

'Are you fond of children, Mr Lear?'

Before he can say anything, the little, bright-eyed Ada runs up and places her left hand in his right. 'You write poems, don't you? Mummy tells me that your poems are very funny. I have read a few. Do you love poems more than stories?'

'Poems are stories too.'

The soft brown leather boots on her feet and matching pair of yellow socks and wide-brimmed straw hat make her look much older than eight.

'No.'

It is ten-year-old Lionel, her dark-haired brother, sitting next to their mother, his face buried in a book. 'Stories always come in books where the lines run all the way from left to right, filling up the page. Poems are lines that go from top to bottom and often look like ink blotches on the page.'

Lear laughs. They are so unlike the two girls at Mr Curtis's hotel!

The massive walls that enclose the Residency glint in the sun through the open door. Only allowed to venture into the garden to sit on the benches and look at birds, the Willoughby children seem so sadly trapped within the Residency's walls. Colonel Willoughby had told him the night before that the two would soon be packed off to an English school tucked away in some bucolic corner of Surrey.

The two children are curious about the Taj Mahal.

'Do you think it is the most *beautifullest* palace in the entire world?'

Ada's eyes are filled with awe.

'It is altogether Indian and lovely – so beautiful as to be impossible for any artist to capture on paper.' Lear realizes that 'altogether Indian' may not mean anything to an eight-year-old girl. So he tries again.

'Do you know what I think about the Taj? The inhabitants of the world can be divided into two classes – them as has seen the Taj and them as hasn't.'

The two had heard about the green parrots at the Taj, perching on the trees in the gardens and sitting on the monument's marble face and minarets.

'The parrots are doubtlessly pretty. But do you know what made my friend Giorgi and I laugh horribly? To see a very small monkey dressed perfectly as a soldier and surrounded by a host of chipmunks, sitting just outside the Taj!'

Lear does not tell them about the cheerful corpse bearers he saw on the way back to the hotel. A crowd singing, all dressed in white.

Ada places her hands on Lear's shoulders. 'Mummy read to us your story about the four little children who went round the world. Violet, Slingsby, Guy...and I forgot the name of the fourth. They made friends with so many strange animals, sailed across the sea in a boat, climbed palm trees on strange islands, played with the pincers of crabs.'

Not to be left out of the conversation, Lionel joins them. 'The small cat steered the boat.'

Ada's dark eyes are fixed on Lear's bearded face. She runs her finger across the top rim of his eyeglasses very gently, as if tracing an invisible object.

'Can you write a story about *us* – about the two of us going round the world, like Violet and her friends did, in your tale?'

'Why, of course, if you are willing to wait for a day.'

'Can we also take our two friends who live in Bournemouth – Cammy and Jerry – on this trip?'

Ada gets excited that the storyteller they see sitting in front – the bearded man with a funny nose, wearing round eyeglasses, a man who wrote books with funny drawings and rib-tickling poems – just agreed to chronicle their *very own* adventures in India.

Short-sighted, Lionel has to adjust his ill-fitting eyeglasses that keep sliding down his nose.

'Grandfather got the glasses for Lionel because he grew a pumpkin as large as the table you see here. He also sent us a new red train.'

Lionel places the book on the table. 'Grandfather Willoughby wrote us a note. It said, "Now go forth, see the world. Just do not get lost." Wonder how one can get lost in a train.'

'When can we read the story?' Ada pulls gently at his cuffs.

'Tomorrow afternoon, if you eat your peas and do not trouble the peacocks in the garden.'

After dinner, the children leave, talking excitedly about what they would do with their rail engine. Lear hears Lionel say, 'If we travel to Agra and get lost, we can always go to Colonel Mathews. He is sure to take us back home. He is in Papa's battalion.'

'But what about the sea? Cammy and Jerry would have to drive their engine from Bournemouth to Gwalior. That is at least eighty-five thousand miles!'

Lionel corrects her. 'It is eighty-four thousand and twenty-two miles.'

Returning to his room, Lear ignores the bottle of quinine sitting on his table and immediately sits down, pen in hand, with the clean sheet of paper placed on the shiny mahogany table.

The Residency is an opulent affair. Room, table, dinner, lights, service, wine, dishes – all of first-rate order and taste. Champagne in rivulets. But he thinks about the two Willoughby children. They seem so cut off from the rest of the world, as if locked in a beautiful tower guarded by swashbuckling cummerbunds. The tall, swarthy, resplendent sashed figure standing very still at the doorway takes shape before his eyes. The man's large nose twitches as someone walks in through the door.

But now, the story he has to pen! The new moon is visible outside the open window. The words appear on paper, moving like the crane he saw a few days back at the lake outside Dholepur.

Once upon a time – on a fine October morning – Ada, Cammy, Jerry and Lionel drive the red train engine that they have received as a gift from Grandpa to Portsmouth and haul it into a big boat. Soon, the green and yellow boat, carrying the red train engine and the four children and their pet walrus, Jinny, moves swiftly through the waters. Jerry and Lionel sit inside the engine and carefully inspect the boiler and the store of coal while Cammy and Ada polish the many brass handrails, cook dinner and make tea – not in a big kettle but in a brass pot. At times, Ada, too, stops by to inspect the engine. She does not trust the boys. The seas are stormy, so the walrus, Jinny, has to jump into the waves to hold up the ship's bow and keep it moving steadily.

Along the way, they see many islands filled with wonders – one with a volcano spilling out molten chocolate and another one with trees full of pink marshmallow sweets. Cammy cries, 'Wait! Can we stop and fill our jars with chocolate?' Jerry says, 'No, if we do, we will be terribly late.' 'Can we stop to pick some marshmallow?' cries Ada, and Lionel says, 'No, we cannot, as the sharks around will come biting. You know how sharks love to feed on walruses.' Jinny trembles, so they keep going.

In seventeen days, eleven hours and eleven minutes, they reach the port of Bombay. The train is hauled out and placed in front of the rail tracks. Along comes a giant elephant wearing a red cap, who says, 'Sorry, no permission to drive the train on our government rails. You will need to sign sixty-four forms and play the accordion to take your train engine to the railhead.' He looks around curiously and asks, 'Ah, I see, only engine. Where are your carriages?! Just for that, you have to pay a fee – ten shillings, sixty-seven coconuts, eighty-one bottles of blueberry jam and five hundred clotted creams.'

The four look at the elephant and say, 'But, sir, we do not have any of these things. We finished eating our last bottle of jam in Suez.' 'What can we do?' asks Cammy. 'Please, sire, let us go,' says Lionel. Jinny joins them and says, 'Please, sire,' and then Jinny's eyes open wide. 'Is it not Jumbo Jackson, my old friend from the Scraggly Waggly Circus?' 'Is it not Jinny, my old friend?' the elephant says. 'What are you doing in Bombay?' Jinny asks. 'I am here because, after leaving the circus, my fourth paternal uncle's brother-in-law's second sister's husband got me this job as port inspector in good old 'OMBAY port.' Soon, the six of them are having veal cutlets for dinner.

Early in the morning, the five get into the train engine, and off they go towards Gwalior. They pass Sillybillypore, Hot-as-hellpore, Hullaballoopore and many towns with unpronounceable names along the way till they arrive at a small station called Dole-kadolepore. They are told that the tracks ended there as the river ahead had flooded and the bridge had been washed away. The four are at a loss. How would they get to Gwalior?

Lear pauses, looking at the large metal mantelpiece. He notices a large picture mounted on the wall, of caparisoned camels trudging through desert sands.

He returns to his story.

Soon, a pack of camels comes trundling along. The oldest one, with a sneery face, says, 'Well, that engine looks like it is stuck. What are we going to do?' Then the second camel with a golden nose ring says, 'Simple. Let us form a chain and carry the engine on our backs till we see the next station across the river.' Soon, Cammy, Ada, Jerry, Lionel and Jinny are sitting in the engine that has been placed on the backs of three camels. The camels walk into the river, holding their heads high, and in no time, cross the waters. Ada sees so many fish waving at them, and Cammy sees a rainbow trout waving a rainbow-coloured flag and singing, 'Welcome to our land of Gwaaaleeeyour!'

As soon as they get to the other side, and the engine is put back on the tracks, a horde of peacocks comes dancing. There are rain clouds gathering in the sky. The peacocks begin singing a song that does not have any English words. Cammy looks enviously at the peacocks and says, 'Can we have some of your lovely feathers?' 'Most certainly,' says the peacock in front, and soon, fifty-three peacocks start pulling out their feathers, and before long, the four of them wear lovely peacock skirts and breeches. Jinny is not interested in wearing a peacock-feather skirt. But soon the wind rises, and the feathers begin to be carried away, flying off their bodies like angels. The peacock says, 'Do not worry; we have plenty to spare.' 'That will not be necessary,' says Jerry. 'Can we have our clothes back, please? It is getting a bit cold.'

But the peacocks run away with Jerry and Lionel's shirts and breeches, and Cammy and Ada's frocks and caps, and Jinny says, 'I warned you. You cannot trust native birds.'

Soon, they change into a new set of clothes, and before long, they are at Gwalior station. What a station! It is all made out of purple and yellow buns and dark brown truffles. Near the exit is a fountain of curry that smells so much that all of them walk past it in a hurry. Outside, the kettle birds are all carrying red kettles and the hairy long-legged goats are assembled in circles and triangles to greet them, some knitting sweaters from their own wool.

The clock strikes ten. The wind has picked up, making the trees outside swish noisily.

'I am done for the day. Hopefully, the remaining part will be ready tomorrow.' Lear turns down his light. He cannot hear Giorgi snoring as the rooms at the Residency are far apart.

The next morning, he is restless, having woken up early, thinking that he has to get down to the business of completing the unfinished story. Giorgi laughs when his master asks him to prepare the table. 'I hope it will not be too long of a tale.'

'I think I will also write a small score for a musical accompaniment for the band playing outside the station. But I need mystery, an element of magic in my tale.'

Lear ignores what Giorgi has just said about stretching tales. Instead, he pushes back the chair and pulls out his notebook.

The view of Gwalior and the city below with all its houses is vastly like that of the Acropolis and the city of Athens, and immensely lovely. So I drew and drew and drew until disturbed by the crows and many children, when we came down to some granite detached rocks, shadow-throwing, and there, lunched quietly enough on fowl and bread and sherry and water and oranges. We left the boulders and the kites and came down that hill of tombs; and so, by long, slow giros through dusty bazaars we have now come inside the fort gates…

The fatigue of travel makes him stop, put down his pen and find his way to bed.

Just as he has placed his left leg over the fat bolster pillow, he hears a knock on the door. Hastily slipping into his dressing gown, he sits on the high-backed chair facing the window. The tall and very blond Mr Willoughby walks in, accompanied by a young, aristocratic-looking native man with a well-trimmed beard and a small black cap on his head.

'Mr Rashid works for the Revenue Department. He is the best man to answer your questions about Gwalior.'

The day before, when Mr Willoughby had visited, Lear had inquired about the small domes of Muslim shrines that stuck out very visibly into the sky. On the same streets, he also saw some quaint-looking Hindu temples with bells hung on the doors. The happy co-presence of two faiths in the same city had intrigued him. Mr Willoughby's knowledge of Gwalior's past was rudimentary, but he assured him that he would seek out a local historian. So, here he was – Mr Rashid, who had a BA from Bombay University, joined the Revenue Department five years back and had been quite recently posted in Gwalior.

'The Viceroy's guest! Have you had the opportunity to meet many Indians?' Mr Rashid's dark eyes meet Lear's. He is impressed by the bearded Englishman's account of his travels in India but bemoans the fact that the artist has had so little interaction with educated Indians.

'I am sure you'll agree, Mr Lear that one can learn a lot about a country by directly meeting people who know their own history.'

Their conversation soon drifts towards Lear's question about mosques.

'You have an eye for things that easily escape the notice of most Englishmen. Gwalior does indeed have its share of Muslim shrines – not major mosques like you see in Agra or Delhi – but local ones dedicated to Sufi saints. The city has the distinction of being the home of a patron saint of Sufi Islam in the mid-1500s – Muhammad Ghawth.'

Lear was acquainted with Sufi Islam, having once leafed through Fitzgerald's translation of the *Rubaiyat of Omar Khayyam* at Tennyson's house and read about Sufi poetry of Persia. When he mentions it, a faint smile appears on Mr Rashid's lips, suggesting that he knew about that translation.

'Sufism inspired many poets in the past. You will be surprised to know that our city of Gwalior has been the home to a more – how should I put it – revolutionary form of Sufism. Ahamduallah, an aristocrat who gave up his worldly possessions to become a Sufi, and then fought against the English during the Mutiny, lived here. He was apprehended hiding in a Hindu home, and sadly, beheaded. Both of these saints are still revered in Gwalior.'

The half-light filtering through the open window lights up Mr Rashid's beautiful face as he proceeds to relate the gruesome details of that story.

'Limbs hacked into eleven pieces, fingers chopped and placed on a platter...'

'Joan of Arc – the young maid who had a vision and found herself engulfed in flames. Burnt at the stake.'

Mr Rashid notices the slight trembling in his fingers as Lear brings up the martyrdom of the maid of Orléans.

'Like *our* own Ahamduallah, a mystical fighter who became a saint. I've seen the painting by your Rossetti. What can be more sublime – a face illuminated by the divine, eyes turned upwards, knuckles white from the grip on the sword!'

The allure of Rashid's face and tight body and the manner in which his lips move make Lear sit up straight.

Revolution is magical. Revolution brings humanity's manly energies. Men of action, of daring, drive the spirit of revolution. Men – and very rarely, women – of revolution are built of steel, raw, their minds and bodies taut like the coils of metal springs that can be released by the simple pull of the finger. Mystery and magic animate their faces and bodies. Garibaldi! They can make things move by the sheer command of voices and arms raised towards the sky.

'I need a mystic for my tale. Ahamduallah it will be!'

The suddenness of his own outburst takes him by surprise. Even children's tales – with or without fairies – need to be fired by the mystical beings. He had learnt that from Gussie years ago.

Soon after Mr Rashid takes his leave, Lear returns to his table and begins to write furiously.

The four friends and Jinny, the walrus, get back into the train engine, and as it chugs along to Agra, they see a river filled with flamingos that are having a festival of kite flying and are engaged in organizing a parade filled with music and dance. There are sitars and flutes and also a few bagpipes. They get off the engine and come up to the river. The grand master of the flamingo parade says to them, 'Come along in our barge. We are all going to see the Taj Mahal.' As they get into the barge, they see a bearded old man singing on the banks of the river. 'I am Ahamduallah, a friend of the flamingos,' he announces. Dressed in a long, white robe with a two-stringed lute in his hand, he joins the children and does not stop singing till the boat reaches the edge of the beautiful Taj Mahal.

Seeing the marble monument rise almost like the peak of a snow-capped mountain fills the children with awe. 'Does it not look like a silver-white crown?' asks Ada. 'It looks more like a white cream cake,' says Jerry, 'a fresh white cream cake.' 'The pillars all around, are they also part of the cake?' Cammy asks. 'I wonder what it is filled with? I would like to scoop it with a big spoon,' and looking at one of the flamingos, says, 'Can we use your bill?'

They alight from the boat, and the bearded man stops singing, puts his ear to the ground and says, 'There will be a battle, my children, and we have to stop it! The soldiers are all around, some waiting in the distant fort that you see.' He points to the ramparts of a great red fort nearby. 'A battle? Well, we have no choice but to fight with our flamingo friends to save the great cream cake!' Ahamduallah raises both of his arms into the sky. Ada asks, 'Why are they fighting?' The bearded man replies, 'They are fighting for the great jewel – the largest plum pudding that is hidden inside the walls of the Taj Mahal.' 'A plum pudding?' says Jinny. 'What a waste of time! I do not even like plum pudding!'

Soon they reach the front archway, and facing it is a beautiful garden that stretches out to the pool that reflects the white cake standing majestically against the blue sky. Gardeners tend to the flowers that grow in long lines and circles. Suddenly, there is music, and the fountains begin to dance. One gardener, dressed in gold and red, begins conducting an orchestra, and the beautiful flowers sing:

Oh, lovely Mary Donnelly, my joy, my only best,
If fifty girls were around you, I'd hardly see the rest;
Be what it may the time o' the day, the place be where it will,
Sweet looks o' Mary Donnelly, they bloom before me still.

Jinny stands dancing, flapping his fat tail on the ground. The bearded man plays his lute, and the flamingos show off their red and pink feathers. The dome of the Taj begins to swing, and Ada is afraid that the big cake will fall and crumble in front of their eyes.

While this is happening, they suddenly hear the roar of a cannon and the stomping of elephant feet. Jinny rushes up to bolt the gate of the great archway.

Lear stops. Time for a cup of tea. As he sits in the large drawing room, he finds the mounted heads of deer, leopard and tiger staring vacantly from the walls. Deep tropical forests with trees through which the sun struggles to enter. A sudden movement and distant roar shake the trees, and unknown birds rend the sky with their screeching.

Agatha Chilcot. I need Agatha Chilcot in my story.

The lady who had introduced herself to Lear that afternoon had been Mr Willoughby's half-sister visiting from Gloucester and on her way to Hongkong. A small woman, with sharp eyes and dark, curly hair, she had reminded Lear of a literary character, but as hard as he tried, he could not place her, until she started speaking. Her every utterance opened with a *no*, unconsciously but emphatically articulated, even when she was in agreement with her interlocutor. 'No, India is not a country but a continent. *No*, I think you have a reasonable point, Mr Lear. *No*, the high clouds mean that there will be no rain. *No*, I have been quite comfortable, thank you. The journeys have been quite exhausting, but John made the best arrangements.'

After Mrs Chilcot had taken her final sip of tea, she hurried back to her room, saying that she had to pack her bag and get ready for her trip to the fort. Her *no* rang out loudly when Mr Willoughby asked her – as she hurried down to her room – if she would care to join them later for an early dinner.

Agatha Chilcot was a living incarnation of Andrew Forrester's Miss Gladden. The hardbound copy of *The Female Detective* that belonged to a friend of Emily Tennyson had remained in Lear's study for months. On a warm April day in 1865, he had spent the entire morning glued to the book's riveting account of the daredevil exploits of the female investigator, 'G', a woman so sceptical about everything she saw or heard that the word 'no' crept into every sentence she uttered! He chuckles, remembering the manner in which 'G' addressed the reader directly as she went about her sleuthing business. Agatha Chilcot would be the perfect character in the travel story, her 'nos' would be the perfect counterpoint to the overt exuberance of the story.

Lear's hands tremble with excitement.

Who do they see entering as the gate is being shut? Aunt Chilcot! Agatha Chilcot is Britannia, with silver armour and a gold spear. A silver helmet studded with precious jewels sits on her little head. A white and gold robe covers her little body. The children are startled by the sudden appearance of the aunt from Gloucester! More startling is the fact that, for company, she has a band of peacocks dressed in trousers and frocks, flocking around her. These were the very peacocks that had run away with the children's clothes a few days back as they made their way to Gwalior! Raising her spear, Aunt Chilcot proclaims, 'No! No! Never. They will NOT defeat us. As long as I stand with you!' They can hear the soldiers marching outside. Cammy says, 'Oh, what can we do to stop them?' The bearded man says, 'Do not fear.' Aunt Chilcot joins him as he raises his lute high up to the sky with his outstretched arms and begins to strum it with one finger. Almost immediately, music from the skies, a kind unlike anything they have heard before – certainly not like the music of 'Oh, lovely

Mary Donnelly' – fills the air. Aunt Chilcot begins singing 'Rule Britannia', and they all look with wonder at large alphabets swirling around them – letters that fly out of the beautifully carved drawings on the arch of the Taj Mahal swirl in the wind to form long lines that curve around and drape the trees like garlands. Almost immediately, the jumbled alphabets of the English language follow and arrange themselves as 'Trespassers will be Persecuted' all along the gateway. The bearded man utters with heavenly gusto, 'Stay! Those who wish to kill the spirit of our old Emperor. I command thee! Vaporize!'

And out of the Taj Mahal emerges a shadowy figure – an old man with a white beard wearing a crown. Ahamduallah is joined by Jinny as he goes up to him. He is the Emperor of India. Bowing down before the shadowy figure, Ahamduallah says, 'All your troubles are over, Your Majesty.' Then a wind comes through that shakes the trees so violently that Ada looks very worried. 'Oh, I hope the cream cake does not crumble. I so want to taste it.' The wind whistles for an hour but eventually calms down, and the four suddenly realize that the stomping of elephant feet, the march of boots and the clash of bayonets have ceased. Instead, there is complete silence.

Ahamduallah laughs aloud, a laugh that rings all around, and out of thin air, he produces, in his right hand, a shiny Christmas ornament – with the Taj Mahal inside, glittering like a jewel. 'Oh, I love it,' says Cammy as the old man hands it to her. All of them flock together to have a closer look. Each little detail is visible. The minarets, the glittering gems in its marble inlay, the golden spire at the tip of the dome giving out a light of its own. Aunt Chilcot looks at it and says, 'You will find it being sold in the markets of Agra.' But when they turn back to thank him, they realize that Ahamduallah has vanished into thin air, and with him, the sad Emperor with the grey beard and crown.

Lear stops and looks out of the window. The sun has set, and the growing darkness has swallowed the view outside his window in one abrupt gulp.

'Not particularly happy with the ending,' he murmurs to himself, noticing a single bat flapping between the trees outdoors.

But *how* does one conclude a story that has turned out to be little more than a mixed-up adventure tale growing out of the sights and sounds that had struck him in his travels, almost like a colourful sea polyp? He twirls his pen between his fingers, thinking. How would he get the children back to their train? How would he describe the return journey to Portsmouth? Would Cammy and Lionel stay back? Could he end it like *The Story of the Four Little Children Who Went Round the World* that he had penned years ago, where the rhinoceros was killed and stuffed directly? That was impossible. Besides, what a mercilessly cruel ending that was! The poor, poor rhinoceros! What *was* he thinking when he wrote it? Must have been Miss Greene's awful Yorkshire pudding!

Giorgi comes up to him. 'Master, it is late; time you went to bed.'

Lear turns to Giorgi and asks, 'Do all stories about journeys have to come to an end?'

Giorgi answers in a deep, meditative voice, 'Not if the end of the journey is unknown.'

He then lowers the flame of the lamp and melts into the darkness.

For a moment, the image of the skinned rhinoceros looms like a flickering shadow on the wall. In that story, the poor dead beast had been set up outside the door of the children's house as a *Diaphanous Doorscraper*. It was the same creature on whose back the four children had *cooked* in the *most satisfactory manner.* The more he thinks about that skinned animal, the more the darkness around him feels real. Then, somewhere, he hears the gentle melody of a distant harp being played by a fair-haired girl in blue and is gradually lulled to sleep.

The next day, he learns that the children had been sent to the fort early in the morning. So, he leaves the sheets neatly tied in a string on the mantelpiece.

7

'NUNKOO LAL IS LATE.'

Lear looks at the moving hands of the lantern clock on the wall. The large ficus tree outside allows the late winter sun to filter gently through its translucent leaves, making the shrubs below gleam among the dancing hues of gold and yellow. A cold draught blows across the room, making him shiver. A turbaned man sweeping the floor lets out a loud sneeze.

Giorgi must have opened the window when he did my bed, Lear thinks, putting down his cup of tea on the table.

Quite late. Very surprising, indeed. Nunkoo has been as punctual as the thrush that sat outside my window merrily whistling at five every morning in Kurseong.

Two days ago, they had arrived at the *dak bungalow* from the railway station, dusty and weary from another exhausting train journey. Cases, bedrolls and a sketching stool carried by the hunchback gatekeeper followed the two as they made their way through the creaky old iron gate. The gatekeeper handed Lear a note.

Please come to tea between five and six any day if you are available.
It was signed Colonel T. Cracroft.

Your guide, Nunkoo Lal, is at your service for the next three days. He has been instructed to show up at eight every morning.

At the bottom of the slip of paper were Cracroft's hastily written words:

Worked as a professional guide for ten years, comes with the best recommendations. Lady Penelope, the wife of the Eastern Command's Colonel West, appreciated his good English, excellent manners, and impeccable personal hygiene.

Lear places his empty cup on the table.

'Could he be ill?'

Giorgi pours him more tea.

That day, barely an hour after they had settled into their room in Delhi's spacious but somewhat rundown *dak bungalow* and put their cases on top of a wide table placed next to the window, a horse-driven coach pulled into the driveway.

'Nunkoo Lal. Myself guide.'

A man in his early thirties, dressed in a spotlessly white long shirt, narrow white trousers, a brown knitted waistcoat and a native cap, walked up to the veranda and introduced himself.

'But we were not expecting you until tomorrow morning.'

Lear noticed that the man had already taken off his shoes and left them at the bottom of the stairs. 'I am glad you are here. We are not occupied, so perhaps you can take us to the Cracroft residence in Ludlow Castle.'

He had woken that morning craving homemade sandwiches, pie and tea. A good steak and ale pie would be most welcome.

The man bowed very politely before sitting on the edge of a wicker chair placed at the far end of the veranda. Eyes set wide apart, with high cheekbones and a prominent chin, the man pulled down the sleeves of his shirt as soon as he saw Lear staring at his long, dangling arms.

'I was instructed to meet you.'

'A kind face.'

Lear turned to Giorgi, arching his back a little.

'I feel I am up for a visit. Aren't you, Giorgi? Quite a miracle that my back does not hurt as much after that bone-rattling train ride!'

'A good evening tea will be most satisfactory.'

Giorgi helped Lear with his overcoat and reminded him to change into more comfortable footwear. He was concerned that the raised sole riveted to the underside of the patten he had worn during the journey was falling apart and might give way any minute.

Lear asked for his croquet shoes to be taken out of the wooden case.

Soon, the horse trotted happily towards Ludlow Castle. Sitting at the front of the open horse carriage that was fitted with blue silk and wool tufting, Nunkoo cleared his throat several times before speaking. The wheels creaked menacingly when the carriage went over uneven patches.

Nunkoo's commentary, delivered in flawless English, seemed straight out of a textbook. Events, dates, people. He *did* take his duties very seriously, thought Lear, seeing the young man raise his arm from time to time to point towards an archway, a wall or an obscure, dark lane.

'Nothing like what we saw in Calcutta.'

Lear's eyes gazed at the line of official buildings that they passed, his face bearing a tinge of disapproval. But as soon as the sandstone walls, gateways, domes and latticed verandas – interrupted by an occasional *bungalow* with shaded verandas and lime-washed walls – came into view, he sat up.

The latticed upper verandas of the houses were familiar, quite similar to what he had seen in Gwalior.

'Strange that I do not see any signs of what Evelyn Baring calls *Indo-Saracenic*. They were visible almost everywhere in Calcutta.'

'What you see around here was inspired by the late Moghul style. Sadly, many of the early Moghul houses were destroyed by the great fire.'

Nunkoo's tone changed almost immediately, and Lear was taken aback by the force with which he enunciated the word 'fire'.

A line of camels sat on the greens along the side of the road. A sharp right led to an avenue lined with wide-canopied trees.

'Calcutta is the seat of the British Empire. This, sir, is the seat of the great *Moghul* Empire.' Like a conductor facing the orchestra, Nunkoo sat upright, his right arm sweeping across from left to right. From his lips flowed the names of Moghul emperors, their wives and concubines, architects, poets and painters from Persia. Some familiar but the rest new and foreign-sounding.

'All patronized for nearly three centuries by the unparalleled Moghuls.' Pausing, he continued, enunciating the names of Moghul emperors with startling precision and passion. 'Now we have the English, of course. History moves, but in all honesty, I see our present age as the great falling off from that glorious era.'

They were right in the middle of a busy street when baskets of pomegranates toppled from a cart in front that had swerved too quickly. The carriage driver hopped down, picked up a few and placed them back in the large wicker basket.

'I hear that His Excellency, the Prince of Wales, has a visit planned to Delhi later this year. If he had come before the fire, he would have seen a *truly* glorious city, rivalling Rome.' The carriage had just turned to another avenue lined with copperware and brassware shops. This time, Lear's ears picked up very clearly the word 'fire', but before he could ask, he saw Nunkoo raising his right arm and pointing his delicately shaped finger to a gateway behind which lay a pile of ruins of an intricately designed archway.

'Kashmiri Gate, sir. This is where the Punjab Infantry broke down the barriers to enter the city.' The ears of the horse flicked back at the sound of a bleating goat.

'Terrible battle, sir. Terrible. More fire. Many lives lost.'

The shattered sandstone pieces and fragments of latticed window frames, all stacked and placed along a tall, shattered wall, cast strange shadows on the ground. In front were horse carriages, bullock carts, jostling crowds selling and buying oranges, scarves, combs, cooking pots and sundry objects laid out in carts pulled by recalcitrant camels. The spectacle was on a scale grander than he had seen before in India, the shadows more intense and sharply defined.

Giorgi had remained silent all along, taking everything in with a kind of stoic indifference. Seeing a shiny fruit fly sitting on his master's shoulder, he flicked it very gently with his large handkerchief.

The air was filled with smoke coming from a flaming pile of wood and bramble lying on the side of the road. Two official looking carriages came up from behind very noisily and went past in great haste, the wheels raising a cloud of dust.

'No one talks about the fire these days. It is as if it had never happened.' Nunkoo's words were lost in the motions and noise of the busy street.

While we have been hanging upon the next Indian mail to tell us whether or not the Mutiny had been extended or suppressed, a much larger question has arisen – whether our Indian Empire is to be retained or abandoned?

As Lear sat staring at the two carriages speed past, he recalled the lines from *The Spectator* that Fortescu had handed him that July evening in London. He had recently been made the Under-Secretary of State for the Colonies. 'England will certainly choke on the great bit of muffin she is stuffing on, don't you think?' Fortescu's words had seemed strangely ominous. A warm, almost blustery breeze had wafted in through the open window. That summer in England, the sense of utter shock was apparent. The unspeakable stories of the horrors of the Mutiny seemed to be on everyone's lips, and so were accounts of grit and valour at the manner in which British soldiers had 'met the emergency with equal strength and wisdom' – words Lear remembered reading on the pages of the *Saturday Review*.

Sixteen years on, the memory of the Mutiny produced different reactions among the English stationed in India. One in particular had stood out on a hazy winter afternoon, soon after he had returned from his stroll by the canal in Calcutta.

'The insurrection was the result of a deep conspiracy hatched by misguided loyalists of the ageing and half-blind Moghul emperor.'

Evelyn had brought up the topic of the Mutiny, but Lear had chosen to remain silent. After all, what did *he* know about the loyalists of the Moghul emperor? They had a quiet evening, but after dinner, when he mentioned that earlier that day he had walked across a large mosque in the outskirts of Calcutta, Tollygunge, Evelyn's reaction struck him as being somewhat excessively dramatic.

'No one can doubt that the mosque is very picturesque, but in a cold, *bloody* sense. Many of the murderous rebels found refuge in it.'

The look on Evelyn's face had reminded him of the fair-haired English soldier who had led Lear and Giorgi to the spot when they visited Lucknow. That woodland was where, he claimed, the bloodthirsty rebel Nana Sahib had led the slaughter of innocent Englishmen. Encircled by charming green grounds, the area was covered with tufts of grass where stray goats grazed and the tall trees around cast deep shadows.

'Bloody, diabolical', the soldier's words, 'a terrible bloodbath' – rose once more as the carriage rolled past a broken archway bordered by two wide-canopied trees. Almost instantly, Lear's thoughts went to the giant tree he had sketched, sitting on a wall in Boyle's compound in the sleepy town of Arrah. Only a day before they arrived in Chunar, he had been introduced to Major Elliott, a large, florid Englishman with a penchant for storytelling. Standing next to a broken wall, Elliott had elaborated, with much relish, the story about the district engineer Richard Boyle defending his house and the railway money chest concealed in its walls. While Elliott spoke about the stench emanating from the body of one of the mutineers shot dead by Boyle and left dangling in its branches, Lear kept drawing. More details followed – about sudden attacks and reprisals, about the brutality of the natives, and the valour of the English. There could be no doubt that the Major relished repeating what seemed to Lear to be little more than the now-familiar features of Mutiny folklore. What had surprised him the most was how attentively Giorgi had listened to the tale.

As the carriage made its way to Ludlow Castle, it appeared that the very air that stirred the elegant *peepul* trees and touched

Giorgi's face carried with it the unmistakable stench of death. It had, in fact, seeped into the crumbled shapes around him, into the cracks of the dilapidated walls, filling each crevice with lost echoes and undetectable savagery, coiled like an unknown sleeping serpent. More blackened archways, more burnt-out debris on the side of the street. It was only then that the word 'fire' leapt up, with its curled tongue shooting into the air above.

1857. Sixteen years ago. The not-too-distant past had tunnelled its way into the present.

Before long, the carriage made its way through high metal gates to a large, white stucco and brick house. A long line of gently swaying *peepul* trees along the driveway slid past them. On both sides were rows of petunias, poppies and perfectly laid-out and well-looked-after ornamental shrubs. 'No broken grounds here,' Giorgi heard Lear murmuring. Servants scurried around, popping in and out into the large, glowing paved verandas, walked around with large brooms, while agile gardeners swung their arms, gripping the handles of shiny metal watering cans. Out of the freshly watered shrubs wafted the smell of jasmine.

'A place of ruin, that is what I call it – Delhi,' Mrs Cracroft announced as they stepped into the spacious living room. Pouring Lear a cup of tea, she continued, 'Oh, the Mutiny! As a ten-year-old, I was fortunate not to be here at that time, thank the Almighty Lord. Leeds – that is where my parents had a house with a large garden where we grew up. Here, alas, women and children virtually lived in a prison for weeks on end, in pure dread every waking hour, fearful of being attacked, killed or worse.' A shiver ran down her body as she served the beautifully carved sandwiches arranged on a bright green japanned tray. The shaft of the afternoon winter sun danced merrily on a sea-green japanware tea caddy.

The next hour was spent with the pale lady describing the many teas and luncheons – both official and unofficial – that she was in charge of organizing ('Just had one yesterday after three consecutive ones last week'), the frequency of visitors stopping by ('Five from Birmingham only last week – all unannounced'), the unending task of explaining each little detail to workers ('The tailor is almost half-blind but is an excellent craftsman'), before moving on to a detailed description of the tribulations of life in exile ('The Colonel is away three weeks every month, leaving me alone with my daughters for months at a stretch'), their fourteen-year-old daughter's rashes and boils ('The young doctor replacing Dr Hodge does not really know much about skin rashes'), the unreliable supply of household provisions ('Specially good claret and pure English lavender'). She ended, somewhat abruptly, with the topic of *kamsamah*s and the insolence of Indian servants ('Just you wait and see their expressions when I look away').

The talk about the serving staff led Lear to mention the excellent mutton he had been served in some of the *dak bungalow*s he had stayed in. 'True that it is often hard to understand what goes on in their minds. But I have nothing but praise for their cooking.' The conversation about the trials and tribulations of women living in exile in India continued unabated. Not unlike Major Elliott, Mrs Cracroft seemed to have a special penchant for detailing each misery – from food to foot disease – with the ardour of a storyteller.

But as the relentless ticking of the clock reached their ears, Lear could see irritation cloud Giorgi's face. Saying that he wished to catch the light for his first drawing of Delhi, he excused himself and bid Mrs Cracroft farewell. Nunkoo was sitting by the gate, looking intently at a bush with a single orange hibiscus dangling from its branch.

It had struck Lear that Nunkoo Lal's finely cut features made him look like the men he saw on the streets of Gwalior. After they had departed from the Cracroft *bungalow*, Nunkoo told them that he did, indeed, come from a village situated not far from Gwalior. In Delhi, he lived with his younger brother, who was preparing for a job in charge of keeping accounts at the army barracks.

'No wife,' was his response when asked if he had any children.

After a few minutes of riding through a long avenue of trees, the famous Observatory came into view. The carriage stopped, and Nunkoo pointed to a low hill and the terrain around – grey and stony, filled with acacia, their leaves almost fern-like, with a few taller ones rising like abandoned ships in an old dockyard. No high canopies, just a web of low-hanging branches, tortuously contorted in places, that cast a pale green light on the rocky ground. The vast plains stretched out gradually as they ascended the ridge, the delicate undulations of the red gravel road leading to a spot at the very top. Visible against the horizon was the dome of the mosque they had glimpsed on their way to Kashmiri Gate. One large dome across a line of smaller domes that looked very much like the lesser peaks of the Kanchenjunga rearing their heads into the sky.

After alighting from the stationary carriage, they followed Nunkoo on foot through an unpaved track to a Gothic-style tower. With four tiers rising from an octagonal base, there was nothing appealing about the 'Mutiny' monument. The worst kind of *Britishized beauty* – as Lear noted in his notebook – it had absolutely no redeeming features. Turning away, Lear sat on a rock. 'Methinks I will rest here, read and draw.'

Giorgi walked away as Lear pulled out his Bishop Heber from the satchel and began reading.

In the history of the world, nothing is more wonderful than the acquisition by England of her Indian Empire, except her retention of it. That, at a distance of some thousands of miles, a population of thirty-five million should control the destinies of some thousands of a population of two hundred and fifty million is a fact the romantic and extraordinary character of which cannot be wholly explained away.

He put Heber's book away into the bag and stared at the monument. Syllablubbery – that was what Heber's big words sounded like, sounds rising like the vapour of a glorious English destiny, fatuous and so utterly empty of meaning. Tempered by the steady buzz of insects and bee-eaters that hovered around the branches, the sounds faded as rapidly from his mind as the February sun that was gradually setting in the western sky. The Heber had been a gift received from the manager of the Government House in Calcutta. 'The best book on India, in my view. I am sure you will enjoy it. Heber was also a traveller,' he had said. Seeing Heber in Lear's hands, Evelyn had pulled out a book chronicling the adventures of General Sir Charles Napier.

'Napier said that he had *sinn'd,* meaning that he had captured and annexed *Sindh.*' Lear had chuckled at the pun but listened with rapt attention to Evelyn. How effortlessly a pure verbal felicity could transform the thrill of adult military exploits into a lad's excitement of being part of the great game of Empire. Could anyone doubt the fact that long before he had set his limericks on paper, the nonsense of the *Caledonian Mercury* – about the sun and the British Empire – had cast its spell of wizardry on the minds of the English!

After writing a few lines in his notebook, Lear began to sketch silently, observing from the corner of his eye the rocks that were shrouded in a gauze of green and grey. Nunkoo was watching him from a distance.

'How old were you during the Mutiny, Nunkoo?'

'About fourteen.' Nunkoo cast a stone at a lizard, which made the creature disappear under a rock. 'Gwalior's Rajah Scindia was loyal to the British. An uncle – my mother's own brother – hiding in our house was taken away by British soldiers one evening. Never seen again. My mother cried for days.'

Nunkoo looked at the sky and at the pigeons perched on the tops of trees.

'Sir, have you ever heard about the poet Ghalib? Delhi was his home when the city burned in 1857.'

Raising his head, Lear looked all around across the horizon. All he could see were the domed heads of innumerable tombs, and interspersed all along the horizon were ever more minarets, slender, jutting into the sky like the fingers of the dancing women he had seen in pictures.

'No, never.' He put down his pencil.

'*The trust of training the peoples of India to self-government, of raising them to the level of Western civilization...*' Heber's words lingered in his mind as he held up the pencil.

'I have an hour or so of good light.'

'We will leave when you are ready, sir.'

From the corner of his eye, Lear saw Nunkoo sitting on a rock, turning the pages of a small book.

All Lear could think about as his eyes scanned the dome-filled sky was a once-great city that was now little more than a vast cemetery, a sprawling habitation of death, where Death's bony fingers reached down like a mother's hands running gently over the heads of her sleeping children. Death, it appeared, had absorbed all the light and radiated it back at the city, dazzling the eyes.

'Did your excellent poet write lyrical poems or epics?'

'Ghalib composed the most exquisite lyrics in Persian, and in Urdu.'

'*Green shoots from walls and doors, Ghalib wanders in a desert while his home blooms in spring.*' Nunkoo's lips quivered as he uttered the words in English. Pausing, he proceeded to wipe his eyes with his white handkerchief, and then, the Persian words began to flow like liquid alphabets distilled out of the shimmering sky. The soft vowels and sibilants of Persian and the hard, syllabic sounds of English. Lear thought about the broken walls, the crumbled masonry that he had witnessed earlier but also of fields of swaying mustard and green pastures where long-legged goats grazed.

Suddenly Mr Discobbolos
Slid from the top of the wall;
And beneath it he dug a dreadful trench,
And filled it with dynamite, gunpowder, gench,
And aloud he began to call – 'Let the wild bee sing,
'And the blue bird hum!
For the end of your lives has certainly come!'

The lines popped up like tiny filaments of mycelium he had tried sketching during his walks in Cornwall. And the words soon turned into a cluster of shadows – of the great Queen pacing the halls with a sketchbook in one hand and the globe in the other, repeating, 'Empress of the Realm.' Willoughby had told him the Queen's son had been promised that his proposed visit to India, planned later that year, would be the grandest thing, beyond the imagination of her subjects. Buzzing around the Queen's crowned head was a most annoying bee: 'dynamite, gunpowder, firework'. Unable to rid his mind of that strange vision and voices, Lear asked to be led up to his carriage so that they could return to the *dak bungalow*.

Giorgi, who had been sitting on another rock close to Nunkoo, sensed his master's weariness.

'Been a long day. We must return without further delay. You must have a quick supper and go straight to bed.'

Nunkoo finally arrives at nine, apologizing profusely. On his head is a black cap embroidered in gold and his leather shoes gleam.

'The clock had stopped, and my brother did not wake me up.' They hurry into the waiting carriage, and after a short drive, reach the crowded market of Chandni Chowk. The dome of the great mosque rises like the head of a turbaned caliph, dwarfing everything around it.

'Is this the dome we saw last evening?'

Nunkoo nods and points to the *bazaar*, teeming with people.

'The market of the magnificent Moghul princesses.'

'The Square of Glittering Silver' looks so dark and dilapidated that no royalty can be ever imagined walking its streets, ruby-encrusted robes trailing on the ground.

They alight and walk through the maze of shops, through narrow streets where the sun barely pierces through the walls of houses and inner courtyards. Children and men gawk at them, breaking into laughter. Giorgi cannot take his eyes off the fresh fruits laden in piles in hand-pulled carts. In the very heart of the walled city lies a world wrapped in unending layers of broken mortar, half-visible arcades that were once adorned with blue and white tiles of exquisite beauty, flashy silks fluttering in the breeze and brightly decorated bridles swaying from poles. And between them there are people, horses, camels, dogs, goats and some audacious roosters.

They stop at another archway and make their way through a narrow alley to reach a door.

'Ghalib lived here. The great poet I mentioned yesterday died about six years back.'

Nunkoo pulls out a slim book from his bag.

'A broken man when he died. Full of pain and yearning that he expressed in his poems. He lived through the blazing fires of Delhi. Entire neighbourhoods went up in smoke and embers. People fled with whatever they could collect. Cries in the air that lasted for weeks.'

The sunless alley is filled with voices.

'Taken away from his beloved Delhi, the old and blind Moghul emperor breathed his last in Burma, thousands of miles away, friendless and poor.'

Lear is startled by the story he hears. Only a week ago, the story he penned for the Willoughby children had featured an ageing Emperor who was conjured up by the robed mystical saint! Had some invisible Muse whispered the story into his ears as he slept? Did Delhi also have its own Ahamduallahs?

More shattered archways and decaying walls meet their eyes, under one of which sit two women with a large metal can in front. The occasional jangle brings people to drop a coin or two into them.

'You must have heard about Havelock, the great English hero of the War.'

Lear faces Nunkoo, who stands in front of the door running his fingers over the broken mortar on the walls.

'Havelock, why, of course! Cawnpore burning, and the siege of Lucknow. Havelock, the hero of the British Empire.'

'And John Nicholson?'

Nunkoo notices Lear's raised eyebrows. He has just taken off his eyeglasses.

Havelock's name had been etched in Lear's mind in the autumn of 1858, just before he returned to Corfu from London. The English newspapers were already full of reports about that siege: how, at first, Havelock's force was too late and too weakened by casualties to save Cawnpore, but his victories in July and August brought him acclaim. In September, the valiant Commander had successfully broken through on the fourth try to relieve the Residency at Lucknow. What jubilation! Even the fruit vendors on Holloway gave out fresh apples from their carts. Walking through central London, he saw women breaking down in tears and weeping uncontrollably by the wayside. There were reports about the Queen writing to Lord Canning that she shared *his feelings of sorrow and indignation at the unchristian spirit shown towards Indians in general and towards sepoys without discrimination.* But John Nicholson? Who was he?

Nunkoo sums up very briefly the story of Nicholson's hard-fought recapture of Delhi. 'The man responsible for setting the city on fire was himself killed in action.'

They walk back to the carriage after Lear has a last look at the broken door of the poet's house.

Ghalib's lament about Delhi: Lear wonders if the Queen, who had spent so much of her time choosing the right shade of red – the red that would give the roses more of their rosiness – would have really cared about the plight of an unknown Indian poet who saw his home and city turn to ashes. Beyond the stain of black soot on the collapsed walls, scavenging death appears to nuzzle on leftover scraps of food. Ravenous stray dogs sniff around in the alleyways. The flames leap high up in the sky, spread like a burning sheet over the distant horizon. An ocean of fire threatens to wash ashore. The city's viscera is strewn on its devasted streets, blood streaming down the drains.

Does he not feel now, as he did on the way from Purnea, listening to the driver of the *garry* talk about the thousands of dead and homeless escaping the *dead* land from the dreaded famine?

Giorgi is pointing to what was little more than a receding thin, grey line glowing in the distance, waning with the light of the setting sun. 'The famine must be happening in that place just beyond the distant horizon.' Death and devastation on a scale he had not imagined before.

Lear's fingers are freezing, and his mind wanders off. This *is* the heart of Britain's Empire in India, where one cannot avoid sensing devastation in its rawest, most immediate, forms. He can tell from seeing Giorgi's pursed lips that he is also thinking about what may lurk behind the broken walls – can it be the story about the world turning into heaps of ash, about *nature red in tooth and claw*, about the cruelty of man against man and the killing of the rhinoceros? In his mind, they begin to converge into a single zone, a pulsating nerve point in his brain. He fears another attack and is relieved to see the carriage pull up at the gate of the *dak bungalow*. Making his way to his bed, he lies down and shuts his eyes. The sun is beginning to set in the western sky, and the familiar buzzing of mosquitos makes him ask Giorgi, 'Will you please pull down the nets?'

Giorgi has been complaining about unbearable stomach pain.

No doubt the Albanian could not stomach the stories of death that Nunkoo had related nor the water he had accidentally sipped from the copper bottle he had found lying on the seat of the carriage.

'Diarrhoea!' By the time Lear offers Giorgi a generous

dose of quinine, he feels that the affliction is creeping up in his bowels, too.

Two days later, the diarrhoea strikes intermittently, but that does not stop Lear from visiting a few remaining places on his list – the tall, carved pillar at Qutab and Safdarjung Tomb. The wild gardens of the latter are no match for the beautifully patterned gardens of the Taj, although the wild, untamed foliage reminds him of the forests he strolled through in Kurseong. But so utterly tropical – the canopy of a giant deciduous tree casts its shade so wide that Lear can sit and draw under it while being surrounded by several men, women and children lying on their sides, deep in slumber. The half-visible mynahs and parrots flit from one branch to the next. As Lear and Giorgi leave, a band of half-naked children follow them, screaming, 'Baksheesh, baksheesh.' Two nearly naked boys sit on a plank of wood placed over a rock, moving up and down, screaming at the top of their voices. What a remarkable thing – an improvised see-saw, placed right in the middle of a tomb in ruins!

Their gleeful screams fill his ears with half-remembered sounds.

'Shadow and Light on a see-saw, Flinging their hands high up in the air. When not doing their classroom sums, they roam the forests, Soundlessly and without a care.' On one end sits Eleanor, moving up and down, screaming with excitement, and the young boy sitting on the other end is nervously holding on to the plank.

Giorgi sees his master looking in the direction of the two children who repeat, 'Baksheesh! Baksheesh! One pice only, one pice.'

Standing among the red stone ramparts of the fort at Tuglakabad later that day, Lear's eyes fall on a cluster of carrion birds perched on top of the crumbling ramparts. Dark, ungainly, their large wings flapping noisily, the vultures are visible even through the branches of the trees. Some glide through the air and land with wings outstretched to join the group. With sharp beaks, hooked on the end, and their bald, featherless heads, these birds occasionally let out rasping, hissing sounds. Giorgi is so captivated by the sight that he nearly stumbles as he makes his way up a broken staircase. *'Singularly ominous. A child's mind will most likely be filled with dread seeing your pictures.' Lushington sits at the table looking at some of the drawings he had made of fantastical winged carrion creatures.*

He couldn't muster the courage to tell Lushington that when he sat unmoving in his chair with that impassive look on his face, his companion felt only fear and panic. In fact, there was more emotion on the face of the grasshopper he had drawn that breathed down the back of the Old Person in Black and the Floppy Fly than on his dear juror friend's countenance. Unlike him, his ominous creatures stood by his side through joy and pain, held his hands when he craved solace and comforted him when the world seemed dreary and bleak. What's more, the juror only helped in depleting his entire stock of claret in one week, a stock that he had procured and saved over months.

Nunkoo sits on the crumbling ramparts, gazing at the horizon.

Another day ends with the ticking of the clock in the room and the smell of Giorgi's tobacco that wafts in through his open window. Before going to bed, Giorgi faithfully offers him the concoctions from the numerous bottles that they have been carrying in the brown metal case.

On their last day in Delhi, Lear and Giorgi wait for the *garry* to take them to Haridwar. Taking off his glasses, he looks once again at the handwritten words of Ghalib, translated by Nunkoo himself into English. A neat cursive hand fills ten pages of a small notebook. Two starlings chatter in the trees. Lear pulls out his notebook and begins to write, sitting on the creaking bench: *Ruined sepulchres all over the land.* The thought of Sarah – the news of her death came to him earlier that month in a letter – makes him go over what he had written the evening before:

Early life is becoming remote though ever clearly remembered, not as Little Milly L. said, 'I have lived too long to remember so far back ago,' and as nearly all with whom quiet moments used to be passed are either gone or changed. To think back is merely sadness, and mere sadness is what one can't afford to entertain here in India.

Death, dying and silence.

Not a single word comes out of Lushington's lips as they walk over the cliff. His stiff body moving across the rocks gradually disappears from view. The music drifts into the room from the Mussulman fiesta in Fatehpur Sikri and mingles with the sound of crickets; the shrill, tremulous band of kites fills the skies, and beyond the jungle, the jackals, the lords of the feast, slink in the shadows. And somewhere in that muddle, a maimed face.

Lear turns, once again, to Nunkoo's beautiful hand.

My heart, only my heart, not unfeeling stone,
So why this despair as it throbs with pain,
The heart was made to suffer ten thousand darts,
What is one more torment?

The words are like the land itself, binding its secrets tightly in the folds of looping cursive alphabets while the air is filled with mysterious noises.

The Donati Comet suddenly flashes across the sky. It is autumn of 1858. Stepping into a half-lit room, his eyes fall on a silver locket placed near the mirror. It is the same locket that shone on Fortescu's aunt's throat when they visited Bath. Placed within its little chamber is a single strand of hair. Very blond but turning white. The tiny Xs appear, a long endless string of Xs, on the margins of his notebook, where he has been recording the dates when he suffered his fits. 'Forgive my grief for one removed, Thy creature, whom I found so fair.' Walking through Hyde Park on a grey December morning, Tennyson's voice rings out. The old childhood house in Highgate is being torn down, brick by brick, giving way to rows of shiny, new houses. A dead woman with eyes painted over her closed eyelids is a daguerreotype placed on the window of that tiny shop on Regent Street. A tiny price tag is placed next to it. A metal paperweight sits on the neatly folded letter bearing the news of Ann's death. The crocuses are just beginning to come up from the frozen ground.

Are these visions merely bits of fine dust flying around in the air and settling on him noiselessly? Or are they real – as real as Hunt's *The Shadow of Death*, the painting with the shadow of Christ's arms raised, falling on the wooden spar behind him? *Crucifixion Prefigured*. Just like the lull between the flash in the sky and the thunder. 'I am all at sea and do not know my way an hour ahead. I shall be so terribly alone,' his words to Fortescu soon after the news about Ann reached him on that bright, cold day in spring. The bits of detritus crawl like the fat worms that feed on the shrivelled petals of roses strewn on the ground.

The *garry* arrives, and the two set off for Haridwar. His last view of Nunkoo is that of a beautiful man wearing an oversized shirt, his large cuffs concealing his long, elegantly shaped fingers. The figure with his right arm raised in final goodbye gradually recedes into the mist. Nunkoo had, indeed, turned the terrifying fires that he saw raging around him into the placid, quiet beauty of blue glazed tiles glinting in the sun.

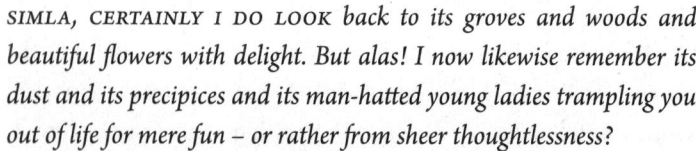

8.

SIMLA, CERTAINLY I DO LOOK back to its groves and woods and beautiful flowers with delight. But alas! I now likewise remember its dust and its precipices and its man-hatted young ladies trampling you out of life for mere fun – or rather from sheer thoughtlessness?

The *S* in *Simla* stands up like the squiggly band of hair adorning the head of 'The Young Lady of Firle', Lear reminds himself as he runs his pen on a blank sheet of paper. Only four pages left in his notebook! Raising his head and looking up, he notices someone pulling the blinds of the large sitting gallery. Almost instantly, he draws back from the glare of the sunshine. Except for the repeated chirp of an unknown bird, there is no sound, not even the now-familiar swish of the wind rushing through the pine trees. His face lights up with joy seeing Giorgi walk through the door carrying in his left hand his eyeglasses.

'I must send a note to Mrs Campbell thanking her.'

'Mrs Campbell's man had them delivered this morning. The repairs took longer than expected.' Lear looks very pleased to see the mangled arm of the eyeglasses straightened.

'All I could see this morning as I stepped out was the bright sun shining in the perfectly blue sky, but it was so still and silent outside that, for a moment, I thought no one was around.' Wiping his eyeglasses, he puts them on.

'You are short-sighted, *very* short-sighted, Mr Lear, but I had not realized that you are getting hard of hearing, too. The children have been out in the garden since daybreak, playing hide-and-seek and screaming like parakeets.'

They are sitting in the dining room of the *dak bungalow* in the little town of Solan, surrounded by a steady stream of servants going about their business silently while children dart in and out of the door into the gallery. The thought of returning to the hot plains after spending two weeks in Simla fills him with a certain dread. After having enjoyed the cool and quiet of pine forests, it will be time to resume the journey on a sweltering train carriage. Solan is the last station in their descent to the plains, a place where he can still feel – in April – warm and cosy in woollen socks.

'I am six days short of sixty-two.'

Picking up his cup of steaming tea, Lear gazes out of the window at the military barracks in the distance, against which the mountains rear their sparkling heads, the sunlight drenching the lower slopes with dashes of gold and white. Not a speck of cloud to be seen anywhere in the vast expanse of the skies.

A box of paints sits on the table. 'I quite dislike painting with colours from these miserable tubes, Giorgi. I am told that they are the rage in Calcutta. But honestly, I can't tell why. When I tried them last week, I found the entire tube of blue just full of air bubbles!'

Giorgi looks at Lear as he holds up the unfinished wash of the mountains from Mashoobra.

'Don't you think that when you see from a distance, your eye picks up details that get strangely altered as you come closer?' Lear's nose almost touches the surface of the paper, so close that Giorgi wonders if his master has detected a strange and unfamiliar smell in it.

'The closer you are, Giorgi, you notice things that had escaped your eye when you observed them from a distance.'

Giorgi picks up the sock he has been darning and marvels at the way in which Lear goes through socks almost every week.

'True. That makes logical sense, but...'

Lear pauses and looks across the room.

'Being in these heights alters the way the eye sees, Giorgi. When you stand up straight and look, the imagination is caught up in the vastness of the world that lies in the distance. When you bend down to look, the perspective changes. The little grains and the spots on the grass begin to matter. A simple idea, I would think, but to a travelling artist like me, whose knees creak with every step he takes and whose back is as stiff and crusty as a five-day-old loaf of bread, it makes a world of difference.'

Holding his newly restored eyeglasses carefully in his left hand, he walks slowly up to the doorway.

'The vastness of the world, seen from a distance, is as real as the grains you see in this block of wood.' Lear runs his fingers on the door. 'I know, Giorgi, from being born short-sighted.'

Three men – military men – sitting in the far corner of the room are discussing the changes in Simla that resulted from the decision made a decade before to turn the town into the 'summer capital' of the Indian Empire. Their conversation piques Lear.

'The changes have marred our lovely Simla utterly and irrevocably,' says one.

'The building of the Hindoostan–Tibet Road was, indisputably, a crowning achievement, but the move to bring the competition-*wallah*s from Calcutta … ah! That has already started ruining things for men here,' says the other, winking at his friend, who is holding a large drink in his big, ruddy fingers.

'You know what I mean. Fewer local lasses to be seen around at the Ridge these summer days.'

The three fall into a laughing fit. Lear is struck by the sight: the very men whom he had observed at a distance from the window approaching the gate – gallantly attired in their dashing military uniforms – now seated across from him, seem so crass, in fact, ugly, laughing while feasting on eggs and beefsteak, bits of mashed potatoes stuck to their lips.

'The disparity between seeing from near and afar compels us to think about *what* is real.'

Bemused by Lear's words, Giorgi remembers the late-evening conversations the two used to have in Corfu – about Locke and Bishop Berkeley. English lessons over, they argued about the difference between the three types of empiricism. *Poppycock!* Lear's own word to describe the theory about the sound of falling trees when one was absent.

'Poppycock is what makes the world shine in all its majesty,' he had remarked.

Just then, the manager walks in, and seeing Lear with his eyeglasses on, says, 'Ah, well. You have them back. Whatever happened?'

'Luckily, the glass did not break. They slid off my nose while I was making my way up to Mrs Campbell's last Thursday. The frame got bent, so I left them with her. She graciously agreed to have them repaired and delivered.'

Lear does not mention that one of the *jampan coolie*s had inadvertently stepped on his eyeglasses.

'Mrs Campbell from Mashoobra?' the manager exclaims with unusual passion. 'I hear she has a breathtakingly beautiful mansion up there, overlooking unending forests of cedar, pine and deodar. In fact, Mr Scott did most of his paintings of the Mahasu Peak while he stayed with Mrs Campbell.'

'A.E. Scott, the painter patronized by the Simla gentry, I presume?'

'A man of great ability, I may add. And very popular with the ladies.'

He nods before making his exit.

Retiring to his room, Lear puts away his sketches and sits at his table.

Simla – the summer capital of the Empire – a little Europe tucked up in the hills! Darjeeling was a far more diversely interesting place than this, as to its European elements – the tea planters, though of different grades socially, being more or less men of intelligence and gentlemanly. Here all is either civil or military, one large sanatorium.

His face breaks into a smile. He thinks of eager Edgar Ware and the rare orchids of Darjeeling, Peter Hornsford with his feathered cap, Christopher Perry on his grey pony – all men of Empire – true blood, loyal subjects of Her Majesty. The smile turns to a chuckle, thinking about Simla's sun-drenched Mall filled with blond children, baby carriages being pushed by frantic *ayah*s; the two-storey house of the famous Charles Napier that had been turned into a school filled with the titter-tatter of girls; the room filled with an expanse of glittering curios and china, and his friend Le Mesurier and his gallant friends gathered around the mahogany table on which lay the furry hide of a long-deceased tiger!

An old Eurasian guest leaves the gates and waits for his *garry*. Giorgi notices that his master is deep in thought, turning the pages and squinting at the little sketch of the spire and the slanting roofs of Simla.

All along the valley we got on, till, at 1.15 p.m., we were deposited at Mrs Lowrie's hotel at Kakkerhutty... Later, I went out, wandering about to discover something to draw, but although Simla is visible to the naked eye, it is only seen over the crest of other hills, themselves hidden by nearer ones.

Lear is thinking about 'distance' as he reads his own words. The amazing anomaly – the greater the distance, the sharper the view – Simla, with its spires and tall spruce and pines, sharply glimpsed as a miniature picture on a cameo hanging from the neck of an elegant lady riding in a London brougham. Thinking about that view from the little village brings up no tangled thoughts about the great enigma of the middle ground, only about the minor obstruction caused by the high conifers standing in the foreground. In fact, the mystery of objects is often heightened when viewed from a distance, Lear thinks as he sharpens his pencil, allowing the shavings to drop to the floor. Oddly, it has little to do with how much detail you capture on paper.

The journey from the village of Kakkerhutty on a hand-carried *jampan* to that fabled hill town founded by the celebrated Lieutenant Ross was another story.

The steep descent to the river and then the ever-steeper ascent along the ridges, the occasional view of the vast, undulating sea of mountains as the jampan *moved in its own rhythm.*

It made one eternally grateful for the service provided by the four sturdy bearers. The storm and driving wind along the way had taken him totally by surprise – a feature of the region that the two would experience many a time during their subsequent sojourn. Giorgi was shivering like a poor mouse, his hands placed tight on the knees, quivering like an aspen tree. Then, who would you expect to show up as the *jampan* reached town? Lear's old friend, Mr Philip Le Mesurier and his daughter.

Giorgi looked curiously at the large man getting off a horse that had a canvas apron buttoned around its neck and waist, entirely covering the fore and hind legs. When he stood before them, all Giorgi noticed was a dark-haired man with very long arms, dressed in military uniform, pins and all. What happens if you have to get off the horse in a hurry, he wondered, seeing the flaps on Philip's cap beat furiously in the wind. The fourteen-year-old girl accompanying her father carried a small parasol that flapped noisily in the driving wind and rain.

'Just imagine, it has been twenty long years since we last met!'

No one could have been happier than Lear to see his friend. The Major shook Lear's hand vigorously, and almost immediately reached into his overcoat pocket to take out a photograph. It was of a woman with heavily lashed brown eyes, a fine chin, generous lips and a head of lovely dark, curly hair done up in a neat bun.

'Mrs Le Mesurier. This is my dear wife, taken the year we arrived here by Mr Jennings, who owns the Crescent Studio. Marjorie is from Chester. You remember Ralph, don't you? She is his younger sister.' Although Lear had spent time with the Major on several occasions when he visited England and had also met many of his friends, he had no recollection of ever meeting Ralph. All he did was pat the horse on the neck.

'We will see you at my residence, my friend, and very soon, I hope. Sorry, have to rush; got to meet the postmaster on urgent business.' The Major dashed off, holding his daughter's hand and leading her in the direction of a large stone house. The policeman, whom the Major requested to direct the *jampan* to Beatsonia, came up to Lear and shook his very cold hands.

'The light is still good, Mr Lear.'

Giorgi knows when he sees his master flipping lazily through the pages of his notebook that he needs the occasional nudge to return to his sketching. Perhaps, he has forgotten that his eyeglasses have been restored, or perhaps, this is yet another wool-gathering day.

'Did you know that a frog can starve to death if its prey does not stir.' Giorgi points to the garden seat overlooking the foothills.

'Am I the frog or the prey?'

Giorgi just gestures towards the large canvas bag placed on the table.

'The Mountain View Pharmacy just delivered the dentifrice you had ordered.'

'Odd. I paid for only one.' What could I possibly do with four tubes of Trotter's Oriental Dentifrice!

Giorgi reads the note that came with the package: *To Mr Lear. With my kind compliments. Your ever-devoted servant, Stephen Orr. MV Pharmacy.*

That day in Simla, the young man, Mr Orr, who had stood behind the counter, had said, 'I simply adore limericks and do scribble a few lines now and then when there's time to spare between work and home.'

Clearing his throat, Mr Orr had proceeded to recite:

'How pleasant to know Mr Lear!

Some think him ill-tempered and queer.'

That was such a striking opening to an amusing poem, Lear had thought, looking at the earnest, chubby, clean-faced pharmacist wearing eyeglasses that were too large for his little ears, his eyes full of anticipation, and eager to impress a poet–

client. But before he could think of the next line, Mr Orr was called away by an aggrieved customer who was irked to know that the English shaving kit he had ordered two weeks before was stuck in a warehouse in Calcutta.

Mr Orr returned to the counter after a few minutes to apologize.

'It's so hard to let one's creative juices flow unhindered while serving irate customers.'

Lear was not sure if the young man had the necessary talent to think beyond an arresting opening line. The open, earnest face he saw in front appeared to mask a head teeming with poetic ideas and clever rhymes. Additional lines began to crystallize inside Lear's head as he saw Mr Orr's hands resting nervously on the counter and the fingers tapping the tops of the bottles in front.

> There was a Young Person of Simla
> Who thought he had a magic formula,
> Of bottling potions, with his wildest notions,
> That lovable Young Person of Simla.

After putting together the lines silently in his head, Lear left the pharmacy, marvelling how poetic inspiration could be found in the most unlikely of places – even in a draughty apothecary in Simla, heavy with the odour of carbolic acid, lavender and metal polish.

Looking at the four tubes of dentifrice lying in front, Lear decides to go indoors to brush his teeth.

Returning, he sits very still and runs his tongue along his squeaky-clean teeth.

It is hard redoing a sketch. He squints, and with his pencil, begins shading the vertical lines of the cedar forest. From the corner of his eye he sees a young, bearded man walking in the garden, with a half-familiar gait, his eyes transfixed by his own shadow on the ground.

Lushington's long strides. It's his day off from court. He has been practising shooting with a five-barrelled revolver after returning from a day out on the sea yachting and will ride his favourite horse after lunch.

The son of the eminent Edmund Henry Lushington, a man known for his physical prowess, Lushington's physical frame showed that he was built for the outdoors. But sadly, a dull and tedious career dealing with legal disputes of petty farmers on an Ionian island was what he had settled for. As for himself, Lear could barely hold a rifle straight, let alone get a flying goose to fall from the sky. He suddenly remembers that the last time he picked up the letters from the post office in Simla lately, they consisted of Lady Waldergrave's short note about Fortescu, another from his publisher, a few from Lady Wyatt written nearly two months back, and another from Mr Fairbairn. Not a word from Lushington! While he was in Mussooree, he had dreamt of Lushington walking in through a brightly lit doorway. He woke up convinced that he would hear from him that very day. A few hours later, as he sat on a bench outside the hotel, picking out the watercolour tubes he would use to start colouring a picture of a hibiscus he had sketched, a middle-aged Eurasian man walked up to him and announced that an 'urgent' telegram had just arrived for him at the hotel. The hibiscus, it seemed to him, had been touched with the tip of an unseen paintbrush, the red just oozing out of the colour tube he held in his fingers. That very instant, a wave of thick clouds crept up from behind. In great haste, he had rushed towards the post office through a thick wave of clouds. Fifteen minutes later, Giorgi noticed his master's faltering steps as he returned to his bench and took up his paintbrush. Concerned, he had asked him, 'Were you expecting a telegram, Master?'

The telegram had been for one Mr Spears, a botanist from Leeds who was studying Himalayan conifers.

Across from the *dak bungalow*, the hill dipped down and spread out like one of Ann's quilts embroidered in scarlet and pale yellow and blue. In front of him are wild geraniums and less intensely coloured rhododendrons, mimosa and wild grass. The young man he had noticed earlier sits on a boulder gazing at the hills, his back to him. The figure appears to glow in the light filtering down from the open sky through the surrounding oak trees.

Lushington and he are walking up to Mount Panachaikon, past meadows of poppies, wild roses, irises, viola, sand lilies, and Ranunculus. He looks intensely at the horizon ahead, as if his destination is beyond the terrain ahead. Although they have spent hours walking, frequently stopping to look at the flowers, Lushington does not seem very aware of his companion's presence. Lear stops to rest on the grass while the man keeps walking, and soon, his figure turns into a lone, distant shade – speechless – just a mere shape in the midst of other shapes.

Over the dinner table, they had so many conversations – about Greece, Patras, the arrival of political refugees and the nation's future. The interest in political events unfolding in Europe certainly stemmed from Lushington's familiarity with matters about law and jurisprudence. Trinity is where he had picked up Greek, although he often said that he felt like he was no more than a passing stranger among 'real' Greeks. Lear knew that his own knowledge of classical Greek was rudimentary. Most of the tutors he had hired to instruct him were either themselves amateur teachers or they would spend hours sitting with him arguing in Ionian dialects they claimed to be the closest to ancient Greek. The evenings would fly reciting lines from Aristophanes, Euripides, Sophocles. When he playfully inserted his own Latin inventions, Lushington's forehead would often scrunch up. The juror had little patience for silly, childlike 'gerund grinds'.

'The fireflies have lit up the garden corner. Let's wait and watch.' The late spring air caresses Lushington's face.

To this day, he has not been able to understand why the man who didn't quite enjoy wordplay agreed to stay back for dinner!

The man sitting on the boulder has left.

Lear realizes something he had known all along but had been slow to acknowledge and accept. His young friend certainly took great pleasure in his company, especially during cold evenings when they discussed and debated the intricacies of classical Greek over a glass of fine brandy. He enjoyed the physical exertion involved in going for long walks on Corfu's shores with him. He certainly knew his place in the world. But that was *all* there was to their relationship. *Nothing* more. It had struck him long ago that he read a lot more into Lushington's wistful look, his smile and the ease with which he would settle into the sofa in Lear's living room than the poor man ever intended to convey. For the juror, the fireflies were just six-footed beetles whose mating instincts made them light up to repel predators. Nothing more.

Giorgi removes the pencil and paper from Lear's desk and arranges the watercolour tubes in a circle.

'Nothing that really catches my eye today.'

Giorgi hands him his unfinished sketches and his notebook.

'Perhaps these need some touching up. Perhaps a wash or two.'

Lear's eyes run over the hastily sketched domes of Delhi, and he remembers the journey that brought him hitherto to Simla –

the departure from Delhi on a gentle spring morning, the perilous journey on a boat to Roorkee, where he nearly died after the arch of an overhead bridge tore down the boat's roof, the *bungalow* on an island in the Ganges just opposite Haridwar's bathing *ghats*, where he spent the night watching the lights twinkle on the banks of the river. The motion of six able-bodied *coolies* pushing and pulling on the winding road of the Sivalak Hills had made him think of the flow of a certain poetic metre that he was sure Tennyson would not approve of. A line of peacocks strutted by just as the fading light of the late afternoon sun became visible on approaching the valley of Dun.

Nearly a month had elapsed since he had walked the promenade in Mussooree, the European hill station up from the valley. The beauty of Landoor, the highest part of Mussooree, had taken his breath away.

The most sublime view all across the snowy Himalayas, a long, long range, quite unlike what one saw from Darjeeling, where Kanchenjunga, a sort of mountain epic, controls and absorbs every interest.

He leafs through the pages of his notebook as he retraces his steps through Landoor.

All that side of Mussooree is very fine, even sublime, where it is not cut up and hashed by rails, palings, roads and Anglo-Saxonism.

Amongst all the signs of European civilization, nothing seemed more offensive than their intrusive presence in the Himalayan wilderness. He remembered Le Mesurier's friend Bayley's reactions to that term when they met at Le Mesurier's residence.

'Is Anglo-Saxonism bad?' he had asked, filling his pipe.

Lear often felt – and he shared his opinion with Giorgi a few times – that church spires, archways, and neo-Gothic or Indo-Saracenic monuments built in pristine Himalayan locales and admired by all were, in fact, *wrong. Completely and utterly out of place.* Much like the new roads intended to make the world more accessible; they were built by hacking away and destroying old forests and slicing off entire sides of the mountains. Even Giorgi understood his master's abhorrence of all that imitation and ostentation. Did he not, like him, share the same kind of aversion for absurdly elaborate English hats, skirts, ruffles and parasols and the wrong kinds of shoes? What was the point of all that preening, modifying, elaborating and needless adornment? The wilderness, palaces and ruins they had seen offered the most astonishing spectacles ever, without any embellishment.

A lone eagle circling in the sky above that has several other birds gathering around and settling noisily on the branches of the oak trees suddenly draws Lear's attention. A Himalayan carrion bird sits among the foliage, his giant wings flapping vigorously. Can a carcass of a wild ibex, such as the one he had seen in Simla, be lying somewhere – an animal that had missed a step and been hurled down a steep cliff? Lear tries to rid his mind of the ibex's unmoving eyes.

As the day passes and cups and plates are filled with tea and sandwiches, Lear is reminded of what Giorgi calls *trivial matters* so starkly visible in the sun-drenched Mall. The outrageous hats worn by self-possessed Simla ladies looked like plump, overfed pheasants roosting on human heads. The frenetic pace with which people entered shops. At one end of the Mall, the curio shops were crammed with only-too-eager customers running their fingers over stoles and carpets, and at the other, the shops selling cheap pendants and Chinese vases had little doors choked with customers thronging to enter.

But now he notices the morning coat of worsted wool and pale brown trousers that Giorgi wears. 'Did you buy the horn buttons on your coat from the shop in Via del Corso?'

'You remember very well. You were still at home waiting for the cook to show up.'

Giorgi's smile borders on mild disdain mixed with a touch of tenderness for the man who never took to his cooking.

Buttons! *Horn* buttons! Lady Le Mesurier, Philip's devoted wife, and her missing priceless button. It was the day when they had walked nearly two miles to reach Philip Le Mesurier's house. Situated behind a large garden on the upper road of the Ridge, past the Union Church, it was a large cottage with dried-up wisteria vines draped over the front veranda. They found Mrs Mesurier at home, very upset about a button missing from a silk blouse sent by a friend from China. She had discovered the loss – she told Lear – while putting away the clothes that the *dobie* had just delivered.

Sitting on back-tufted chairs with gold buttons sewn over the deep blue damask upholstery, Lear had listened patiently to Lady Mesurier's long protestation about her *dobie's* reckless washing. 'These buttons are priceless cameo buttons that I found in a shop in Chester that I had put on the blouse.'

Her vexed eyes darted from one item of furniture to another.

'These people have no value for such things.'

The 'real cause of the problem', she went on to elaborate, were 'petty shopkeepers, poor clerks, peons, coolies, rickshaw pullers' who had taken over the lower *bazaar*, many of whom engaged – sadly – in the 'nefarious trade of opium'.

'Of course, there is the thriving *good* trade in honey, borax and potatoes. All sanctioned by law. But the rest, the less said, the better.'

Her beloved Simla – once a quiet, remote town – had

suddenly become the focal point of sixty-three routes meeting from different valleys spread through the Himalayas, 'leading to the rapid deterioration of the town's standards of respectability'. Her teeth showed quite prominently when she spoke. Like Mrs Cracroft, she was unstoppable, launching, the next moment, into yet another peroration of the moral decline of the resident Europeans – and the immediate need to be more vigilant about the visiting functionaries from Calcutta.

'How long do you intend to stay here?' she asked, offering tea, her chest heaving as if she had just walked uphill.

The afternoon sun had moved between the towering cedar trees visible from the open window as the lady proceeded to list all of the balls, archery contests, fêtes and picnics that were on the list of activities that she had initiated and that she encouraged the two to attend. 'Not to forget our amateur theatre,' she said, closing the window to keep away the draught, 'and, of course, my daughter is playing sweet Miranda in *The Tempest*.'

The deservingness that stuck to her body and face, and even the way she sat in their silk upholstered chair, with the soles of her elegant shoes barely touching the carpet, seemed to conceal something. A closer look at those eyes, the dark, nervous eyes, flashing with restless irritation, lips closed tightly, a non-existent chin held up by the ruffles of a white silk blouse, revealed that Mrs Le Mesurier scarcely bore any resemblance to the photo her husband had pulled out of his pocket to show the visitors that rainy afternoon.

'You will be more comfortable here. It has a window with the best view of the town but without the draught.'

As the three walked up to the window, Lear's eyes were dazzled by the spectacle all around the room. Gilded and silver plated vases, innumerable papier mâché objects of different sizes, delicate ivory carvings with silver inlay, silk and woollen shawls in intricate designs draped over the chairs, Tibetan prayer wheels and sceptres studded with semi-precious stones, extravagantly embroidered saddlery, an ivory table with a decorative carved base, wool *durrees*, silk carpets with dazzling patterns, grinning demon masks on the walls sat on all of the visible surfaces, and a large spoonback armchair with buttoned backrest and carved legs was placed at the far corner. Placed on top of a chest of drawers was a framed photograph of the Queen sitting in her carriage, surrounded by several photographs of the Le Mesurier family and a poorly executed painting of Hadrian's Wall. What an absurd medley of objects! An insane collector's treasure trove, Lear thought, running his finger over the carved table.

Taking off his eyeglasses, Lear placed them next to the photograph of the Queen. Giorgi stared at the carpet. Of course, he wanted to make sure that his shoes had not left any marks. The sun, entering through the pimpernel chintz curtains, and flapping gently in the breeze, made everything glitter like the cave that Aladdin had walked into with a fire lamp in hand. Seeing Lear absorbed in studying every little object that met his curious eye, Giorgi excused himself and left the room, taking out his tobacco pouch as he walked through the door to the garden. The weary Lady Le Mesurier ordered tea and left the room.

As the sunlight poured through the open window, the photograph of the Queen appeared to acquire a magical glow. Touching an inlaid brass bowl ever so lightly with his right finger, Lear peered at her face.

Windsor Castle. It is a warm afternoon in August. Moving slowly through her collection, the Queen holds up a two-inch carved deer, the antlers studded with tiny garnets. 'How exquisite! How did you get these beautiful things, Your Majesty?' There is a pause.

'I inherited them, Mr Lear.' The Queen sweeps out of the room, places herself at a table and says, 'It is time for tea.'

Outside, in the garden, the wind chimes let out joyous sounds like the distant ringing of church bells. Major Philip Le Mesurier appeared through the door accompanied by three of his friends – Peacock, Daley and Bayley. Lear was greeted with a warm hug.

'Let us sit where there's a patch of sun.'

The wicker chair made funny, squeaky noises every time Lear moved his arms.

From the top of a large, carved mahogany table, the head of a tiger, attached to its yellow and black skin, stared at him with wide-open jaws, the sharp fangs sticking out of gigantic paws.

'Philip and his artillerymen fired and killed the beast only six months ago. No one had heard of tigers before in these parts. Some villagers attacked it thinking it was a leopard, till it sprang and attacked them back.'

While Peacock patted the head of the dead beast, Lear ran his fingers over the soft fur.

At that point, Philip was summoned to the garden by the gardener, so he left hurriedly, leaving the door slightly ajar.

The three men in the room spoke to each other in hushed voices.

'Philip wishes to be Commander-in-Chief, and there is a good chance that he will be. In less than a year, I imagine.'

Peacock drank from his scotch.

'A military man of exceptional skills with a passion for rare dictionaries,' Daley responded, picking up a beautifully preserved copy of *A New Dictionary of the Terms Ancient and Modern of the Canting Crew* from the mantelpiece.

'Truly a collector's paradise, Simla is. And a treasure house for rare objects.'

Bayley held the mask of a grinning demon in his hands. 'The old man in the Lower *Bazaar* supplies me with unusual ritual vases. The man undoubtedly has important connections in the monasteries.'

Peacock helped himself to several pieces of cheese from the plate while Daley drew his chair noiselessly up to Lear.

'You are a poet and an artist. Quite certain you know the value of things oriental. Did you meet Mr Kipling in Bombay?'

Lear had stared at the fine lines around Daley's handsome jaw and his receding hairline until Peacock rose from his chair.

'Lockwood spent some time here about three years back working with a craftsman, mostly wood. He certainly has an extraordinary eye for things oriental.'

Peacock finished off the last piece of cheese and wiped his lips with a handkerchief.

'So did Francis Firth, but he was a photographer. Went up to Kullu and Spiti. A daring man. The finest sensibility, I dare say, that I have encountered in these parts. A few years ago, Marjorie bought a photograph taken by him of Simla. A lovely view of the Ridge.'

The sun has begun to lose its intensity. The view of the mountains is getting dimmer with each passing minute. Looking down, Lear realizes that the young man he saw before has not returned. A broken wheelbarrow and a rusty spade lie on the grass. He moves to the outside gallery, just as some guests arrive. Three ladies, an infant with her *ayah*, four girls and two boys, accompanied by three military men. The family he had seen walking along the Ridge the day after they arrived in Simla – he recognizes them instantly.

Seeing so many European children running around the Mall in Simla, all squealing and screaming under the watchful eyes of their *ayahs*, was so delightful that he made sure to note down a few words just before he went to bed the night before:

Simla beginning to fill... numbers of jampans, each with eight or ten liveried servants are on the road; also infinite lots of delicious, little, fair, lovely ducks of English children.

It is the third week of April. A strange emotion passes through him while reading the words he had written the day after they had arrived in Solan.

Returning to the town, wished I could draw one exquisite landscape of immense depth and distance; the delicacy of its farthest horizon, the mountain in the golden haze of evening was sublimely lovely when all the detail was lost and only space, colour, glory and mystery remained.

The sounds of the buzz and chatter at the Mall, the spires that unflinchingly asserted their towering Englishness, English children running around, screaming, their cheeks flushed and stained from eating strawberries – everything he saw and sensed in Simla appeared to exist in a haze, encircled by another world, where the aura of Englishness, so painstakingly cultivated in this little Europe, was subsumed by something bigger but quite ineffable.

Where was the glory, he asks himself, looking once again at the rusty wheelbarrow in the garden. Is Englishness just like the gleaming but motionless iron tracks that he had seen criss-crossing the vast expanse of India, the pathways that allowed the iron monsters to just chug along belching so much smoke that it made you splutter? One platform after another, the destinations just slide past as you sit motionless inside the guts of these monsters.

Strange questions swarm in his mind. He looks at his sketches again.

Here, among the mountains, the abiding sense of expansiveness had touched his very core. The dense forests fading into the skies on his way to Narkanda and Mashoobra offered the most desired scenery one could have, the perfect light and angle, so he had sketched feverishly all day. Every wash made from those sketches offered to the eye a new realm of perception. A swirl of light furrowing through the depths of the scenes appeared, like an epiphany, a single pine tree standing amidst a pile of rooftops, with a lonely figure stooping among the fire and smoke to stoke an evening fire.

Meanwhile, what he sees outside, in the garden of the *dak bungalow*, makes him smile. Next to the rusty wheelbarrow now stands a carriage bearing an infant throwing an epic tantrum. The screams rend the air, making the squirrels scamper away in alarm. The two girls standing near the rose beds sulk, while the women sitting in deck chairs complain about the behaviour of *coolies*. The *ayah* stands alone, staring at the bawling baby and looking helplessly at the valley down below. On the table in the gallery sit the men, lounging in large chairs, laughing, holding large mugs of beer in their burly hands.

'Infants will cry, and helpless *ayah*s will look on. That is the order of things.'

Lear's ruminations about the world amuse Giorgi, who sits in the sun reading an old edition of *The Civil and Military Gazette.*

'Do you remember how we escaped the tantrum of another baby on the Mall?'

'I have never seen you walk so briskly as on that day, Mr Lear.'

Lear shudders.

That day, in the sun-drenched Mall, they had run into Mrs Parker – the lady from Scott's Hotel in Mussooree, who, without any warning whatsoever, had entrusted the two with the care of her infant and the *ayah*.

'Back in a jiffy.'

Before Lear knew it, the lady in the wide-brimmed hat had vanished into the crowd.

Fifteen minutes elapsed.

They looked around anxiously. The baby had begun to scream, squirming violently. Another fifteen minutes passed. No sign of Mrs Parker among the hats bobbing in the throng.

The Indian *ayah* sat on a bench with another young woman, chatting.

Lear promptly signalled to Giorgi. Leaving the howling baby, the two hastened off in the direction of Elysium Hill.

Elysium Hill – they had been told by the manager of the hotel – was where Napier's house once stood.

It was the perfect time to make an escape.

'Hard to miss. A two-storey brick house, with many windows and a large portico in front, and surrounded by tall rhododendron trees. It is now a school.'

Giorgi never quite understood the allure of Charles Napier. There was no doubt that Napier's book had captivated his master. But to be so insistent on visiting the residence of an almost forgotten military general seemed to him to border on pure obsession – especially for an artist who spent so much of his time contemplating the beauty of landscapes and mountains and mocking the pompousness of military commanders.

But unpredictability was one of his master's strongest points – a feature that made him stand apart from his friends and acquaintances.

The walk up to Elysium Hill took nearly an hour and a half, until Giorgi paused at the sign that read 'Punjab Girls School'. Seeing a young girl walking up to the gate, he handed her Lear's handwritten note, seeking an audience with the mistress of the school. The girl took it willingly and disappeared behind the gate.

'Napier's residence became Lord Auckland's private house and then turned into a school for girls, I presume.'

Lear ran his fingers through his beard and steadied his walking stick, which Giorgi had handed him that morning.

Shortly, out of the gate appeared a middle-aged lady who introduced herself as 'Mrs Neely, second mistress'. Dressed in a long, black gown, a white blouse with little black bows, puff sleeves narrowing down to the cuffs, she invited the two to follow her through the gate and up a flight of stairs, past portraits of people and framed pictures of the Himalayas. Girls were hurrying down the stairs. Mrs Neely looked at them disapprovingly, without saying a word.

'Our very own Carlyle.' She stopped on the way up the stairs and nodded at the portrait of a venerable-looking man with greying whiskers and a beard staring out of the grand, gilded frame.

Lear was out of breath and needed Giorgi to hold him before they made their way to the top gallery. As they climbed up the stairs, Mrs Neely continued to point out the 'extraordinary features' of the unframed portraits and pictures hanging on the walls. One was a sketch of a cluster of wooden houses that she explained stood on the grounds of the school before they were pulled down to make way for Napier's house. The next was a photograph of shaggy horses standing next to a lady all dressed in black and – most astonishing of all – of a young Englishman attired in 'the local costume', sitting on a donkey and flanked by three Englishwomen in frills and hats.

'Simla from the time I arrived from Kent, nearly fifteen years ago.' Mrs Neeley gathered her skirt as she went up yet another flight of stairs.

The exhaustion on his master's face was beginning to show. Giorgi pulled up a chair for Lear as they reached a small room on the top gallery. Mrs Neely's lecture continued, about the history of 'this remarkable school', which included a small sermon about the importance of girl's education, a short eulogy on the founder, Reverend J.B. d' Aguilor, and the educational principles he espoused about imparting 'proper Christian education to European girls'.

But not a word about Napier. The two followed Mrs Neely to the open window, where she pointed to a cluster of buildings nestled in a grove of conifers.

'Our school was first established at Holly Lodge. It has been only six years since we moved into these premises.'

As Mrs Neely spoke, Giorgi interjected, 'Surely, the school is meant for the students of the region of Punjab? Are the girls all local?'

'All local but certainly *not native.*'

Mrs Neely straightened her long skirt.

'A few come from families of regular residents. The rest come from elsewhere. Others have parents who reside in Simla only during the summer months.'

As they left the gates of Napier's house – thanking Mrs Neely profusely for giving two hours of her valuable time – they saw behind them a group of fair, blonde girls, laughing, carrying their bags to the carriages waiting under the trees.

'Why do they call the school *Punjab* Girls School?'

Lear responded to Giorgi's very earnestly expressed question by letting out a sigh and then steadying his cane.

Leaving the iron gate of the school, they took the road that wound through a forest filled with cedar and pine. Without warning, Giorgi abruptly stopped at the turn.

Through the gaps in the dense foliage that lined the road, the foothills stretched out, and in the fading sunlight, their gentle folds rippled over to the far horizon, where the peaks appeared as if carrying the multi-hued skies on the tips of short, stumpy fingers.

'Another grand scene of the mountains.'

Lear stood still for a few minutes. After they resumed walking downhill, they found themselves entering a small garden. The walls of the small cottage at the far end of the garden were built from planks of partly rotting pine. A crumbling slate roof sat precariously on top, and two open windows had pink and white curtains flapping noisily in the breeze.

A young woman dressed in a green sarong and a cap walked up to them and gestured with her hands. It soon became clear that she wanted to show them something.

At the bottom of the sheer cliff next to her garden fence lay a goat-like creature with small striped horns and a little beard. At the base of its neck was a patch of congealed blood. Flies buzzed around the motionless body. No doubt, the creature had fallen from the top of the cliff that rose above the cottage.

A few young boys joined them, one stroking the unmoving head with a long stick.

Lear peered down.

'Ibex! Must be a Himalayan ibex! Sure-footed creatures. Odd that it fell from the cliff.' The sharp-edged hooves were intact, but one of the horns had split open.

Giorgi turned his eyes away while Lear directed his attention up to the mangled branches of the dense rhododendron bushes growing on the sides of the steep cliff.

'Must have slipped. They are foragers, and it is early spring.'

A pile of gravel lay next to the body.

'The weight of falling bodies is enough to kill even a mouse, I reckon.'

As they walked back to their hotel that day, Lear's thoughts were fixed on the brownish-grey coat of the dead animal, the wide-open eyes, as if it had been startled by the unexpected fall.

'The weight of falling bodies. Newton or Galileo?' he had remarked unmindfully to Giorgi when the latter helped him put on an extra pair of socks.

The men have finished their beer and walk back to their rooms while Lear sits at his desk and turns the pages of his little notebook of expenses. The watercolours lie in a pile around his sketchbook. A golden birdwing flutters by and settles on a rhododendron bush with a single remaining bloom. After staring at the tubes of watercolour, Lear changes his mind, picks up the pen and begins writing.

The Himalayas, barring Darjeeling, are mighty uninteresting! Compare the Cumberland or Welsh hills and their lakes. The Alps, their lakes and glaciers; the Dolomites and the Tyrol; the varied forms of Greece and Italy; and then think of the hundreds of good-for-nothing, weary miles here, remarkable only for hugeness-magnitude.

Cleft-hooved animals and the colossal mountains all around – the sheer effort to keep one's sense of balance but also the real possibility of falling. A sharp ache runs through his knees; his chest throbs, and he begins to feel – and not for the first time – that the journey is beginning to tire him out, that enormous effort would be required of him to just be able to walk back to his room.

As hard as he tries, he cannot keep his mind from thinking about those *weary miles* and the *hugeness.*

The sheet of paper before him shows that his brush had left a semi-transparent layer of colour over the lines of the drawing. Pausing, he picks up his pen again while Giorgi places a woollen blanket on his knees.

There is still enough light to figure out the shapes in the distance. Outside the dak *bungalow in Teog, the path to Mrs Campbell's mansion is steeper than expected. Suddenly, he feels Giorgi grasping his left arm very tightly. The hues in the farthest visible distances are changing rapidly, as if the skies are being steeped in a fresh coat of wash every minute by unseen hands.*

Towards sunset, however, this immense landscape became very lovely, all pallid as it is beyond the dark ilex trees. The next range is the palest green; and then the rest fades off into the Chour, which is hardly darker than the sky. A beautiful drawing may be made by washing it out into almost nil, if you could only keep the purity of the remote ranges. Be the idea absurd or not, it is very much like an enormous Claude. Just before reaching Teog, the cluster of native huts down below from the ridge to Mashoobra come into view – the tiny sloping roofs of slate, the ring of bushes all around them, the smoke rising from the little chimneys. The coolies are milling around, so Lear walks a distance, followed by Giorgi, and sits on a boulder. His knees are about to buckle.

Lear looks intently at his paintbrush, now standing very still in a small tumbler of water. Claude Lorrain often spoke about the power of colour to both embody and dissolve the solidity of the world – to hold the lines between the distant and inaccessible and the near and tangible. But in India, the solidity of the world is so often marked by an ever-moving screen made up of objects, faces and the blurry outlines of bodies. Often, it took an enormous effort to be close to things that caught one's attention. Who were the people living in the tiny huts partly visible that day when the clouds drifted away and became shadows? He recalls the picture of a native Himalayan village in a studio shop in Simla. The distant huts must have been home to the men and women portrayed in that picture. Women in bright black and red sarongs, their necks adorned with beautifully embroidered fabric belts, large earrings hanging from their ears, strings of metal beads attached to the head wrap and falling over the forehead, and men in long coats and starched turbans. Perhaps, the villages were also home to orange-robed monks twirling their prayer wheels, lips moving in silent prayer.

After they had reached another village very similar to the one he had viewed from the Ridge, he was confounded by what he saw – in place of the picturesque rural scene he had imagined, there were decrepit wooden shacks with broken slate roofs and makeshift, half-decaying doors. In fact, the village seemed abandoned, with only a few ragged children sitting idly by the roadside, some bone-weary women piling the firewood in stacks. The little gardens at the back looked as if no one had ever tended them, and the rhododendron bushes he had seen before were sick and dying, with stacks of rotting firewood placed all around them and covered with old, rotting rags. The view when you get close to the object – things do change!

Later that evening, after they had reached Mrs Campbell's residence in Mashoobra, Lear sat gazing from the window at the fires being built below by the *coolies*. He learnt from Mrs Campbell that most of the villages they had encountered on their way were now deserted. The new route had diverted the existing trade route that had, for centuries, enabled the mountain caravans to journey across the mountains from the remote regions of Ladakh. New roads promised better revenue. The caravan trade had dwindled rapidly, and consequently, the inhabitants were without work.

'Many of the men you saw in the village now work as *coolie*s in Teog while many families have simply abandoned their homes and gone down to Umballa. A sorry lot, these folks, Mr Lear!'

Mrs Campbell's story had taken Lear by surprise. They had arrived at the large house that very afternoon after their second attempt as the existing road had been blocked by a landslip. Lear had sat for hours looking out at the vast blue hollow spaces between the receding mountains while Mrs Campbell narrated her story. The outlines of the distant mountains were gradually being erased before turning into the hazy outlines of a giant death mask.

A distinguished resident of Mashoobra, Mrs Campbell's husband, Edward Campbell, had fought in the Mutiny, and she had spent many years in Simla before retiring to the Mashoobra woods. After dinner, when she began reminiscing about her glorious days in Simla, Lear pulled out a picture he had sketched of a group of monkeys sitting on a crag.

'Not a single day passed when my Simla gardener did not have to use his slingshot to rid the *langoor*s that hid among the branches of the trees. They would ravage the fruit trees and raid the kitchen. But I was always captivated by their faces. So human-like!'

Here was a lady who had spent nearly forty years of her life in the mountains, attending military dinners and going for balls and now lived alone in a large mansion that was literally inaccessible to most Englishmen. No *langoor* ever visited her in her splendid isolation. All that remained were empty rooms and long curtains that reached down to the floor and swung when the windows were left open. The mountain owls hooted all night.

Lear shuts the notebook and looks out at the garden. The young *ayah* is playing with the baby girl. 'Missy *baba*, missy *baba*, I will take you to village, and we play with monkeys.' The *ayah*'s voice reaches Lear's ears. She is cold and wraps her green shawl over her head. Outside the gate, the three *coolies* are stretched out on the back of the *garry*. Lear takes off his eyeglasses and rests his head on the back of his chair. Soon, it will be dark and the howling of mountain wolves will resume. Giorgi puts away his paints and brushes silently as Lear returns to his room. Outside the window, a man carries a pile of wood for the fireplace in the gallery. The fire in the gallery dims, and someone at the far end of the gallery bolts the door noisily.

9

The Cummerbund
An Indian Poem

I

She sate upon her Dobie,
To watch the Evening Star,
And all the Punkahs as they passed,
Cried, 'My! How fair you are!'
Around her bower, with quivering leaves,
The tall Kamsamahs grew,
And Kitmutgars in wild festoons
Hung down from Tchokis blue

II

Below her home the river rolled
With soft meloobious sound,
Where golden-finned Chuprassies swam,

In myriads circling round.
Above, on tallest trees remote
Green Ayahs perched alone,
And all night long the Mussak moan'd
Its melancholy tone.

III

And where the purple Nullahs threw
Their branches far and wide,–
And silver Goreewallahs flew
In silence, side by side,–
The little Bheesties' twittering cry,
Rose on the fragrant air,
And oft the angry Jampan howled
Deep in his hateful lair.

IV

She sate upon her Dobie,–
She heard the Nimmak hum,–
When all at once a cry arose,–
'The Cummerbund is come!'
In vain she fled:–with open jaws
The angry monster followed,
And so, (before assistance came,)
The Lady Fair was swallowed.

V

They sought in vain for even a bone
Respectfully to bury,–

They said, 'Hers was a dreadful fate!'
(And Echo answered 'Very.')
They nailed her Dobie to the wall,
Where last her form was seen,
And underneath they wrote these words,
In yellow, blue, and green:–
Beware, ye Fair! Ye Fair, beware!
Nor sit out late at night,–
Lest horrid Cummerbunds should come,
And swallow you outright.

Pouring rain outside, so Lear lies in bed watching the fine filigree of shadows on the wall. A handwritten copy of 'The Cummerbund' he had sent to the *Times* lies on the table beside his bed. Raising himself slowly from the bed, he picks up the *Times of India* and begins flipping through the pages. Just below the 'Notice to Shippers' and 'Passengers to Europe' is 'Bentley's Favourite Novels', where two novels by Wilkie Collins are listed.

Poor Miss Fitch is one of them.

Poor Miss Fitch! What a silly, sentimental novel! Just the kind that will sell in Bombay.

He looks at the clock. It is almost nine.

'By my Uncle Arly,' he mutters, 'I hope I haven't missed breakfast.'

Luckily, the *kitmutgar* arrives as soon as he has placed himself on the table at the far end of the breakfast room. There is just another lady in a white frock and hat, sitting and drinking her morning tea. Monsoon rains beating down, what a force of nature. The windows shake, and the gusty wind beats on the door like an impatient visitor waiting to be let in.

It is only the third week of July, the second week of the monsoon season in the Deccan. With all that water and wind packed in, sweeping across from the Arabian Sea, the last five days have been just grey, gusty, damp and chilly. Not unlike the days of the frightfully thick glum sirocco of Corfu.

Hope that I am not coming down with a fever. Perhaps, I should remind Giorgi to pour some quinine in my gin. Lear scrapes up the remaining egg and steak from his plate, picks up a piece of papaya with the fork and looks at the copy of *Humphry Clinker* that one of the guests had left lying on the sofa. What an intelligently crafted epistolary work it is: six characters writing about the same events but what interesting variations of the same story! On his last journey by train, he had skimmed through Scott's *The Surgeon's Daughter*, but left it unfinished, taking up Smollett instead.

'Numbingly tedious and utterly banal' – words he had used to describe Scott's India novel to Giorgi.

He returns to the *Times*.

'I dare say, "The Cummerbund" looks quite lovely in print.'

The suddenness of his words startles the lady sitting across from him.

'I am sorry. Did not mean to startle you. The *Times* has just published my poem, which I sent just two weeks ago!'

There is astonishment on her face.

'In a week? How did you manage that? I imagine it takes much longer for the mail to travel between here and London.'

'The *Times of India*. Printed in Bombay. It is an Indian newspaper.'

'Oh,' the lady responds with mild disdain and resumes cutting her steak.

Giorgi has just walked in.

'Giorgi, my friend. Here is "The Cummerbund" – in flesh and blood – on page six of the *Times*. They actually printed it!'

Just a few weeks ago, Giorgi had given the poem five readings before taking it to the post office to be mailed.

'I am so delighted. So nonsensically Indian your new poem is, Master! Fantastic animals, odd people and even odder trees – all so…colourful and *ominous*.' Giorgi is unsure if *ominous* is the appropriate word to describe a poem. Holding the spoon up to make sure it is clean, he asks in an earnest tone, 'Is "The Cummerbund" a poem meant for children?'

'Fiddlediddlety. It is a poem that is aimed at scaring, soothing, educating, confusing, and certainly, at titillating, my friend. Remember the man standing behind the lady at the Residency in Gwalior? A handsome, besuited creature, the cummerbund is. But his modish good looks are very, very deceptive.'

'But how did you compose the poem?'

Outside, the gentle pitter-patter has given way to a steady drumming. Giorgi is busy rearranging the bottles of medicine.

How can he possibly express to Giorgi *how* the poem came into being? The man hasn't the faintest idea about Rossetti or the painting of Lilith – the lady with the red curls cascading down her shoulder. When he stood in front of the fiery deity on the walls of the Buddhist shrine, Giorgi was waiting outside, smoking. Sure, he had been served by competent *kitmutgars* and been carried in *jampans*, but a detailed explanation of how these entities turn into a swirling mass of flying objects may just be too bewildering to the man now looking intently at the label of a small, brown bottle.

He is right. The next thing he hears from Giorgi is, 'Will you require your quinine now, Master?'

Lear holds up a metal dish to inspect his face and mutters,

'Good grief. I am looking pale, very pale, indeed!'

Giorgi peers down, once again, at page six of the *Times*, bringing the paper up very close to his nose.

'The monsoons have made the paper almost porous. Even the ink has an odd smell.'

He wants to explain why one of Lear's undershirts is missing but holds himself back. Have to move beyond this endless talk about quinine, housekeeping, counting and accounting, darning, and packing, he tells himself. He would rather Lear give an opinion about the poem he had begun writing. Titled 'Waiting in Silence', Giorgi is still uncertain about its poetic metre. Could he seek his master's aid?

But Lear's eyes are shut. He seems to be in deep contemplation.

With his eyeglasses held in his left hand, Lear pinches his nose with his right. The images and sounds that inspired and shaped the poem are once again beginning to flock around his head like the herd of buffaloes he saw walking on the narrow road in Jubbulpore. The constant beat of the pouring rain, the thunder crackling, the lightning flashing across the sky – a rabble, a throng of shape-changing creatures, the *jumblies* hustle past the Old man of Melrose, followed by Mrs Cracroft's brightly attired *kamsamah*s who nod and smile like marionettes in a London Harlequinade. Bright blue demons baring their fangs creep out of the crevices on the wall. On the large mirror is the misshapen body of the childhood mummer flinging himself high in the air, wild with frenzy, the purple colours of his garments glinting in the bright sun. The twittering, moaning and howling follow, and then the winds beat relentlessly on the roof of the quiet house in Margate, making the glass panes tremble. A man waves his little, dark-haired boy goodbye from the garden gate, and soon after, the lad sits at his desk, squinting at the book he holds in his tiny hands. Outside, on the empty road, the *bheesti* sits, staring listlessly at the blazing sun in the sky. On a dry and warm day, he could be seen watering the dry, red soil, his glistening *mussak* slung over the shoulder. In the distance, Lady Lilith reclines in blazing white under a bower filled with bright squawking green parrots. She is combing her red, flowing tresses. The *dobie* counts the soiled clothes that lie in a pile at his feet. All around, the mynahs shriek, flitting from one branch to the next.

Shaken out of his reverie by the sound of a teaspoon falling at his feet, Lear opens his eyes to see the lines of the printed poem in front slowly dissolve into muddy spots. Giorgi has vanished from the scene.

The more the din of the hammering rain intensifies, the harder it is for Lear to free himself from this unstoppable spectacle that his mind has set into motion. One after another, faces appear: the wizened face of the Simla *dobie* uttering, 'You paid for thirty-two items and you have thirty-two here, not one less'; the silent *punkahwallah* at the *dak bungalow* slowly pulling the cord while on the walls around him, two shadows sweep from one end to the other; the *ayah* draped in a bright green *saree*, watching sorrowfully over the wailing infant in the garden full of the dancing heads of poppies; *kamsamah*s and *kitmutgar*s floating across the brightly lit room carrying trays filled with cream pies; a bloated *mussak*, glistening on the back of the *bheesti,* moaning like a child in pain; two lean *coolie*s of the *jampan*s resting under a tree while the remaining two walk away, holding hands.

In one unexpected flash, the nib of his pen had moved, almost like a golden serpent making its way out of a dark hole. Without crossing out a single word, he wrote, while outside, the blazing, hot sky had turned into a theatre of dark clouds and lightning. It was still summer. When the poem was finally done, the skies had cleared. Holding up the sheet of paper in his hands, he had brought it close to his nose. Just then, a branch of a giant *peepul* tree outside came crashing down, the leaves scraping noisily against the windowpane. From somewhere, a sulphurous vapour filled the room. All he was left with was the memory of Evelyn Baring handing him a copy of *The People of India* on a cold winter morning in Calcutta and saying, 'The people of India, indeed, present a maze to English eyes.'

Meanwhile, he notices that Giorgi has returned with a steaming cup of tea.

Faces and more faces. Limbs and shoulders. Photographs. He is leafing through the thick, hardbound copy of The People of India. *The freshly cut pages leave a faint scent on his fingertips. A Series of* Photographic Illustrations. *London: India Museum.*

'The magic of photography.' Evelyn beams at the shiny new volume. 'It should run into a few more volumes, I reckon. Lord Canning's idea – to produce the annotated photographs of all of the native castes and tribes in India, with details about their hereditary occupations.'

The editors, Watson and Kaye. Watson, a professor of medicine in Bombay, the printed words on the title page.

Evelyn pours more brandy into his empty glass. The Calcutta winter sun moves between the branches of a giant peepul *tree.*

Wordlessly, Giorgi sits on a chair, gazing out of the large window at the dark clouds billowing in the sunless sky. He picks up a pen to write.

'The magic of photography. Ah, I wish I had a photograph of Lushington.'

Both hands on his knees, Giorgi faces Lear. His lips curl upwards as he speaks.

'You did sketch Mr Lushington once while he sat on the chair reading the fat book you offered him. The last time I saw you take that unfinished sketch out from the box on the mantelpiece, all you did was run your fingers over it and put it back. If I remember right, the box also contained an unfinished sketch of a woman sitting under a tree.'

'Ann.'

Lear's single word, uttered with emphasis, is followed by the sound of a young man walking in with soaking, squelching gumboots. Taking off his large coat, he shakes it and places it carelessly on the sofa. The *kitmutgar* promptly picks it up and puts it away on the coat rack.

'I thought the sketch was of a younger woman, the one from fairy tales.'

Lear does not utter a single word.

Photography. The revolution of our times. The camera obscura. The shaft of light entering the tiny hole in a darkened room. Why conjure up a shadow? Is life not already a parade of shadows? You see embalmed bodies in coffins, mute faces painted in the gold of eternity. They pass like the occasional roar of the ocean that wakes you up in the middle of the night. A face flickers in the half-light but dissolves as soon as the first shaft of light enters through the window.

That cold winter day in Calcutta. Outside, the sparrows gather on the grass. The sound of scissors clipping the tops of the tall hedge reaches your ears while you flip through the pages of the large book. Evelyn mentions stereoscopy, about which he knows nothing. The People of India is replete with faces – of all shades and shapes. People sit, squat, stand. A child stares blankly at the distant horizon. The gaze of a dark-eyed woman wearing a large nose ring. Farm workers huddle around a fire, warming their hands. A young man is perched on a village well.

A cluster of women huddle on a bullock cart. A large, tall man with fingers gripping a spear. Long-robed figures. A naked fakir. *Turbans folded like serpents on the head. Giant camels. Towering mountains. Haystacks. Sand dunes.*

Bits of his conversation with Hunt come to mind about Fox Talbot's calotypes of rural scenes. They had found themselves in a small London gallery while escaping an unexpected shower.

A sudden bolt of lightning lights up the walls of the darkened room.

Evelyn's clearly enunciated words return to him.

'The Sikh gentleman I introduced you to on the Maidan yesterday belongs to the Sindhoo clan.' He had placed his long finger on a photograph of a swarthy, tall man with a sharp nose, a full beard and turban, his right hand holding a sword.

'Each warrior clan in India has its own story and history. A learned friend tells me that the Moghul Emperor Akbar, while on a hunting expedition, had fallen in love with the beautiful daughter of a landlord after seeing her balancing a pitcher of water on her head while holding down with her foot the rope tied around the neck of a runaway heifer. He asked for her hand in marriage, which was granted, and in exchange, the community was rewarded with land. The clan descended from that union are known for their martial prowess.'

Warren Hastings's face had stared down from the large portrait hanging on the wall.

'Part history but mostly myth, I reckon, like most things here and elsewhere.'

Amused by Evelyn's comment, he had walked towards the tall mahogany shelf, where he could see the works of Carlyle arranged neatly.

'Much like most aristocratic English lineages, I imagine.'

Evelyn had walked up to the tall bookcase by the window and pulled out a copy of *On Heroes, Hero-Worship, & the Heroic in History*.

After breakfast, Lear goes back to his room. The wind is still howling outside. He cannot help thinking about *The People of India* as known and half-familiar faces slip in and out of his mind while he sips the special concoction offered by Giorgi. Then, sitting under a pool of light cast by the large lamp, he readies himself to write. Placing his left hand on the blank pages, he absent-mindedly flips back to the pages that he had filled with details of his last train journey.

The train carriage stands still at Ghaziabad station. Destination: Allahabad, back to that city on the Ganges. Blazing hot. Giorgi's diarrhoea doing its mischief once again. The cool mountain breeze is turning into a distant dream. Just days since we left Simla, and we are in the middle of a cauldron. Handkerchief and collar already soaking wet. More perspiration dripping down my ankle.

Cooler as the train moves out of the burning station and gathers speed. The carriage shakes incessantly, and the copper water bottle falls to the floor and rolls towards the feet of the man sitting across. The tall, statuesque man has been sitting very quietly. Picking up the bottle, he hands it to me. Notice his long, chiselled nose and proud chin and luxuriant beard! Seems very familiar. The Sikh man whom Evelyn introduced to us on the Maidan: can't for life's sake remember his name! Could he also possibly be a Sikh from the Sindhoo clan? The likeness, could it be just my illusion? The heat. Train goes rattling along at an easy pace, and the tall man begins undressing very leisurely, slipping into nightwear. Can't help but be utterly dazzled. The powerful arms move so sinuously as he combs the beautiful black tresses and

applies a pomade from a small container on his lush beard. Beautiful
fingers return the comb back to the small red bag. Thighs visible under
thin cotton pants resemble large, knotted ropes descending from belly
down to ankle. Pencil and paper, ready to do a quick sketch when he
is not looking.

Hear him say, 'The Bengal Army, served for over ten years now.'

Our eyes meet. An awkward silence.

'We are travellers from England.'

All quite tricky.

Man straightens sleeves and places slippers under the seat, getting
ready to lie down.

'Do you belong to the Sindhoo clan?' Cannot help asking.

Loud clanging of the metal wheels going over a narrow bridge
drowns my silly question. Giorgi takes no notice, absorbed in some
book about seafaring in the Indian Ocean. The train has quite suddenly
come to a creaking and clanking halt. Chirping of crickets fills the air.
Understandably, the man does not answer. Put away my pencil and
paper.

Suddenly interrupted by a servant asking if he desired a cup
of cocoa, Lear sees Giorgi standing in front of a row of framed
photographs hanging on the wall, his eyes fixed on the portrait of
a young boy in a sailor suit.

'Photography fixes the shimmering but impermanent image of
the camera obscura and pins it down so that it is no longer a mere
flash of appearance.'

Giorgi does not hear Lear's words, continuing to walk down the
length of the wall, stopping and then moving on before returning
to the chair.

'Sadly, I am too old to learn a new skill, Giorgi. Do you know
what Hunt once told me when I told him about my interest? His

exact words: "On no account should you venture into taking photographs or doing human portraits. It's the fashion, but far too many of them do it these days. Your mind is more attuned to producing inflated realities, not real objects."'

Giorgi simply nods.

"'Even in the picture you drew in Suez, the camels appear to have better expressions than the Arab men standing around, who – anyway – have their backs turned. You should stick to doing landscapes. Your watercolours and washes sell like hot cross buns!'"

True, landscapes have always captivated him – of seascapes and coasts, long vistas of hills and mountain ridges interspersed with a cluster of huts, a ruined wall somewhere tucked away behind a clump of trees and shrubbery. But during his journeys by train, he saw mostly flat, barren landscapes flashing by, along with fleeting images of people, goats and cows. On his way down from Simla, for the first time, his eyes were caught by the vision of four singular women walking in single file along the side of the road. Was it their clothes that had struck him or their hair, the toe rings or the way their eyes remained fixed on the ground even though they were moving quite rapidly on their bare feet, swinging their arms, the baskets resting on their heads? Or was it the colour – the hues of the world, the garments that draped their bodies, the single dot on the forehead that had blazed forth? *Kalka is full of picturesqueness* were the words he had written in his notebook. Yet, when he had sat down to draw those sights, all he got down on paper were unmoving stick figures, never the movement of the arms or the glint of the toe ring. Just blank faces mirroring the blank spaces on paper. In his drawings, even the panorama of human bodies he had witnessed in Banaras months earlier – of bathers flocking to the *ghats*, their wet bodies glistening like seaweed on the rocks – appeared as mere strokes on paper. Were the objects he saw bobbing up in the water really bodies of the dead brought to the *ghats*? In his drawings of the gardens at the Taj, the skeletal bodies barely bore any discernible faces or heads. All of his early efforts to draw human figures had resulted in producing more stick figures, which occasionally would turn into twisted bodies with contorted faces around which he arranged in his nonsense poems.

But the likeness that photography nudges you towards is the grandest of all illusions that singes the brain – the mirage of reality that, strangely, like nonsense, leaves one yearning for more when, in truth, there is little beyond the trace that a pen leaves as it moves frenziedly on paper. The only difference is the way the finger moves. A shutter click here, two fingers gripping a pencil there.

Giorgi can tell that Lear is agitated by his own cogitations. Although he is turning the pages of the notebook, adding a few sentences along the margins, and using his pencil to touch up a drawing, his forehead shows deep furrows.

It is a wonder as the pages of scribbled lines on the notebook have led Lear into the path of retracing the train journey from the town of Ghaziabad barely two weeks earlier. Every word triggers images that make him think of photography and the grand illusion it conjures. All through the night, the train had moved through a tunnel of darkness, but a shaft of light appeared to enter through an invisible aperture as the first light of dawn seeped into the skies. The Sikh gentleman sitting across had already gathered his belongings and stepped out of the carriage onto an empty platform. The train heaved itself out of the platform, and after a few hours, pulled into Allahabad station. The huff and puff of the engine subsided, and they alighted onto another platform. They were met with hot winds that rocked the metal signs on the platform. Six months ago, they had braced themselves against the cold bluster of late January. A police band was playing under the blazing sun as they made their way out. A pony cart waited outside to take the two to the Lauries' residence.

'Curtis Ellsworth? You stayed at *his* hotel?'

A look of utter disbelief moved across the face of Mrs Laurie, their hostess in Allahabad. Hair done up in a top bun, she had joined Lear, Giorgi and her husband, Howard, on the well-shaded veranda after lunch.

'I remember last seeing Curtis at the club more than three years ago.'

Mr Laurie scraped the remaining custard from his bowl. They all sat in planter's chairs, but Lear preferred not to place his legs on the extended arms, knowing well that the feat would take an enormous effort.

'Rumour has it that the Indian girl who is the daughter's companion is really *his* own.'

Mrs Laurie waited for Lear to say something.

'Two utterly charming girls.'

Lear noticed a crow hopping on the grass, pecking at something.

'Of course, all of it could be sheer gossip. Nonsense, much like your words, Mr Lear.'

She handed Lear her personal copy of *A Book of Nonsense*.

'Tony loves to throw a limerick challenge when there is nothing much to do indoors in the heat.'

Sitting on a rug on the floor, the two Laurie children were applying watercolours to some of the drawings. The girl chuckled at the picture of the young girl from Majorca, whose frock had been painted in bright red vertical lines alternating with bright green. The aunt's face was a pale green, her dress orange and the sky yellow and blue. Purple and pink stripes ran down the breeches of the Old Man and over the floor. *There was an Old Person of Bangor* had squiggly lines drawn all around the chair he sat on.

Piled up on the table were several large, lifelike porcelain bisque dolls clad in taffeta, silk and lace, their hair spun from wool. Just before the Laurie children began colouring the drawings, they had spent an entire hour playing with them. All around the walled garden stood trees with branches laden with large, unripe mangoes. Someone on the street behind the wall was playing a flute. And then, they heard a vigorous rustling in the branches as a pack of black-faced *langoors,* large-limbed monkeys with mighty tails that looked like serpents, descended from the trees. They were much larger than the ones he had seen in Simla. Before their astonished eyes, a female *langoor* crept down and made off with one of the dolls, climbed back up the tallest tree, sat on a high branch and began nursing it as if it were an infant. Meanwhile, the children screamed in alarm, forcing Mrs Laurie to take them inside.

He had never seen anything like it before. While the children were still shrieking, the old gardener appeared from the back of the garden. Standing quietly under the branch, the man tapped his fingers on his own forehead, and with folded palms pressed against his chest, he bowed. Much to Lear's surprise, he began to speak, very gently, to the monkey perched on the high branch. He hummed, cajoled and made soft clicking noises with his tongue. In less than a minute, the mother monkey descended very cautiously, left the doll near the gardener's feet, stared at the man and climbed back up.

In the gaps between the treetops, he can see patches of the deep blue sky.

Lear feels Ann's hands resting on his shoulders.

A day after his sixth birthday, they are walking in Highgate Park. A small crowd has gathered around a metal cage. 'Mummy, look at the bunny with the long tail,' the youngest of the two girls screams excitedly. Two pairs of deep brown eyes and mouths wide open, as if in a motionless grin, baring sharp, pointed teeth. The mother with the long tail picks up the little one in its arms and walks away. 'They are so much like us, don't you think?' They are back home, sitting at an empty table on which lie two broken cups. 'Where do their mama and papa live, Ann?' 'Somewhere very far way, I imagine. India or Africa.'

The room darkens as a thick band of clouds sweeps across the sky. Blue and black, the two colours bleed into each other. His mind is tugged from one scene to the other – enormous mangoes swaying on the branches, the gate of Highgate Park swinging open, the dark brown branches on the trees outside the gallery swaying violently. He wonders if he would ever be able to capture, on paper, the drama he had witnessed in Allahabad. The powerful movement of the animal's limbs as it climbed down the tree, the expression on the gardener's face, the gentleness in his voice and the slow motion of his fingers as he cajoled the animal. What skills would he need as an artist? Could he replicate the look on the young girl's face as she peered at a monkey trapped in the cage or the beauty of the fingers running down a comb through dark tresses?

Lear's thoughts are interrupted by two *kitmutgars* chatting excitedly about a guest who had just arrived. A military man, Lear learns. The next moment, the gallery is filled with voices that ring out as the visibly annoyed manager calls out, 'Ratan! Ratan! Where could he be? Said he would be gone for a few minutes.'

The manager's voice dissolves into voices he had heard at the Lauries' residence.

'Bhuliya! *Burtans.*' A voice from inside summoned the gardener into the Laurie kitchen. He had reappeared from the side door with a pile of pots ready to be scrubbed on the platform placed at the back of the garden. In his little arms, the Lauries' young boy carried the abducted doll.

The children gathered around Lear as he began reading from *A Book of Nonsense.*

> *There was an Old Person of Bree,*
> *Who frequented the depths of the sea;*
> *She nurs'd the small fishes, and washed all the dishes,*
> *And swam back again into Bree.*

'Aren't you going to ask Mr Lear how the lady of Bree nursed small fishes?' The little girl sat on her mother's lap, waiting for his response.

'An artist has magical powers, and the lady of Bree was a magician.'

The little girl had been very happy with his response.

The drizzle intensifies, turning into sheets of water that leave a large pool where the lawn once was. Giorgi notices his master pencilling in the details on the sketch he had made earlier, of a *bheesti* walking down the road. He adds a line here, a shade there, pausing in between. How could one possibly sketch the chatty water carriers seen on the streets of Jubbulpore who moved so quickly, swinging their hips from side to side, carrying the two pails of water hung on a stick placed over the shoulder? The *bheesti*, on the other hand, moved very slowly under the hot sun, great sluices of water coming out periodically from the goatskin bag that was strapped over his sunburnt shoulder.

'Do you remember when you had me pose as a *bheesti* so that you could get the shape of the back correctly?'

'The sketch I had made earlier did not seem quite right.'

'You got it right but after your *fourth* attempt. By the time you finished, my spine had begun to bend!'

Lear just smiles back.

Putting away his pencil and taking off his eyeglasses, he holds up the drawing.

'In his isolation, the *bheesti* seemed to demand his own space, and his body, though bent, was fully absorbed in the action. That, and nothing beyond, which is what I intended to get on paper. No detailing of the turns of road, no tree canopies, no clouds floating across the sky.'

The clock strikes eleven. Two young men are moving black and white squares on a large checkerboard. Screams come from a group of children playing Crambo.

Among the cluster of large and small portraits of men in uniform and women in frilly hats, fans and gowns are photographs of rural scenes that feature an odd assortment of farmers driving bullocks through fields, women weaving baskets and children fishing with little nets. Among them, Lear's attention falls on a cluster of wooden huts and a large bullock cart under a tree. 'Neral Village, October 1864'. Words etched at the bottom. Another picture quivers in his mind's eye as he gazes at this scene. Yes, Neral, the stopover he had glimpsed very briefly on their way to Matheran from Bombay. A few wayside shops selling tea and savouries and a few huts scattered over the edges of the hills. The view from the *garry* had taken his breath away. Dots of distant villages set against the sky that soon began to look like miniature brown and green cushions set on a blue bed. It had been a long, hot journey from Bombay, but luckily, the air had turned cooler as they began their gradual ascent. The clinging humidity had suddenly given way to gentle winds, and wisps of cloud were seen wafting across the road.

Accompanying them was the young babu, Mr Desai, a Maharatta, from the Irrigation Department in Bombay, who had been sent to escort them at the special request of Evelyn. The *garry* heaved itself along the slight incline of the road, stopping frequently to allow cattle and the occasional flocks of goats and ducks to cross. After they had passed a banyan tree, whose giant canopy resembled a lady's hat, a tight knot of men and women came into view. Tattoo, thread and brass amulets and nose rings, the women seemed almost naked – and so were the men, except that their upper bodies were wrapped in coarse woollen shawls. Pots made out of what looked like dried gourds and a few spades and shovels, all quite primitive looking, lay on the ground.

'People from local tribes, native distillers who work as agricultural labourers in the fields you see below. Not long after the government had allowed men from Poona and Bombay to buy land, forests turned into fields of rice, wheat, banana. The tribes were brought from the forests to work in the fields.' Mr Desai's slow and measured voice suggested that these changes had brought much-desired civilization to these remote, long-forgotten regions.

But Mr Desai broke off mid-sentence.

'All good, but needless to say, they are poor, very poor. The fields produce a lot of crops, but the tribes remain hungry.'

Unlike the garrulous Chimariote people he had encountered in Govno years ago, the men and women seemed mute, little more than figures drawn on the pages of a book. The passing carriage aroused some curiosity. One young man stirred and called out to another, but the women, sitting on their haunches, stared vacantly at their spades.

'Neral village.' Mr Desai pointed to a cluster of thatched huts and crumbling mud houses.

It had occurred to Lear that he and Giorgi belonged to the world of constant movement, of ceaseless departures and arrivals. That was the world he had actively chosen for himself. At some point, the life he had led seemed too hurried and unsettling. Unlit and dank rooms in makeshift homes in London, the frequent back and forth on rickety carriages between the city and the sea, the rough seas, sailing between England and the Mediterranean. But over the years, the nightmare of the unknown had changed into a dream of exploration and discovery, of stumbling upon new mosaics that lay concealed under the floor of an old, tumbling house. All of his art – drawings, paintings, musings, words – in fact, grew out of those encounters with the unknown.

But deep inside, he knew that beyond all of that fabulous spectacle of the world that he drew and painted was a world swirling in the eddies of the age, and it was that lingering consciousness that had made him ask: Did the men and women they saw standing so still near the tree truly belong to their homes? Were the valleys nestled somewhere in the hills, beyond reach, the place they had once called their own? If the very lands they tilled for ages had been lost irretrievably, what could they call *home*? Was it possible that their vacant stares meant that they were simply biding their time, waiting to return to the lands they had lost to the new hosts? The words of a half-remembered song echo in his mind, 'Because the grove is below us, the pickers slide further into the shade.' The house built under the startlingly blue skies of San Remo surrounded by tall cypresses – but so distant from England or Corfu – could it be called *home*?

The journey he had undertaken that day was unlike anything he had experienced before. The wheels of the *garry* creaked as they kept moving, and with each successive lash of the whip that beat down on the backs of the giant bulls, the carriage moved up the gradient of the hill. Before long, the figures standing near the tree moved away from view, disappearing into the cool, misty air. A strange light descended on the distant hills as the rain and wind began to sweep down with increased force.

Lear finds himself wandering so far off in his thoughts that he does not even know when Giorgi had placed a blanket on his knees.

'Thank you, Giorgi. I needed it.'

Lethargy seems to have invaded his entire body. He wishes he could just sit there, not stirring all day. While the driving rain keeps hammering on the windowpanes, through the window glass, a face comes into view. It was not of Ann but his sister Sarah, when she was about seven or eight. That morning, he had overheard an exchange between two military men sitting in the long gallery – about New Zealand, its beautiful landscapes and pastures, and about the Irish who were emigrating in droves to settle there. Nearly fifteen years ago, Sarah had travelled to New Zealand with her new husband, from where she wrote him long letters describing her new life among the pastures and the albatrosses that flocked around the house. A temperate climate, lush pastures perfect for cattle rearing, small trade in fishing gear that brought in handsome returns, Sarah's letters were full of everyday details about milking and shearing sheep.

Fortescu had once responded angrily to the stories he had conveyed to him about Sarah's pastoral 'new home'. All was not as he imagined. The New Zealand 'bothers' were recommencing. The newspapers were full of reports of insurrections, the wars and treaties with native Maori, and about the spread of diseases and epidemics. The leadership of Governor Browne had worked for the most part, and things were 'under control', the *Saturday Review* paper had reported. But what did that *really* mean, Fortescu had asked? The Maori uprising was 'a challenge that could be dealt with by rapid and imposing display of force'. *Terrify the natives into submission?* They were words that Fortescu had pointed out in that report, which he could never forget, even ten years later. Strangely, not a single word about these troubles found mention in Sarah's letters that, over the years, became infrequent. But he always yearned to visit her and see for himself. After a few years, the letters stopped coming, and he did not know the reason.

Like Ann, she was now lost to him forever.

Something about the incessant patter of the rain easing makes some faces wind in and out of the screen lodged in his mind. Sitting in the warm room shielded from the deluge outdoors, Lear realizes that figures at Neral were, like the Maori thousands of miles away, 'terrified into submission'. The very authority that had made the people of the land into *kitmutgars* and gardeners, *chuprassies* and *ayahs* was also the entity that sent relief to famine-stricken villagers, made picturesque plantations and tea gardens out of their forests, built schools but also locked people up in distant garrisons when they turned mutinous. The unending vistas of pasturelands in the far corners of this splendorous Empire, the rippling folds of the mountains that unfolded in front of his eyes, the unfamiliar names – *Matheran, Mahabaleshwar, Wai* – through which they had made their way were all bound by the great abyss, the one he had merely glimpsed sitting on his stool on the ridge in the Himalayas.

Lear is not sure why these questions have begun to spring in his mind but realizes as he sees the clouds billowing in the sky that they are like vapour rising from his own ruminations that once crystallized into his funny verses. But the dream that had truly inspired him – of pinning down the world he was traversing and the scenes in it that his ears and eyes had apprehended so sharply – still eluded his fingers and pen. They were like the flashing image that vanishes once the ray of light is turned off. All he has left to show are lines scribbled on paper and a dab or two of wash and ink.

Lear is surprised to see the lamps being lit one after the other, and as the shadows begin to emerge, he flips back the pages of his notebook, stopping on the page marked *Wai*. Nearly four pages of details! He had certainly seen many beautiful landscapes before – in Albania, southern Italy, Crete, and many others whose names he can barely remember, but the sheer elegance and poise of a small town encircled by the blue Sahyadri Mountains had taken his breath away. The reflections of temple tops on the glistening waters of the river Kistna, the river winding in gentle loops through the small town, the houses in the distance set like gems against the pure azure sky.

Wai was not on their itinerary. From Matheran, they were to make their way directly to Poona. But struck by the first view of Wai, he had asked Mr Desai if they could make an overnight halt. They were lucky. A certain Mr Dossabhoy, a hotel owner known to him, would certainly be able to provide rooms, Mr Desai assured Lear, instructing the driver to follow the narrow road lined with scarlet flowering trees.

'It's the beginning of the monsoons. I am quite sure he has rooms to let.'

Elated by the sight of a small sign – *PEARL HOTEL. Estd. 1854* – Lear took off his eyeglasses and peered at the colonial bungalow that appeared on the left. With a low-hanging veranda in front, and a well-tended garden and an old stone well surrounded by low bushes, Pearl Hotel was like a picture of bucolic bliss.

Mr Rustom Dossabhoy, it turned out, was a Parsee gentleman. Bearded, wearing a white turban, his loose-fitting muslin calico pants and shirt flapped in the breeze as he opened the garden gate.

Lear found himself facing a grandfather figure with a hooked nose and receding chin.

'Mr Desai, my friend! What a splendid surprise! Welcome! It has been at least six years since we last met! Was it in Poona or Bombay?'

His voice carried a slightly clipped musical accent.

'I have the best rooms for the three of you, all overlooking the river. Pity no one visits Wai during the monsoons, but this, really, is the ideal season.'

Straightening his crumpled sleeves, he urged his guests to follow the smartly dressed porter carrying the cases.

Soon after he led them through the door, Mr Dossabhoy began talking about the Parsee community.

'Panchgani and Mahabaleshwar. Mostly hotel owners. All bought from the English.'

On a small table in the corner were several curious-looking brass snuff boxes next to which was an elaborately carved hat stand.

'My father moved to Wai from Bombay. The hotel business is not easy these days, but we Parsees have a knack for it.'

The porter continued his steady march up a flight of stairs when Lear stopped to catch his breath.

'Do you know the Parsee family that owns the Calcutta Docking Company? The Banajis, I believe – or is it Banerjee?' Lear hoped that Mr Dossabhoy had not seen his chest heave.

'Oh, the Banaji, not Banerjee. Banerjees are Brahmins of Bengal.' Mr Dossabhoy laughed out loud, and upon reaching the floor above, led the three down a narrow corridor into a well-lit gallery whose windows offered a perfect view of the river in the distance.

'Yes, I have heard about them. They are an eminent Calcutta family. Run a reputable shipping company; business in China, I am told.'

Several shelves with books sat on one end, and on the other, a large teak *almirah* with a pile of pillows placed on top.

'I visited their beautiful home in Calcutta last December.'

Lear was struck by a framed portrait of Prince Albert hanging on the wall facing the window.

'Tragedy, that is what I call it. His Majesty's untimely passing away has come as a great blow to all of us. No one expected a healthy man in his early forties to die so early in life.'

Mr Dossabhoy's adoring look confirmed what Evelyn had shared about the Parsees – that they were some of the British royalty's most loyal subjects.

Giorgi was shown the door to his room by the porter.

The three had finished drinking their second cup of tea when Lear turned to Mr Dossabhoy and asked if he could sit for him.

'Just a sketch, Mr Dossabhoy, and it will not take more than an hour, an hour and a half, at the most.'

They reassembled downstairs, and Giorgi, who had been looking out of the window at the sun moving through a band of clouds, remarked, 'Did you know, sir, that Mr Lear was the Queen's personal tutor? Drawing and painting.'

The old man's face lit up instantly.

'A tutor of our beloved Queen! How remarkable. What a privilege to have you as my guest, Mr Lear. I welcome you, too, Mr George. I am so very glad that our paths crossed.'

Then, Mr Dossabhoy turned to Lear and said, 'You mentioned a portrait. I will be more than happy to sit for you. But I have a special request. Can you include my manservant in the portrait? Naresh is like the son I never had.'

Then, raising himself from the chair, Mr Dossabhoy walked towards the door leading out of the room.

'That's settled. We will sit in the afternoon after you return from your stroll by the river. Here are the keys to your rooms. If you need extra blankets, please let Naresh know.'

After an early lunch, the two stepped out for a walk by the river. While strolling along the banks of the river, he noticed a small temple in the distance, and in front of it was assembled a small crowd of noisy devotees. The brass bells that hung on the doorway rang loudly as the devotees raised their arms. A few carried small brass trays with flowers and smoking incense.

Ah, a festival. Lear immediately took out his pencil and paper before striding down towards the arched gate. Huddling together on the steps was a throng of Brahmin men, all dressed in white, with shaven heads, chanting hymns. They were all bare-bodied, their bellies glistening with oil. But as soon as Lear reached the gateway, a fat old priest rose swiftly from the steps and began waving his right arm with signs of extreme disgust. Foreigners were not welcome there! Hastily stepping back, Lear made his way back to the top, where he sat down and asked Giorgi for his drawing board.

'Insanity of priests cannot deter me, Giorgi. I have got to get a drawing of the scene, priest or no priest.'

Lear held up the drawing for closer scrutiny and winked at Giorgi. 'Even the sight of a score of Arabs in Petra was not more petrifying than facing the frothing fury of a fiercely indignant Brahmin.'

In less an hour, as they sat on a bench in the little town square, they found themselves talking to a sombre-looking man, senescent, dressed in a white calico cotton shirt and a *dhoti* with a pale orange border. Mr Bhave rose from a bench on the other side of the path that ran across the square. 'I am a local schoolteacher with a lifetime interest in learning.'

Noticing Lear's expression of curiosity mixed with delight, he proceeded, 'I belong to the Chitpavan Brahmin caste. You two are from England, I presume?'

Lear had been told by Evelyn that the Brahmins were divided into innumerable subgroups, with each group claiming ancient lineages.

'Yes, indeed. Quite a variety I am told, some known for their questionable behaviour and lack of civility.' For Giorgi, the scene of a hatted and booted Englishman being shooed off by an ill-tempered and half-clad Brahmin had been most amusing.

Surprised to hear about their extensive travels, Mr Bhave was doubly delighted to learn that Lear was an artist *and* poet.

'Quite remarkable,' he said in a low voice.

Drawn to his well-formed features and good grasp of English, Lear ventured to ask. 'Can I request a favour from you? Will you allow me to do a quick sketch of you?'

Mr Bhave's face broke into a disarming smile. 'Certainly, I would like that, but before you begin drawing, let me tell you a bit about our history. It is a story that will certainly intrigue you.' Cautious about being compelled to listen to storytellers whose tales often went on interminably, Lear guardedly looked at his watch.

'That would be most welcome but got to hurry back to our hotel as soon as we can. Have an invitation to tea from our gracious host.'

Giorgi, who was walking away to look at the bathers, saw Lear getting ready to sketch Mr Bhave and promptly handed him his sketching notebook and pencil.

The grave gentleman took a few minutes to decide where he should sit and in what position.

'The posture is very important, Mr Lear, for us who practise meditation and yoga.'

Mr Bhave cleared his throat as if he was getting ready to sing as soon as Lear placed the sheet of paper on the drawing board. In the next half an hour, the venerable Brahmin related what could be best described as a chronicle – about the historical origins of his caste ('We go all the way back to the ancient Puranas, although more recently, we were important prime ministers for kings and potentates'), moving to discourse on the complex etymology of the word 'Chitpavan' ('Many of us still speak variations of a language called Konkani, from a region near the coast'), then to the size of the community ('There are four hundred and forty surnames'). He ended with a very short account of his wife and two daughters, both of whom, he noted, attended school, learnt to recite sacred Sanskrit verses from memory and were happily settled in their married homes.

It took about ten minutes for Lear to outline Mr Bhave's broad forehead and even broader shoulders. It took longer to sketch the hands that were resting gracefully on the folds of his calico garments. When Lear held the sketch in front of him, the man's face broke into a smile.

'Do you wish to keep this one – to remember this day of meeting on the banks of the sacred Kistna?'

'*Krishna,*' corrected Mr Bhave in a soft voice, 'that is the correct way to pronounce it.'

Then, looking at Giorgi, he asked Lear, 'Is this gentleman also from England?'

'I am from Bristol,' was Giorgi's brief response.

They parted and took the now empty road back to Pearl Hotel.

As they sipped tea, Lear began his pencil sketch of Mr Dossabhoy, who was seated on his beautifully carved chair dressed in his native hat, a black jacket and bow tie, and a lovely blue silk shawl placed over his thighs.

'A gift from my grand-aunt, all the way from Persia.' He ran his fingers over the shawl.

The servant boy, the young Naresh – who was possibly not more than fifteen – dressed in white trousers and a loose-fitting white shirt, stood at the back, with his right arm placed over the top part of the chair. Mr Dossabhoy had difficulty keeping still.

'Of course, we knew you were a poet but did not know that you were such a famous artist. Perhaps it will not come as a surprise that my neighbour's ten-year-old daughter has learnt some of your rhymes by heart.'

Mr Dossabhoy raised himself from his chair and sat next to Lear.

'Are you personally acquainted with the commander in Poona, Mr Hoskings? The journey by ship from England to India must have been very taxing on the nerves.'

He poured himself another cup and sipped his tea rather noisily.

'Parsees are the engines of India's industrial progress. However, some educated Parsees in England, I hear, are raising questions about the legality of the British Empire, which fills me with grief and anger.'

After an hour, Lear stopped and gazed at his sketch.

'I think the drawing is complete. Just needs a few finishing strokes. I am up for tea, or perhaps some sherry?'

All of them gathered around to look at the portrait of Mr Rustom Dossabhoy.

'Your rendition of me is splendid, Mr Lear. Perhaps, you could share a quick limerick with us, your favourite one? I am very keen to hear your recitation. It will go well with the sherry, don't you think?'

Taken unawares by this request, Lear looked out of the window, wiped his face with his handkerchief and began his recitation:

There was an Old Man, on whose nose,
Most birds of the air could repose;
But they all flew away, at the closing of day,
Which relieved the Old Man and his nose.

The silence was palpable after Lear paused at 'his nose'. Giorgi looked away. Mr Desai, sitting near Giorgi, picked up a book on the Ajanta Caves that was lying on the table. Mr Dossabhoy continued to stir his cup of tea noisily.

'Wonderful! Unsurpassable humour! A truly royal nose for harbouring such delightful creatures of the air!'

The next day, soon after they reached Poona in the afternoon, the clouds moved in and the winds began to pick up.

'This is the most well-kept *dak bungalow* I have seen in all of India.' Holding himself straight as he sits in a large chair in the drawing room, Lear looks at the walls. There are no crawling creatures with tongues flicking out of their mouths. Just as he is about to enter his room, he feels a gentle tug. 'Would you like to play a game of Crambo?' It is a small boy with a head of dark, black curls.

The sketch of Rustom Dossabhoy sits on his desk. Looking at it in the half-light, Lear is struck by the details he was able to capture that day. Nothing stick-like about the robed figure. In fact, he can almost see the man smiling back at him, whispering, 'Your sketch is so lifelike, almost as if you had caught me posing for a photograph.'

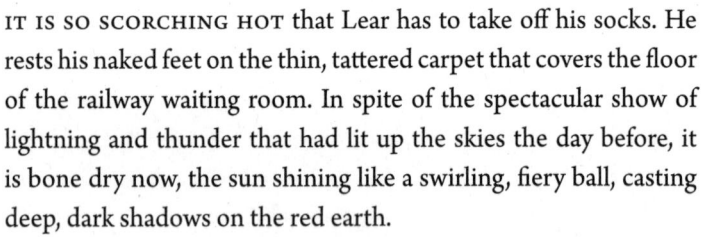

10

IT IS SO SCORCHING HOT that Lear has to take off his socks. He rests his naked feet on the thin, tattered carpet that covers the floor of the railway waiting room. In spite of the spectacular show of lightning and thunder that had lit up the skies the day before, it is bone dry now, the sun shining like a swirling, fiery ball, casting deep, dark shadows on the red earth.

The Beypore–Madras train is due to arrive in two hours. A tiny black bird perches on the branches of a large tree, wagging its little tail, but inside and all around are innumerable, almost invisible, eye flies. It is September, exactly ten months since they first saw the swaying palms of Bombay Harbour. In a few hours, they will be on their way to Trichnopoly. Taking out a sheaf of papers from his bag, he looks at his half-written letter to Fortescu.

'It is time I finished writing the letter,' he murmurs, taking out a pen from his pocket.

Giorgi nods, leafing through an old newspaper. The air in the room has a faint smell of roasted groundnuts.

Lear's eyes go over the first page of the unfinished letter. He crosses out the date on the top left-hand corner and begins afresh.

~~September 8, 1874~~

Dear C.40scu,

The good intents of the above date never bore fruit. It is September 8 today. On Saturday, your last letter was delivered to me, so I shall finish writing to you today instead of going for yet another walk in the blazing sun!

All the better, my beloved Fortescu, to set forth the varied subjects which I shall bring under your consideration. I shall first proceed to look through your letter carefully and reply more or less to the heads thereof. In short, unlike many of my previous letters, this will not be a scribbledibble so that you may feel it borne upon you that you are a letter in my debt & so that I may the sooner hear from you, at least before I leave for Ceylon.

You make no mention in your present letter of the one that I posted in Poona, inducing me to think that the red postbox sitting quietly under the neem tree outside the green-tiled post office into which Giorgi deposited my last letter may have been just a bin for discarding rubbish. But a handsome one, I must say.

That said, I must tell you that after I posted that letter I have been on more trains (all shaky and horribly delayed) than I care to count, all the way to my current destination – beginning my journey in Poona, and frequently getting horribly confused between Bombay and Madras times, as I moved through countless junctions between the Bombay–Madras and other lines that I can hardly name. I have passed through a series of gentlemen's waiting rooms in states that defy description. Starting in the central highlands of the Deccan, I have now criss-crossed large swathes of South India – Sholapur, Gulbarga,

Hyderabad, Bellary, Cuddapah, Bangalore, Madras, Conjeeveram, Srirangam. And yes, I forget the dash we made to Mahabalipooram from Madras, where both Giorgi and I nearly died of exhaustion.

But a truce to the growling on the vicissitudes of Indian travel. Lord, does it rain here! When it gets steamy after a rain shower, you are tormented with prickly heat of the kind that one can only imagine striking the inhabitants of Borneo! I am tempted to compose a limerick dedicated to describing different ways a gentleman in my state deals with that constant annoyance. However, I shall not allow you to be deceived into thinking that my misery is unredeemable. Quite the contrary, South India, the region that I am passing through, is truly another India, a remarkable land of varied topography and even more varied languages and sounds.

Lest I lose my thread: your reply to the letter I posted just before I left Simla arrived before I departed from Poona, much sooner than I expected. In it, you asked me to send you my opinion about the cogs of the machine that I have been witness to in our great Indian Empire. In the Simla letter (put in the post in Allahabad on my way to Bombay), I provided you with some of those reflections – which although personal – did indicate my assessment of the way the English conduct the business of Empire here. You asked about the state of public feeling, a question not easy to answer. For myself, I avoid as much as I can speaking directly on the subject. Some of what I saw can be best described as unending comedy. First-rate theatrics, right in the heart of our Empire in the Deccan, Hyderabad and in other places.

The service has been, for the most part, satisfactory, and at times, quite exceptional. Dear Giorgi has been impeccable, to say the least. More importantly, he has served as a valuable interlocutor and timely intervener in conversations from which I desperately needed to be delivered. Bless his soul. Friend, valet, dragoman… except for a few times when I have actually seen him sulk, he has been like a mountain – unmovable and utterly dependable. Who better than he to spy the invisible hole in the sock as soon you take off your shoes and begin his laborious darning, even if it means missing the second cup of tea! To my utter delight, I have discovered that he, too, loves the company of young children and often uses clever tricks to entertain them with his word games. I, however, worry about him, particularly when I see him read letters that arrive infrequently from Corfu.

Now my questions: as you have quit the office of the President of the Board of Trade, how do you manage to be privy to all the dark secrets of the Cabinet? Or have you settled into a life of taking long walks in the morning with Lady Waldergrave and sipping sherry in the afternoon, gazing out of your large windows at Westminster and reading Mrs Gaskell's latest novels? Mrs Gaskell's novels! I must admit that I still remain fascinated by her, and although I met her only once, about twelve years back, at Stephen Lushington's, I still remember her broad forehead and kind face and the manner in which she talked about her life in Manchester. (About the F Lushington – and not S Lushington – the less said the better.) In fact, he has gone so mum that you would think he has taken a vow of silence in a lamasery in the highlands of Tibet.

I do read the news from England as often as I can get my hands on the newspapers. Except for the Factory Act and the decision to replace all bronze green postboxes with red ones, the present government in England appears to be taking its strides unhurriedly. In India, on the contrary, the endless charades, the shows, the pantomimes continue unabated; in fact, now with more spectacular fireworks. More later about this – and the comedy parts that I mentioned earlier.

Back to my travels after July the sixteenth – I will not tire you out with the nitty-gritty details about my itinerary. Instead, I will chronicle

– if you will – my observations, some – as you will soon discover – I have written to you about before. Here, I will pepper those with newer insights that you most certainly will find amusing although a few bits may leave you passionately furious.

First, about the servants – red-liveried and unliveried – of England's emissaries of light. Odd, that this should be first on my list! I have gone through more English drawing rooms in India in the last ten months than a local clergyman would in his entire lifetime attending to the needs of his parish! I have been served so many cups of tea and plates of sandwiches by so many that it would easily fill the kitchens of all the lords in all of the counties of England. I began my journey from Poona about three weeks ago. At the head engineer Henry Wendon's bungalow in Sholapur, I thought I would be literally trampled under their busy feet. So many whizzing around you, crossing and recrossing the floors in rapid motion, appearing at your back and in front – a retinue of kitmutgars, kamsamahs and bearers. Mrs Hendon looked as if she were conducting an orchestra, complete with subtle finger movements and accompanying facial expressions. Just when you thought the musical piece had come to a satisfactory conclusion, you find one of them handing you a fresh plate of cutlets! And then the show continued. Thackeray – whom I met for the first time on the Folkestone steamer thirteen years ago – would have quite fancied these details for the Indian novel he intended to write (but never did; hard to believe it has been ten years since he passed on).

Even the 'boys' assigned to serve as guides – as I do now – behave as servants, except – in my case – they cannot follow any of the instructions due to their limited understanding of English. Of course, my abysmal abilities to comprehend, or speak in, any of the thirty Indian languages severely limits my abilities to direct them! Do I think that Giorgi is the best as servants come in this world? Abysmally bad at cooking even a simple stew, he nonetheless speaks four languages, three of which I understand completely. But he has also picked up more Hindoostani words than I have over the past one year of travel. Enough to bring a smile to the faces of other (young) servants.

There were occasions, however, when I wondered what went through his mind when some of the servants at the dak bungalows *showed him utter disrespect – like the time in Poona when he was told curtly that no second cup of tea was available when we both saw the other servants bringing in new pots to the tables. I remained a silent spectator. Perhaps because caste feeling is so entrenched among Indians that one liberal Englishman getting livid about the treatment meted out to his servant was not going to take us anywhere. I may also have inadvertently given the servants the impression that Giorgi was in my service, and therefore, not on my level.*

So many questions! Looking back, I sometimes wonder if I am even what I am. A penniless man who now is obsessed with thinking about servants! I only wish I could dub and scrub myself into what I wish to be! But what is it that I wish to be?

Now, before I get metaphysical, let me alter the direction of this letter and take you on a tour of the gardens and rocks I have encountered in South India. I know how passionate you are about gardens, especially after hearing you speak about the ones you saw in Cornwall a few years back. In India, just when you think you have seen an English garden replicated perfectly, you are delightfully greeted by the view of a temple – complete with brass bells and chanter – and a sacred tank placed at the centre! As in Moti Bagh in Sholapur. London should experiment with this innovative form of garden planning, perhaps get the Church of England to take an interest! Now, about Bangalore's Lal Bagh – the Kew of India – never saw a more beautiful place, terraces, trellises, etc., not to speak of some wild beasts. Exquisite flowers … There is something very rural and quiet about this green place. Sadly, I have no Dr Hooker to provide details about all of the species of flora I saw there or about the 'wild beasts' (I think I recognized a leopard, but it could have been a large feral cat).

As far as your eyes can reach, granite rocks are a common feature in the Deccan and most parts of South India, even incorporated into gardens, palaces and forts. Parts of this region – and it is fairly vast – are also exceedingly verdant, so profusely green that they can rival the unparalleled glory of the verdure of the Himalayan foothills. Rocks and greenery. Now, the rocks I mention are solid and immense, rising from the ground, and often, when seen from a distance, their shapes resemble the bodies of large, ossified hump-backed sea creatures. To see massive forts and tombs built around and on top of boulders is to think of the victories and defeats of so many warring kingdoms, of the stories of conquest and settling of new peoples in alien lands. In Hyderabad, one senses that entire civilizations were built and rebuilt over generations on these rocks. Fort Rock in Bellary is a wonderful bit of grand granite, highly picturesque in form and colour (but could not draw as the rains descended yet again just as I pulled out the pencil from the bag).

Bangalore and its precincts have their share of these awe-inspiring sights – and I now have at least ten or eleven drawings of rocks, set against the skies or on the tops of yet another crumbling tomb celebrating the life of a half-remembered prince or general. How different from the rocks of Jubbulpore that I visited last November (although calling cliffs of sheer marble 'rocks' may seem a bit disingenuous).

The way marble reflects light, its whiteness also shimmering so wondrously on water! I must add that the rocks of Jubbulpore encircle a lake almost as large as Lake Windermere, their jagged edges standing over the waters. Giorgi had been entirely enraptured by the boat ride when we visited Jubbulpore November last. No such pleasure in Hyderabad – of navigating silently, gliding on water, looking up at the sheer marble cliffs that built the Taj Mahal. (My friend here tells me that the marble for the Taj actually came from another source, about three hundred and fifty miles west of Jubbulpore.)

A traveller through the Deccan encounters so many of these forts and temples – some even built on top of primeval rocks, some right in the middle of rice fields, some on seashores and some even at crossroads, where you often encounter the coconut seller sitting with his basket. Seeing them, one would be led to believe that India could not think of life – with its varied activities of birth, death, food, sleep, industry, wonder – without erecting something in the memory of someone, something or in veneration of some rock deity or some force of nature dictating life. The famous Golconda Fort in Hyderabad reminded me of the Valley of Kings, somewhat ill-proportioned and coarsely executed in places. The rocks are all-pervasive. I have travelled through Petra, and I have seen nothing like this. The fort made me think of London Paddington, the Tower, Westminster Abbey, and crumbling Glastonbury Cathedral combined in one muddled confusion of archways surrounded by rocks, and halls with views of more rocks, and I dare say, sixty-foot-high walls built on top of more rocks. Grey, earth-coloured, pink, rocks with yellow grey and speckled tones.

In the perfectly executed temples built out of solid rocks, you may forget that it was originally a rock. In the hands of the sculptors, the rock had simply metamorphosed into arches, domes, pillars and walls with the most striking friezes, some impropriety represented thereon. When we came across the latter, I would find Giorgi taking a quick detour, meeting me at a more appropriate site. Often, when I would think of doing a drawing of one of these friezes, Giorgi would be untraceable (particularly inconvenient, as he is always in charge of my bag of paper and pencil).

Talking about impropriety, I surmised from my conversations with Judge Burnall of Tanjore that the library of Sanskrit volumes housed in the palace in this ancient town is full of unique and queerest books of old Hindu literature, and also includes some filthy enough. Think of Henry Ashbee's collection of The Nunnery Tales, Venus in Furs, The Lustful Turk, and many others being moved to Salisbury Cathedral to be placed next to the Magna Carta! Incidentally, Judge Burnall is a popular figure in these parts, having dedicated his entire life to the preservation of ancient Hindu texts, suffering, for so many years, the heat of Tanjore and the shortage of decent beef.

The thought of drawing the intricate carvings on the massive pagoda in Tanjore occurred to me several times, but I must confess that, given my limited powers, executing such a task would have been next to impossible. I would have to learn a new craft – the craft of fine carving. Even then, I would never be able to get the complicated curves, the depths, the recesses and the shades and the-almost-impossible proportions of the human anatomy that meet human eyes. The rock-hewn temples and the sculptures along a massive rock wall, fifty feet high, in Mahabalipooram, look like a page from a highly wrought illuminated book of relief work.

But, of course, the trip there on a boat navigated by two incompetent boatmen is another story that I will presently desist from narrating. I continue to draw and colour but have not done any significant watercolours, yet. A dab here, a bad dab there.

Now, from the sublime to the ridiculous, from ethereal sculptures dealing with the exploits of epic heroes to bad piano playing by English women. Almost every lady I have had the good fortune of seeing play the piano or sing has worn ruffled cuffs, spoken in peculiar nasal voices, and carried pale yellow parasols when out walking. Miss Peate, whom we encountered at the hotel in Poona, wore a dress with large leg-of-mutton puffs above the elbow, played jiggiously, soon after which I discovered that my watch spring had broken. No sense of melody or rhythm informed Mrs Wendon's playing, although, to be fair, she played with great enthusiasm, her face lit up with an inspirational fervour only to be seen among clergymen's wives in England. Mrs Carey in Hyderabad – whose drawing skills were slightly better than her ability to play the piano, and her singing – how would I describe it? – a foolbegotten, spitmecrackle crashmecriggle insane woman practising howling. The list, my friend, of such brazen-throated, piggish screaming, tearing, roaring goes as far back as my days in Calcutta, where even the men who had tolerable voices could not carry a melody to save their lives.

This triumphal playing and singing reminded me (very sadly) of my dear Tennyson's beating the drums in defence of our great Empire. Think of his dreadful 'The Siege of Lucknow'. My immediate response to the poem was the terrible urge to parody it. But what did I do? I waited for nearly fifteen years to write, 'To watch the tipsy cripples on the beach/With topsy-turvy signs of screamy play' for the lines to be found in his insufferable 'The Lotos-Eaters': 'To watch the crisping ripples on the beach/And tender curving lines of creamy spray.' Needless to say, I never sent my parodies to my friend, although Emily may have secretly admired them if I did send them to her. I will be seen as being boastful if I claim that all of my parodies of these musical performances could easily be added to the series in 'Lays of Ind' but retitled 'Lies of Ind' – 'Comical, Satirical and Descriptive Poems Illustrative of English Life in India.' The over-inflated sense of Christian Englishness that one encounters among so many of our English residents! Quite insufferable. But one suffers, tolerates and moves on.

A single mosquito hovers over Lear's head, singing an unknown melody. Protruding from the sheaf of papers in his bag is a sheet, which he immediately recognizes as the one on which Giorgi has been keeping track of the money spent so far. Pulling it out, he slips it inside the case and then rummages among the bottles inside another case for the bottle of claret that they had bought a few weeks back. It is nowhere to be found. He, then, resumes writing.

My dear boy – you mentioned money. I do not at present want any money, and fresh borrowing would only distress me more. I am thought wrong by some for want of independence in ever borrowing at all, and in any case, Northbrook has been very generous in giving me a handsome allowance for his paintings.

Incidentally, the Viceroy hinted to me in his last letter that there may be changes in the offing on Her Majesty's stature in India. He communicated to me a few weeks back that the Queen's private secretary had already ordered English charters to be scrutinized for imperial titles. From Star of India to what, I wonder? StellaBella Imperium Rectus Indica?

From what I have seen, the mania for inventing new, more glorified, titles is matched by the desire, among the English in India, for putting up ever-more extravagant shows intended to display the might of the Empire. I am thinking about the visit of the young Nizam to the English Residency in Hyderabad, which I was fortunate enough to witness, and which, I dare say, could easily rival the spectacle of any Roman spectaculum. I have the Times of India *14 August in front me and will report directly a passage that offers the official view of the English Indian press:*

> *In a letter that describes the proceedings during the young Nizam's visit to the Resident at Hyderabad (Resident being General Blake about whom I will report later in this letter), a correspondent states that the little boy looked perfectly collected, and coolly*

walked down to the stepladder which had been raised to the side of his howdah, preparatory to his departure for the Residency. Our correspondent also observes that the distinctive title 'Our faithful Ally' adopted by Colonel Hastings Fraser, in a well-known work, accrues to the Nizam (and retrospectively to his ancestors) in virtue of memorable and substantial services rendered to the Paramount Power. The alliance with this State has already entered its second century.

Such magnificent syllablubbery! The parade that the correspondent refers to is the one I witnessed and will describe in some detail. That day, while having breakfast at the Residency, I saw the entire place being turned upside down for the Nizam. All the noise and fuss! Rehearsals of durbars and the interminable movement of men and things around. Giorgi was a silent witness to all of this, but I guessed what was going on in his mind. The day before, we had been moved to a tent by Mr Saunders – our present Resident in Hyderabad – from the place that we were housed in the day we arrived. That very morning, I sat outside the tent – which, by the way, was elegantly furnished with lots of pale carpets and stools and a bed that had too many cushions placed at the head and the foot. Spied a beautiful lizard watching the show and wishing to be away from the hateful bosh.

Giorgi suggested a walk, and so we did – through bazaar lanes lined with vendors selling glass bangles, along peepul-shaded roads, and when we entered the broadway of the bund (a large man-made lake), we were greeted by a bunch of black-coated goats. One little beast came up to Giorgi, who tried to stroke its head, but it shied away from him. Elephants moving about everywhere. 'I like them in the wild,' said Giorgi, noticing that a few were being prepared to join the procession.

When we reached Le Mesurier's house, we were met with General

Blake and a handful of not-very-pleasant men from the 'Subsidiary Force', dressed uncomfortably in their military best and swinging their fly swatters with great gusto. One of the men made a comment about tinned ox cheeks from Australia that had the other two in splits. I missed that joke; perhaps there was a pun in it somewhere. Then the tall man, with piercing blue eyes and tousled hair and a strange habit of shaking his shoulders, introduced himself as 'General Blake'. 'An old soul I am. Joined the army in 1833,' he announced before seating himself next to me. Before you could smile back, acknowledging his presence, he launched into an account of the two insurrections he put down – one in Coorg in 1837 and the other in Golconda in 1847 – in which he was nearly killed. He proceeded to relate his adventures in Burma and his subsequent assumption as the head of the Subsidiary Force in Hyderabad. I heard a peacock's cry and looked around. The General continued. The Subsidiary Force based in Hyderabad is shoring up British power in the Deccan...

While the others helped themselves to croquettes and sandwiches, I could not help but look, somewhat desperately, for Giorgi to come up with a strategy for aiding me to escape the General's onslaught. This was not the first time I found myself entangled, feet up all the way to my nose, in a messy yarn secreted by a storytelling spider. But the verbal onslaught continued. Placing his left elbow on a large trestle table, the General continued, 'An honourable alliance we have between the Nizam and the British. The Nizam has accepted a British Resident, which at present happens to be your host, Mr Saunders.' I wanted to tell him that Mr Saunders had already apprised me of the form and function of this august institution, but the General carried on, in a slightly sinister tone, 'The Nizam is obliged to pay for the maintenance of the Force, and if he fails to pay, Hyderabad will be taken away as penalty.'

You can well imagine the state of my nerves, my dear friend. Perilously near death! Before long, one of the two military men joined us just as the General stopped for the servant to refill his glass.

'Do remember that we inspired the erstwhile Nizam through our alliance to build a railway line to connect Hyderabad with the rest of India. The construction is still being underwritten by the present one, the little lad. And the best part of it is that we get to use the railways to move our goods and our forces. Such reciprocity – in these times – is rare,' he said with great emphasis on 'rare', rolling his r's with such great force that I felt he would follow it up with a shot from his rifle.

Luckily, dear G appeared at that very moment and announced, 'Shall I tell Mr Saunders that you are here? He was looking for you. The parade is about to begin.' I could have hugged my man, but I excused myself and said, 'I am sorry. Mr Saunders appears to have made prior arrangements for my seating to watch the parade.' That was a narrow escape. The General smiled and said, 'I hope we will meet very soon.'

I am so glad that that was our last meeting!

Perhaps, dear friend, you are acquainted with the details about our manoeuvres in Hyderabad – in fact, I am quite sure you are – from your dear friend, John Bright, whom you had succeeded at the Board of Trade. But to the Nizam's parade first, which was such a spectacle! The endless streams of men in various costumes, on foot and horse, Arab, Sikh, Maharatta, and the great elephants above all the crowd outside the Residency. The young Nizam, a little boy, pale and intelligent-looking, dressed in yellow satin, quite perfectly self-possessed – I would have called it a 'wonderful unrivalled towering spectacle' – had it not been for the nagging feeling that all of it was little more than a sham show. What was crystal clear was Britain was intent on showing its position as the 'Paramount Power' – a phrase I heard being repeated several times that evening. What I witnessed – the parade and the conversation earlier with General Blake (should I even call it a conversation?) – was proof of it. In short, the Paramount Power has at its knees a perfectly docile Vassal State, also called 'Faithful Ally'. After seeing the parade, I am convinced that the mood has been already set for the Durbar planned for next year for the Prince of Wales. A new beast – a combination of nabob and sahib – may feature in my next set of nonsense drawings.

But I forget the 'comedy part' that I promised earlier. After the procession had passed, I joined the table where Mr Saunders, his elegantly dressed wife and two men from the Resident's office – I forget their names – were sipping champagne. My heart leapt at the sight of the sparkle spirit in tall glasses. Sitting across from me was a very deaf lady using an ear trumpet, who in replying to something that Mr Saunders asked, said, 'Yes,' still holding her trumpet to her ear. At that very moment, the native servant who mistook the ear trumpet for a sort of glass, instantly poured into her ear a deluge of iced wine, whereby the lady, being suddenly distraught, threw it all back at the military man standing behind her. He stood there, aghast, his satin waistcoat dripping with the fizzy liquid. As can be imagined, vast confusion ensued. The servant disappeared, to be replaced by another one, dressed more extravagantly in an elegantly embroidered waistcoat. A few of the nervous waiters came up to the man who had taken off his waistcoat, but realizing almost instantly that that was not the proper thing to do, disappeared from view in an instant. When the dust had settled on this confusion, we had our first course. Smoked salmon. There is a lesson to be learned from all this.

It is getting late, and the sheer bulk of this letter is getting to be more like my corpulent self, making me wonder where I can possibly find an envelope large enough to fit it in. Before I end, let me tell you a bit about my experience catching the sounds of the English language that I heard spoken by the natives. That should give you an idea of what I perceive to be the status of our beloved English language and how its story fits into the scenario I have just painted for you. This certainly has a lot to do with the present political state of affairs in our Empire. It is hard to believe that it has been almost thirty years since dear Lord Macaulay produced his famous Memorandum. I was only about twenty-three years of age then, but I clearly remember reading about it in the papers. One hailed it as a victory of civilization over darkness.

About a fortnight ago, on the train to Bangalore, I happened to be seated next to a Brahmin, dressed in white, and another native, dressed in green. Both were talking animatedly in English about the construction of the new Bangalore Palace. Curious, I asked them why they spoke in English. 'I speak only Tamil and Telegu,' said the man in green, to which the man in white added, with a gentle smile on his face, 'I only Maharatta and Bengali.' 'Both of us understand English,' the man in green said, looking at me with his eyes wide. 'And, sir, you perhaps have not been in these parts, or you would have learned that the English tongue is very much understood among Indian men.' The man in white resumed, 'You see, sir, English is fast becoming the language of this country.' The conversation continued for over an hour – we discussed the universities at Madras and Calcutta ('excellent teachers' said the man in green), about Macaulay ('a man with great foresight' said the man in white), about better opportunities for natives ('better opportunities for employment in government services' said the man in green), till Giorgi came with his notebook, requesting me to read something he had written.

A country with a hundred languages – I am told – and literature that spans over three thousand years – falling in love with Shakespeare, all because of Macaulay and the beloved Queen! Little to be said about our spreading the warm civilizational light all over the world, dear Fortescu.

While in Tanjore, I had the good fortune of spending hours with Dr Burnell, the man I mentioned earlier. He is in charge of cataloguing a vast corpus on Sanskrit literature, all housed in the Palace. When he told me about this new work – tentatively titled Hobson Jobson *– I immediately got excited, thinking it was a book of nonsense. Seeing the excitement on my face, the honourable judge clarified that the book was a dictionary! Can you imagine? A dictionary of colloquial Anglo-Indian and the highly domesticated terms one encountered in English that had their origins in the languages of Ind! When I asked him what made him turn to writing a dictionary after spending a long career as a sessions judge, he said, winking, 'Aut insanity homo, aut versus facit. If you had any idea of how courts functioned in Madras, you would not ask that question.' I then made some silly comment about Samuel Johnson being reincarnated among the temples of Tanjore, to which the eminent Judge responded by saying that he had a young collaborator, Sir Henry Yule, a military engineering man with vast experiences in India, particularly in Bengal and in Burma. 'I am in frail health,' he added, 'but this new work keeps me alive and excited. English has been given a new lease of life,' he said, 'thanks to our interactions with Indians. Their sounds, their turns of phrase, the literal and the metaphorical coming together in unpredictable ways, a bit like your nonsense verse and nonsense cooking.' I meant to tell him about the variants of the English language I had encountered during my travels in India but decided not to as the Judge was in haste to return to his office to meet his assistant.*

So, here I am, sitting at my table. It is about 1 p.m., and I am thinking about your question regarding the painting of the Kanchenjunga. To be honest, I see the painting in oil as a spectre raised by the denizens of the clouds, a vision of sorts, somewhere between what my eyes witnessed, my fingers drew and what I imagine all noble oil paintings should look like. I still wonder what Northbrook really had in mind. I suspect that he knows that my ability to handle oils is perhaps a tad better than Tennyson's skills at writing Ruskinian prose! Buried in layers of folded cloth, the sketches have been lying like sleeping infants, all snug and cosy, in a brown case that I picked up in Genoa. Only time will tell what shape they'll take when they are made to rise from their cots. If I had my way with the genie, they would be made to just fly out of the case and find their way into a framed canvas, all ready for the jubilee!

The next leg of my journey – to Trichnopoly to see and draw the intricately carved gopurams, or temple towers – involves taking another train. So, I must end here and make sure Giorgi has time to mail it before the train arrives (it is already late by nearly four hours). The clouds are beginning to gather in the southern sky, and I am hopeful that the evil eye flies will leave me and find another victim, preferably the young French Catholic priest sitting across the room.

I have written longer letters – as you know – but this is the first long one that I have ever ventured to write from India. Thank Beelzebub that there are no fleas in India. Do you remember how much I complained about the dead fleas in Avezzano?

Your affectionate friend,
Edward

4 NOVEMBER 1874. IT HAS been nearly a year since he stood on the deck of the ship that had left the shores of Genoa on a late autumn morning, watching the gulls swoop over a shipping boat just before their vessel arrived at the busy Bombay Harbour. The coco palms lining the shore stood in rapt attention with their tops swaying gently in the warm sea breeze. After loading the cases behind the horse carriage, they had gone straight to the newly constructed Watson's Hotel. As he had entered the doors, Lear had paused to look at the newly erected cast and wrought iron frame, eyeing the cantilevered walkways with wonder.

Nearly a year later, he and Giorgi sit on a broken cast iron bench at Tuticorin Harbour on India's eastern coast. Surrounded by deep shadows cast by the sun burning in the pale blue sky, the two have been waiting for over three hours for the ship to take them to Colombo. The gleaming walls of the lighthouse, located to their left along the shoreline, remind him of the pencil and monochrome wash he had done of Tivoli more than thirty years ago. Like now, he was then preparing for another journey – to the

Bay of Naples, when he took a few minutes to sit quietly to sketch. But today, he is unwilling to make that effort. Just the thought of their impending journey to Colombo, one that would take twelve long hours, fills him with trepidation. He had been told by Mr Barrows that the sea would be unusually 'herky jerky' this time of the year.

But Giorgi's attention is riveted on what looks more like a factory chimney than a lighthouse. It has the air of a structure built recently. Certainly not at all like the beautiful conical lighthouse overlooking Corfu Harbour that Giorgi saw every morning from his first home near Cape Sidero. The lighthouse there sat in the midst of a world of soft, ambient light that gently touched the tops of the lush green hills and spread over the idyllic beaches dotted by secret coves. Here, there is little to see – other than the barren expanse of land marked by rows of coco palms, extending beyond the shoreline on one side and the flat, gleaming waters on the other.

Giorgi sees Lear sitting with a book in hand, leafing through the first pages while the ocean breeze plays with his beard. It is his book about Corsica, filled with pencil, sepia and watercolour washes. Peering at the deep green front cover that has the title embossed in silver, he murmurs, 'Ah, it is the book you intended to give Lord Northbrook. Placed under your pile of sketchbooks, it has travelled secretly with us all along.'

Lear notices Giorgi's eyes and smiles back.

The bold letters of the dedication – 'To Frank Lushington' – make Giorgi recall the gaunt and lean face of his master's walking companion, who lived just two doors down and whose servant was so inconsolable after his master left Corfu that he refused to serve another man, preferring to return to his tailoring trade that he had quit years ago. Between sobs, he had said that he was not even sure if he remembered his trade very well after all those years of looking after his master. He notices Lear gazing fixedly at the words of the preface, his forefinger gently running over the printed letters.

The present volume consists of journals written with the same intent and plan as those which preceded them. They describe, nearly word for word as they were written, my impressions of the nature of the landscape in those portions of Corsica through which I travelled.

Certainly not literary, he thinks, reading the lines that follow. But the aim of all these journals should be looked on as the same, simply to be aids to the knowledge of scenery which I have visited and delineated.

Lear's eyebrows knit up as he reads, 'Word for word … aids to the knowledge of scenery', words that were certainly not his but a young man's – the red-headed, freckled editor from Hornby, who had hastily scribbled over the lines that Lear had written, not even waiting for the ink to dry before walking out of the room, leaving Lear with little choice but to wait for an hour, and then, leave. Business was done for the day, and Lear had put on his hat and coat and called for a cab to take him back home.

Yet, from the beginning, Lear felt that the journals were no more an *aid to knowledge* than Shakespeare's plays were 'philosophical ruminations'. If anything, the journals were a record of the movements of his own restless eye, a dramatic encounter with the landscapes of Corsica. But how could he have possibly explained that to the freckled man? Certainly not *word for word*. He remembers the half-recognizable musical strain he had heard from a distance while walking at midnight under a starless sky in Corfu. To him, the travel book was akin to that kind of music: it was not a trophy, not a mirror held up to nature. Like a kaleidoscope, the book was intended to catch the play of ever-changing patterns of light and shapes. Sepia and brown ink landscapes combined with the stories of travel evoking flashing moments of the past, some real and some imagined. He wished the reader's eye to be caught up – as it were – in the magic of refraction, diffusion and dispersion!

A sudden splash interrupts Lear's thoughts, and just as he raises his eyes towards the shore, two dolphins leap up from the waves and plunge back in. The horizon shimmers in the sun, and the dolphins return, cavorting with wild abandon, their backs glistening against the perfectly blue skies.

'Are you thinking about Corsica?' asks Giorgi.

Lear nods back absent-mindedly.

Perhaps his thoughts are with the juror of Corfu. Although it has been so many years since he saw him, Giorgi recalls Lushington's slim moustache and his long and lean face. A man of extreme gravity, bordering on – some may call – cruelty. But the man undoubtedly relished his meals with the master and frequently asked if the sherry in the cabinet needed restocking.

'I have been thinking about doing a book about India after I return – like the ones I have done before – about Greece, Albania, Corsica, southern Calabria. Tennyson thinks that this is my real forte – my skill at combining pictures and words.'

He pauses. The sun goes behind a thin band of clouds, only to reappear moments later with new intensity.

'Of course, Tennyson may have said it to urge me to get on with the landscape illustrations of his poems that I promised him years ago. Nothing works better than applause – howsoever undeserved – to egg someone on to finish a job promised. But laggard as I am, that remains unfinished. But the India book – that is a different story.'

He notices Giorgi looking over his shoulders for signs of the ship coming ashore.

'You mentioned last month when we were on our way to the Government House in Ooty that you intended to produce a landscape portfolio when you returned to San Remo after this visit. Dare I say that you have over two hundred finished and unfinished sketches, if not more! An enormous undertaking if you were to include all of your journals and sketches in *one* book, with *or* without poetical passages. The wooden packing case feels heavier with each passing day.'

Lear smiles, seeing Giorgi's body imitate the action of lifting the heft of heavy boxes.

To imagine that once, incapable of deciding whether life can be cured or cursed, he had contemplated letting go of Giorgi before settling down on the Isle of Wight!

'You are very perceptive, Giorgi. My journals are certainly not commonplace books. I intend to do a lot of sifting and winnowing. Perhaps I will end up with one large volume, if the publisher thinks it will sell.'

Taking his eyeglasses off, he winks at Giorgi.

'And, of course, as long as you can bear the weight of my portmanteau. Remember what my Old Person of Hove did?'

Giorgi grins.

'Did he not disappear into a grove and study his books with wrens and hooks?'

'*Rooks*,' Lear corrects him.

'But why would you wish to disappear into a grove, Master?' Giorgi's voice has the tenor of a child asking his mother why she was unhappy with him.

'The house in San Remo goes if I cannot sell any more of my

books or my sketches and paintings. I worry about the money I have borrowed.'

Lear laughs and hands Giorgi the painted bookmark he had picked up from Calcutta.

'The book trade is difficult business these days.' The last time he entered the door to his publisher, Robert John Bush, the rooms looked so desolate that he knew that the halcyon days of the book trade were almost over. But what would come after, he did not know.

'But will not Lord Northbrook pay you handsomely for the painting of the Kanchenjunga?'

Another seabird screeches in the air.

The painting of the Kanchenjunga, the spectre that rests in the folds of his imagination! But what will be its shape after it rises from slumber?

Presently, a boat arrives and takes in a cargo of cotton brought in big sailing boats.

But it is not their boat.

Somewhere, someone is hammering. The steady sound of metal on metal begins to fill the air, and Lear finds himself back in the carriage of a train three weeks earlier.

Srirangam is just an hour away. Outside the window, the greens contrast wondrously with the red Devonshire soil. The views narrow at the horizon and all around are visible rice fields. The red and orange of the sky reflected on the waters move with the train as if they are stretches of elastic, faintly rippled in places, and in others, still and smooth. The skies open, and the train cuts through the driving rain like a knife.

Light *is* colour – that was the unwavering truth of painting. Frederic Church's *Heart of the Andes*, exhibited in London in the late summer of 1859. The eagle soaring among peaks, the cataract running through the wilderness, spread out like a richly woven carpet of greens, yellows and ochre, the sky glowing in an uncertain light with a tone of pale blue that appears to disappear behind the sheer white light filtering down from a watery sun.

He had been overwhelmed by the way the light had washed over the temple in Srirangam and its profuse architectural details and deities painted in extraordinary colours. The journey had continued – from a train that stopped every ten or fifteen minutes to a hand-carried *tonjon* up the Coonoor Pass into the mountains when he had mentally measured their progress by the tread of four human feet. Turner's landscapes had opened up quite wondrously as he made his way up in Ooty – a town that was overwhelmingly English, and therefore, quite undrawable – to reach Lady Canning's Seat. After a two-hour ride from the thriving hill station, they entered another world – through a hidden fold, a crease that had been pierced. The eye looked out at the landscape stretching way below to the plains and at the skies that had no borders separating the land from the expanse above. Just long streaks of light that made up the clouds suspended over pale pink, and all the nearer heights were dark with thick woods and grey-brown rocks. Like Khani Kastelli, Crete, light and colour seemed incidental to each other, coordinated as if viewed through what Hunt once called his 'two sets of eyes'.

It was at that spot where, standing still after being in motion for over two hours, he contemplated for the first time his *India Journal*. He would have to select the best from his store of sketches and forge words that followed the rhythms of his own walks, the fitful movement of trains, and the heave that he felt while sitting in the hand-carried *tonjon*s, and then, of course, the movements of his wandering eye over the vast expanses. Not an easy task, he had thought, for a man almost half worn with travel.

Suddenly, his thoughts are interrupted. Giorgi, who had walked away, returns, his cap in his left hand.

'Master, the ship may be delayed.'

'If it does not arrive today, we will be compelled to spend the night in the lighthouse. It is just one day past the full moon. If we are fortunate, we may see some dolphins leaping up from the sea under the moonlight.'

'I should like that.' Giorgi sits down after putting the book back in the satchel.

'You deserve a royal medal for the years you have dedicated to travel just to be able to *draw*. Can England boast of such intelligence and grit? The sheer labour, patience and forbearance. Remember our journey in Albania? You once fell off a horse. Another time, the horse you sat on sank into a river of mud. A pack of ten fierce barking and snarling dogs faced you as you returned from your walk, only to find yourself in a room with three aged mules and a pack of geese. We discovered only after finishing a half-cooked dinner served on broken metal plates that you had to share your room with a shrieking dervish who, that day, interrupted your sleep after you had travelled all day crossing the Ceraunian Mountains with his strange humming. The smell of hay in the room while horses outside noisily chomped away. Streams gurgling noisily outside the window that kept you up all night. As we were leaving, you asked the man if an underground stream ran under the barn. Cats tearing about, yowling, and just outside, a party of drunk Albanians who broke into song at midnight and feasted noisily till the early hours of the morning. Mourning chants, unexpected shots of gunfire.'

They both laugh. Lear is amazed by the beauty and eloquence of Giorgi's words. Not the person he remembered who took hours to learn the complications of irregular verbs. But that was years ago, when he had begun his services and preferred to chatter away in Italian.

Giorgi is not quite ready to abandon talking about his master's many escapades. He brings up incidents that had occurred quite recently, in fact, just a week earlier.

'Remember the broken railway bridge? How we had to get off our compartment, walk along the narrow and steep edge of the embankment, and then you had to be hoisted up a ladder! If I had not held you to prevent you from slithering down to the river's edge below, you would have been swept into the ocean that I believe is only a hundred miles away.'

Lear remembers throwing out his stiff arms to steady himself, but there was nothing to hold on to. As he began to wobble, Giorgi had reached out.

Lear proceeds to eat the roasted nuts he had bought from a small shop.

'I was often tempted to hold you back as you plunged ahead. A little daimon seemed to sit on your shoulders, urging you to keep moving. And when you did find the ideal spot, the muscles on your neck seemed to calm down, and you remained on your seat sketching till the sun disappeared. Later in the evening, when I lay on my bed, I could see you sitting under the dim light, scribbling away.'

Giorgi's words leave him with a feeling of inexplicable tenderness.

'The journey is as important as what comes out of it and what *it* does to you. This cannot be more true than this mad journey. I daresay it has altered me. For a person who was happy eating sausages, kippers and tongue, I have grown to relish the aroma of spinach fried with onion and cumin!'

'Fried onions, indeed. Thank our stars we have had the good fortune of not encountering any whirling dervishes in India.'

Lear flicks off an ant sitting on the edge of the paper bag with roasted nuts.

'We did face a fuming Brahmin on the banks of a river.'

They both stop talking, and Giorgi walks towards the rusty old anchor placed on top of a boulder.

Lear remembers the journey to Lamb's Rock from Ooty. After walking for three hours on a mended gravel road that looked more like the dry riverbeds he had seen near the Suez, he had hoped to find a place where he could sit and draw. He could not recall a time when he was so exhausted.

It was among the rocks that day when something baffling stirred in his brain as he watched a beautifully marked frog slowly devouring a grasshopper with one swoop of its tongue. Many years ago he had dreamt of a giant grasshopper chirping in his ear as he sat on a chair, terror stricken. That dream had turned into a limerick. But that day, crouched among the rocks, the grasshopper grew a human face! With a frizzy beard and hat, it gazed helplessly at the menacing frog, whose wet, glistening skin turned into a dinner jacket that quickly covered its short neck, and the flat face, and bulging eye sockets grew into a normal human face – graceful, austere and whiskered. The eyeglasses fell on the grass as the human grasshopper let out a high-pitched shriek before disappearing into the gaping mouth. The deed over, the diabolical creature with a dinner jacket and holding a copy of Aristotle's *Nicomachean Ethics* leapt into a gap in the bushes and vanished. Lear floundered and felt his way among the bushes, breathless, before resting on a large, mossy rock. What an uncanny vision that was – the spectacle of a bearded frog being devoured by a well-dressed grasshopper. He gazed intently at the grass, hoping to find the eyeglasses that he had seen falling to the ground. But there was just a dry old leaf, stirring in the breeze.

Giorgi who was about twenty paces behind, caught up, handing him his walking stick.

'Try to not wander off, Master, without me.'

He hears the waves crashing as he brushes down the crumbs from his coat. Fishing out his notebook from his satchel, he turns the pages. 'October 13' written in bold letters.

The great plain is something too extensive and incredible even to attempt to describe, a world of opal beaten out with a flimsy horizon of light and the long, long scheme of cloud casting pale, pearly blue shadows over great spaces of flat plain. The infinitesimal divisions of the vast immense level, with nearer rivers and the villages nearer still. The huge mountain, dipping, step by step, to the valley below; its deep green, grey and purple wooded undulations and crags! And then the left-hand middle ground of jungle and rocky mountainside; and lastly, the foreground path with the poor, meagre natives in their striped blankets, the ferns and the scattered tree ferns below!

He stops reading. The words he had written make him conscious that each portion of space that came into view that day was nothing but a fragment of an infinite whole, and within it, the eyes embraced an orbital sweep of pure space. Colour and perspective were concentrated into this space, and from an unidentifiable source, the light was bodied forth in each particle, pervading everywhere. There must have been light even in the darkness of the bushes where the frog had carried its victim.

A kind of exaltation runs through Lear's body. Is this what he had realized that evening, when sitting on the veranda of the *dak bungalow* in Mahé, he had seen a single firefly – a particle –

flitting around the bushes before being sucked into the gathering darkness?

The memory of Turner had come back to him that evening, and with such immediacy, that he literally saw himself retracing his steps through the National Gallery from that summer day in 1871. He had spent the subsequent nights reading Ruskin while staying at Tozer's new house in Oxford. The scenes follow in quick succession in his mind's eye – the explosions of colour in Turner's landscapes, the misty hollows of the Kanchenjunga giving way to the light that had pulsated through the hills and valleys of the Malabar. In an instant, he is back in Calicut, walking on an empty road, facing the endless vistas opening through the deep grey-green hollows.

Flipping through his notebook, he stops on the page marked 'October 20'.

It is all but impossible to give any idea of these beautiful Malabar lanes since their chief beauty consists of what cannot be readily imitated; to wit, endless detail of infinitely varied vegetation, and constantly changing variety of moving-figure-panoramic effect. The colour, too, of these scenes – the deep and vivid green, the red soil roads, and the brilliant white and scarlet dresses of the people – make all Malabar drawing a painful riddle.

Puzzle or riddle, he senses a powerful vortex churning somewhere.

He is utterly confounded to be so alone this moment, listening to the gentle murmur of the receding tide, until the aroma of Giorgi's tobacco wafts through the air, taking him back to the question about the *riddle*. What had led him to puzzle over what seemed at first to be just the view of landscape shimmering with colour? As they walked that day, Giorgi had stopped to pull out his tobacco bag, when Lear noticed the Malabar lanes getting narrower. And then – quite unexpectedly – the scene simply vanishes from view, disappearing into a tiny pinpoint! What would it take to get that funnelling effect down on paper – how would one recreate that unusual conjoining of motion and stillness?

Eyeing the words again while watching the waves crash all around him, Lear remembers the play of light as the Kanchenjunga had come into view – how the looming shapes that stood out one moment suddenly disappeared into thin air, and how his restless eye could barely keep up with the scenes that were sucked into that mysterious vortex, a phantom shaft that funnelled through that wintry day.

The pages flap in the dry ocean breeze, and the gentle chugging of one of the cargo ships runs through the air like a murmur.

The precise moment when that riddle – or should he have called it 'mystery' – was resolved returns to him with the clarity of the scene in front – of the waves bobbing up against the hull of the approaching cargo ship.

It was a warm, sultry day in the Malabar. Sitting alone, he had been pondering over whether he should continue sketching or try painting. Sitting alone on the veranda, it seemed to him that the pencil drawings he had done so far – as much as they were painstakingly detailed – could not quite capture the depths, the hidden furrows and the surfaces that corpuscular light brought out in landscapes. He had to catch the weight of that special light!

The wind picks up. The light, reflected on the turbulent waves, flickers as the cargo ship docks in front of the pier.

The shadows lengthen on the quiet Malabar lane. A young mother and her young boy stand in front of a tiny wayside shop under a mango tree. A pile of earthenware pots, of all sizes, lies heaped on a mat. Quite unexpectedly, the young boy – he cannot be more than six – comes up and offers him his hand. Embarrassed by the son's actions, the mother apologizes.

'Your son has such perfectly shaped fingers!'

The mother's smile and gesture show that she understands very little English. The temple bells ring insistently in the distance. The gold border of the mother's bright red and orange saree reaches down to ankles that are wrapped in two delicate chains with tiny paisley-like figures. The boy wears a yellow and green shirt.

He timidly offers Lear two large bananas.

'Plantain? Very sweet,' the mother says in an uncertain voice.

He accepts them and then hands them to Giorgi. Bending down, he pats the boy's shoulders. The boy's small mouth breaks into a smile, revealing his glistening teeth.

Then, quite abruptly, the woman leaves, taking the child by her hand.

The woman is walking away, holding her son's right hand, and soon turns into a bright red dot that melts gradually into the green and grey of the lane turning sharply to the right. But just before the bright red dot dims and plunges into the dark grey hollow in the distance, the redness throbs intensely. The evening bats fly back to their nests in droves – as if scattering the remaining light – and the sky above reveals deep purple folds.

A steam whistle blows in the distance.

A young man sells small sketches on a foggy day, standing by the road in Arundel. A few buyers step out of shops, cast a curious look at pictures he shows them – of cottages by watermills, rolling green hills, a woman riding a pony. A kindly lady in a dark blue bonnet buys one and hands him a shilling. Before she leaves, she asks him how old he is. The sky suddenly turns red, then purple, before it sinks into black. Rain.

How far he has travelled since that time! The motions of his life now arrange themselves across a screen stretched in front – of discrete faces and sights, swinging with the unsteady rocking of a boat on high seas. No sooner did the view appear than it begins to turn into bits of dust, buzzing around the eyes like insects before rearranging themselves, again, in long, elliptical shapes and then slowly dissipating into vapour. A human body is visible on the far horizon, bobbing up and down on the waves, wrapped in red and blue seaweed. Very abruptly, it disappears behind a giant wave. Could that be of his friend? Or perhaps, they were signs of the newly discovered substance, ether, that everyone was talking about? Just where the waves meet the horizon, Robert Houdin suspends his six-year-old son, Eugene, at the end of a pole!

Taking off his eyeglasses, Lear sneezes into his large handkerchief. But when he looks back at the ocean waves, all he sees are seagulls swirling around.

The day after meeting with the woman and her little son, Lear had risen early and noisily sipped his morning cup of tea. While emptying the satchel, a few of his sketches fell on the floor. Exasperated, he sat still for a few minutes, placing them in a small pile. Glancing at one he had selected from the heap, he made a decision and readied his watercolour tubes and brushes. A flock of unknown birds flitted across the sky. There he was – literally – sitting in a pool of light. Then, very gently, he began to work, moving the tip of his brush ever so lightly on the white surface of the paper. It had already absorbed much of the moisture from the air, but he was undeterred. After a few strokes, he held his breath, his brush suspended like the cable of a pendulum clock. Placing the caps back on the blue and green tubes, he waited.

'It is getting hot. Why don't we sit under the tree up there?'

Lear points to a large tamarind tree. Giorgi carries the cases. The branches above form a light, dome-like hollow of green. The coolness seems to come down from the very top of the tree and not from the ocean breeze that is still quite warm. Lear turns to Giorgi, who rests on a rock, panting. He has been chasing after a large seagull.

'I earned my living by painting by the time I was fifteen. I could not afford watercolours, so had to use them sparingly. And I also learnt patience, the value, of holding still.'

Giorgi remains silent. This is not the first time that he has heard about patience.

'I saw Her Majesty for the first time when I was about thirty-three. Now I am sixty-two-and-a-half, and, in the past twelve months, have had my fingers and lower limbs go numb in the freezing cold of the Himalayas, my entire body wracked by the prickly heat of the Deccan monsoons and my entire stock of paper go limp and lifeless in the wet draughts of the Malabar. But it was on that day in the Malabar, when the four tubes of watercolours I had brought from Madras had me fretting all day. I was faced with an unsolvable riddle for which I had no clues, let alone an answer.'

Giorgi laughs. 'But that was just the beginning of another adventure.'

'We are almost at the very end,' Lear says, looking at tiny pieces of broken shell on the ground, mixed up in the dirt. He watches the seagull hovering over his cases using its beak to turn a sea glass around.

The Malabar house with green shutters. He had sat on the floor with a half-finished painting beside him and stared at the tubes of paints when Giorgi had suggested a walk. The road outside the metal gate was empty. They had walked past the pepper garden, and upon taking a sharp turn, found themselves facing a deep valley.

So very remarkable an oriental view I have never seen nor even imagined; for, although the infinite lines of the low hills and higher mountains are all quite à la Claude Lorrain, yet the texture of coco-nuttery is something quite unlike what can be seen except in this, and other, extended tropical coast scenery: myriads of small, white flashes and as many myriads of deep, shady dots caused by the light and shade of the great, innumerable palm fronds. The rivers in this view are wonderfully beautiful while the hot sun is low; and all the colour changes of grey and misty lilac and palest opal shade (not opal, though, for that is clear, whereas here, all is misty and damp), make a world of divinely exquisite beauty.

Reading what he had scribbled that evening after they had returned from the walk, Lear feels the power of those flashes to illuminate the dark corner of a half-defined memory. The enigma, mystery, puzzle. Call it what you may. The colours change and so do the clues to a riddle. Little did he know then that the answer to it would come to him by mere chance the very next day, during an encounter with a venerable native gentleman with a keen interest in botanicals.

When he had sat down to paint earlier that day, the varying textures and lines and flashes of colour, all of which had accrued in his mind during his travels in the Malabar, appeared to have been absorbed into the single pool of light that surrounded him. Although he had made a great effort to work carefully at getting the right tonal intensities and contrasts, the colours he had used did not emit any light at all. An invisible swallow hole appeared to have sucked in all of the colours, leaving little but faint traces.

As he sat staring helplessly at his paintbrush, his mind returned to Dr Suss's drawing school in London, years ago. The freshly painted landscape he had completed that warm summer day had magically turned into an ocean after he accidentally spilt water over it. Arching his eyebrows, the teacher had said, 'Surely, your intention was not to paint a blotch on the sea!' That blotch, it turned out, was exactly the effect he had aimed to evoke in the painting!

All he could do was begin where he left off, on a fresh sheet of paper. Why was he so dissatisfied with his colouring? Was it the moisture in the air, or perhaps the quality of the paint? When he paid a rupee for the tubes about six weeks back, he had noticed that they were lying in a dark corner in an old cardboard box. And it was the only shop in Madras that sold watercolours!

Perhaps, the problem went deeper than the mere question of paints or weather. Was he simply not up to the task that he imagined Turner had set up for himself? Did he have to wait for a recurrence of a new moment of serendipity, or even of careless inattention?

With these questions swirling in his mind, he had returned to the pages of his notebook, leaving the painting unfinished. And quite suddenly, he realized that the words he had used describing the valley themselves contained the clue for moving ahead: the white dots were the points of light for which he had to find the right shade of white (perhaps apply several coats with the fine tip of his brush); the opal in the background needed the right kind of open intensity; the greens and greys had to be alternated to recreate the varying shades of verdure and placed in discrete lines. In some places, they had to simply bleed into each other. The blotch effect!

But the paints – what could he do about the tubes that lay on the floor? Where was he going to find a new set of colour tubes?

How could he possibly evoke that vibrancy of light that he had learned from seeing the illustrations of Turner in *Liber Studiorum*? What could he do about the numberless surfaces that lay all around, upon which light played its illusive tricks?

He rose, collected the sketches and placed them on the table in an untidy heap.

Giorgi arranged them in a neat stack inside the wooden box.

That afternoon, his host, Gustav Baudry, introduced him to a Mr William Barrows, the Superintendent of Schools. The tall, lean man, with a noticeable stoop, had in his hands three strikingly blue seeds.

'I hear you are interested in botanicals, Mr Lear. I wish to show you a plant you may have never seen or heard of before – the traveller's plant. Looks like a plantain tree and is known all over the Malabar for its ability to store pure water. Many a weary traveller has quenched his thirst after days of travel by receiving it from this unusual plant. These seeds come from that plant.'

Blue seeds! Gem-like lapis lazuli. He had not seen anything like it before.

So, when Mr Barrows suggested a stroll to have a look at the traveller's plant, they both readily put on their boots. As they were leaving, a small, dark man, with quick flashing eyes and jet-black hair, greeted them. Dressed in a white shirt and an even whiter cotton sarong, three horizontal stripes lining his dark forehead, the man introduced himself as Sankaran Nair.

Mr Nair was an eminent Malabar native, known for his knowledge of native plants.

They began to talk.

'I am no expert, only collect knowledge that already exists among the people of the Malabar.' Mr Nair's unusually soft voice was very soothing.

'A naturalist. You must be a veritable storehouse of botanical knowledge!'

Taking Mr Nair's hands, he looked at his sunburnt face.

'You must take me on a tour of the Malabar countryside. Quite certain there are plants here that I have not seen before, even in Kew!'

Mr Barrows and Mr Nair led Lear and Giorgi through a narrow road. Just where the road swerved, a tall, palm-like tree could be seen growing in a patch of wilderness next to which was a tiny shrine. A cluster of plantain-like leaves fanning out of a nearly ten-foot trunk shot up into the brilliantly blue sky. Several crows circled around. It was incredible that this very tree with large fan-like leaves bore the bright blue seeds that Mr Barrows had shown him earlier.

'They look like cups, don't they?'

Pulling a short blade out of his satchel, Mr Nair ran its sharp, gleaming edge gently across the base of a leaf and out gushed a stream of water.

'Each holds about a quart of rainwater. The sweetest water you can taste in the Malabar.'

Lear cautiously sipped the water that Mr Nair had collected in a tiny clay cup.

'It is assuredly pure and good in flavour. I have not tasted anything like it before.'

Lear gazed in wonder at the majestic leaves that were just beginning to stir in the breeze like the ears of an elephant.

As they walked back, Lear's mind was preoccupied with questions: How could it store such quantities of water? How could a giant palm-like tree bring forth such small, brilliantly blue seeds?

That evening, they were sitting in the library drinking

coffee. The conversation touched on poetry. An ardent admirer of Tennyson, Mr Barrows was delighted to learn about Lear's long-standing friendship with the poet. Mr Nair stood beside a bookcase, dusting a book bound in deep grey hide.

HORTI MALABARICI. The silver and gold letters of the title stood out.

'If you are as passionate about plants as I am, this will interest you.'

Mr Nair handed Lear a bulky volume. Page after page of carefully illustrated botanicals that included exquisitely detailed drawings of leaves, flowers and fruits in myriad shapes and textures, painted in pastel shades of red, pink, yellow and green. Lear ran his fingers over them, mesmerized by the beauty of the botanicals.

He heard Mr Nair say, 'A seventeenth-century compilation of the plants of the Malabar, it was commissioned by the Governor of the Dutch East India Company.'

Hendrik Van Reede, the name was printed in bold Cresci's Italic style.

'I believe many native scholars worked on this book, although they largely remain anonymous.' Mr Nair's eyes dwelt on the bright gold letters, and he ran his fingers over the cover.

'Isn't that the case with most European scholarship on India? So much of it was derived from the native knowledge that was never acknowledged.'

Mr Nair's eyes had moved to the view outside the window. A tiny woodpecker was busy pecking.

The ensuing talk about plants, medicines and botanical drawings prompted Lear to ask Mr Nair if he would be interested in looking over some of the sketches of trees that he had done in the last few days.

Mr Nair's face lit up.

'A fern tree, drawn the day before, is almost identical to the one I drew in Kurseong. Here is the neem – or was it tamarind, I can't remember which – that I drew in Tanjore.'

'You are, indeed, a master artist, Mr Lear. Queen Victoria's personal tutor – what an honour.'

A mixture of admiration and intrigue was visible in Mr Nair's eyes, which changed quite rapidly when the subject moved to inquiring about the Queen's artistic talents.

'Does Her Majesty have any talent for art, Mr Lear?'

'Not without any talent, I would say,' Lear responded, putting his sketches back into the pile.

The shadows lengthened on the floor of the porch outside. As he moved to the hard-backed chair, Lear brushed against the stack on the table, and the unfinished painting of that day dropped on the floor. Mr Nair picked it up promptly.

'I see you have also tried your hand at painting local scenes. This looks like the view from the hill not far from here.'

Lear nodded.

'My first real effort to paint. All along I have been sketching and putting a few dabs of colour. But so far, I have not been able to get the right effect with the colours I now possess. They are the old tubes of watercolour I bought in Madras.'

Pointing his finger at the unfinished spots, Lear said, 'Not sure what I should do next. I so want to be able to capture the play of light and colours as they are fresh in my mind. I have been writing about the views obsessively but have nothing to show in my own work.'

Mr Nair picked up the *Horti Malabarici*. His eyebrows moved, and the half-smile hinted at something that he had not yet shared. Lear was intrigued.

'Mr Lear, the *Horti Malabarici* is filled with all kinds of information about dyes that come from the catalogue of plants. Many are also used for making dyes for cloth. As far as I know, our temple paintings are done in the colours extracted from their leaves, roots and barks. Traditional remedies are also derived from them.'

Mr Nair began turning the pages.

'This is indigo, or the *king of natural dyes* as it is called.'

He moved his finger over the drawing of a plant with flowers resembling the sweet pea.

'The dye is produced by fermenting the fresh leaves of *Indigofera tinctoria*.'

'*Madder*. Now rarely found in the Malabar, the dye was used extensively all over India. You get a red and pink dye from the root of this plant.'

Lear could not contain his excitement. Each berry, each root was like the squids he had seen being sold in Corfu's markets, each turgid with magic ink. Colours produced by the opulence of the Malabar, all locked into plants that could be seen growing all around, on trees, creepers and little plants that grew on temple grounds and abandoned old houses. A veritable living pharmacopoeia!

Mr Barrows handed him another glass of claret. By that time, Giorgi's interest had also been piqued, and he stood behind Lear as Mr Nair continued, 'We have *harda* or black myrobalan. Its fruit gives out yellow and grey dyes. And, of course, turmeric – called *manjal* in the local language – that you can find in most curries. A most brilliant yellow and orange.'

He turned to the 'Index' and then back to the pages.

'*Manju phal*, prepared from the nuts of the wide-canopied *manju* tree that you see here. It gives cream and grey shades.'

Mr Nair stopped, looked at Lear's eager smile, paused and asked, 'Would you like to try painting with these dyes? Not sure if the colour will hold on paper, but it is worth trying.'

Mr Nair was amused to see a portly man, wearing a strange hat and a large overcoat, clasping his hands in glee like a child eagerly waiting for his new toy.

'I would not find anything more pleasurable!'

'In that case,' Mr Nair said, raising himself from the chair, 'I have to return home and procure some of these dyes for you. It's getting late.'

Placing the book on the table and straightening his cuff, he put on his shoes, which were lying outside the door, and strode out.

'I hope to see you tomorrow at seven sharp.'

'Can you see the seagulls sitting on that rock? They are much smaller than the ones you usually find in Corfu.' Giorgi has successfully driven away the single seagull that had already made several attempts at the bag of peanuts. A few sat on a rock, with beaks raised against the wind.

'I was very restless that night after I retired. Dreamt that I was walking through a lush tropical forest. Purple and green vines and tendrils and watermelon-sized flowers. Blazing colours – yes, I do dream in colour, if you are curious – reds, pinks, greys, greens, some pale lavender.'

Giorgi's restless eye is gleaning the distant horizon.

'You may think of me as a man of sepia inks and gentle washes, but I have always been obsessed with colour and paints – ever since I reached my eighteenth year. Although I was taken in to draw birds and some small animals, my first day as a draughtsman at the Zoological Gardens began with flowers and leaves, which I sketched with great abandon. So enthralled I was by petals, calyxes and the shapes and colours of leaves. When I was little, Ann shook me in bed one day because I was shouting out botanical names in my sleep!' Giorgi breaks into laughter, just thinking about a young lad with unkempt hair and eyeglasses engrossed in drawing botanicals while sitting among caged and fenced animals.

Stray clouds begin to gather in the western sky.

That morning, Lear, while waiting near the gate for Mr Nair, saw the gardener wearing just a loincloth, patiently digging around the roots of a shrub. The clouds were thickening.

'The beginning of our second monsoon,' he was told by Gustav, who had returned the previous night after visiting one of his many pepper plantations in the hills.

The clock struck seven, and Mr Nair arrived, carrying a wooden box in his right hand.

Inside it were tiny glass bottles that held a range of colours. Multi-hued genies were locked in small glass containers, all crying to be let out.

'A local man who works on the loom and dyes kindly spared me a few. Almost all of the dyes you see in these bottles have been mixed in with mordants to help the dye to be used for painting on paper. They are made to be used primarily on cloth, but I imagine they should work equally well on paper. At least, that is what I hope.'

Lear strode back to the room and opened the shutters of a half-open window through which the dull morning sun let shafts of silver flash on the swaying curtains. Dipping his brushes, Lear began working. The landscape began to take shape. The browns first, followed by broad horizontal strokes of blue. Splashes of green and grey and a few bright dots of white between them, the pale colours forming into their deeper shades. As his brush moved, an indefinable aura gathered around and lit up the rocks, trees and a palm-fronded village hut. Further back, the deep vistas began to materialize in multiple shades of green and grey, as if the genies he imagined locked in the bottles had entered every crack and crevice. Their gleeful cries could be heard all around.

When he had finished, Giorgi helped him clean and wipe the brushes using a piece of white cloth.

Lear held up the sheet of paper. It was glowing with an arc of light whose source appeared to be simultaneously inside *and* outside the painting he had done. He waited for some of the paint to dry a little more while letting other parts bleed into each other. With each passing moment, the colours brought out new surfaces that appeared to be beaten out into soft, glowing surfaces; in some parts, the graininess highlighted the light playing on the undulations of the land and the surfaces of rocks, valleys and the verdure; in other parts, the paint was concentrated on half-defined forms and blurry outlines of villages tucked away in the distance.

'The poor artist colours his paintings with light taken from fireflies,' Gussie had once said. 'That light is enough to dispel the darkness of a winter night.' Lear thinks of Gussie's fairy tale, written in flowing longhand, that she had shared with him years ago. The look, that day, on her face was enough to make him feel as though it heralded a voyage through the skies in one of the flower chariots she had described in her fairy tale. Lear had always been amused by Gussie's overripe, adoring imagination as she talked about the world of fairy paintings.

'The paintings are the inspiration for my fairy stories,' Gussie had remarked, seeing a blue jay as they strolled down an avenue of plane trees in Hyde Park. Lear knew that although he had never fancied doing fairy paintings himself, he was always drawn to the wicked grin on gnomes playing around toadstools. He had been struck by the beauty and oddities visible in Richard Dadd's *The Fairy Feller's Master-Stroke*, a gift on his fiftieth birthday from Hunt. The flowers, leaves and stalks of grass unfurling profusely across the pages were also packed with miniature figures in fanciful dresses and crowns thronging around a brown-suited gentleman about to cleave an acorn in two with an axe!

A big wave crashes on the shore in front.

An axe, he wonders. Was a riddle locked within the hard shell that had to be freed?

Gussie's fairy tales and Dadd's untamed imagination!

But that day, no fairy chariots, gnomes or acorns were visible anywhere.

With Mr Nair by his side, he had paused to look at what he had done and raised himself from the chair.

'Mr Nair, the riddle has been solved. Do you see the moving-figure-panoramic effect?'

Noticing the man's curious expression, he continued, 'It is a panoramic image generated from a vertical split moving horizontally on a smooth path, like a long roll painting moved in front of the audience by means of a special apparatus. I could not get that effect with the Madras paints I was using. Perhaps because I did not try hard enough, so disappointed I was when I first applied them.'

'It is like seeing a fairy tale with fireflies being told in pictures.' Mr Nair was visibly excited.

'And when I thought of this effect, I thought it was just what my eye caught at that point, standing on the cliff, but here it is, on paper, right in front of me, made alive by the colours you brought.' Lear picked up the bottle of bright yellow liquid, took off his eyeglasses, and looking at it closely, turned the bottle around with his wrist in a slow, circular motion.

'This is the world of the Malabar, right inside this bottle!'

Just before he left, Mr Nair handed him a small envelope. In it were five strikingly blue seeds of the traveller's plant.

The bright blue curtains in Lushington's room swing in the breeze wafting through the window of the room that Lushington has been emptying in preparation for departure. The framed pictures are on the floor, the books on the large table. The curtains would soon be brought down, folded, and placed inside the large, wooden crate, to be carted away to the harbour one fine afternoon when the melancholy song of the birds filled the air. A dash of that same blue remained lodged in his brain like a stubborn stain refusing to be washed clean.

As hard as he strove to get Lushington interested in his washes and in discussing the power of oil, he would respond by merely nodding and uttering an occasional 'no doubt'. The near-vacant house had made him realize that it was too late to fire Lushington's imagination. When their paths would cross again – he could not tell.

The trick of the colour kaleidoscope, he remembers: refraction, diffusion, dispersion! The night before they reached Tuticorin Harbour, he had lain in his bed, restless. It had been a long day of packing and travel. The call of an unknown bird had woken him just when the early light entered the room. At first, all he could sense was an impenetrable darkness, a blankness of sorts. It was as if his mind had emptied itself of all forms, all shapes, all colours, even sounds. From the half-darkness, he saw a shape. The leviathan surged out of the ocean, awash with colours that he could not recall seeing that wintry day in Kurseong as he sat among the ferns. The glacial whiteness accentuated the sharpness of the icy slopes that seemed to plunge into a haze of blue and white. Instead of the blankness in the middle, there was a shimmering haze, and heaving up in front was a swathe of brown, green, red and turquoise poised over a dark gorge where the black had cleaved down to disappear into the bottom where the edge of a picture frame appeared! On the flat brown surface of ground in the mid-foreground was a cluster of human figures. A hooded figure was bent towards another, whose arms were partly covered in gleaming white sleeves. A necklace sparkled on the throat of another figure. Although dwarfed by the enormity of the peak, each human figure in this cluster seemed to stand out, as if caught up in mid-conversation, frozen in time and gesture.

Was this the Kanchenjunga that had lain buried in his mind all along, a likeness to something that was yet to take real shape?

A giant wave crashes on the shore.

He recalls that all along, the Viceroy had been reluctant to say anything specific about the style and form of the final work he expected, only stating that all he wanted was 'a large oil of my favourite mountain that could adorn the high walls of Stratton Park'. Not very helpful, he had admitted, at first. But he had kept quiet.

The tide is returning. The heat has been replaced by a mild coolness. Hastily pulling out the last sketch he had made of the Kanchenjunga from his satchel, he gazes at it intently, running his forefinger very gently over its fierce outlines. In the remembered dream, the Kanchenjunga flashes, emitting an unknown light. Could it be the lighthouse sending out its first signals to a ship, perhaps waiting in the darkening ocean?

He feels that the dream he had the previous night had evoked the immensity that Northbrook expected in the painting of the Kanchenjunga. It was as if his mind had silently worked out the puzzle that had kept him awake many a night: how to turn the bare bones of a sketch done in pencil into a painting replete with the vibrancy of oil. Had his mind reordered all of his sensory perceptions of India and channelled them into the image? The play of vertical and horizontal lines that he had witnessed on the walls of the Chunar Fort as they plunged into the waters of the Ganges? The shimmering yellow that had lit up the mustard field into which he had seen the battalion of maimed soldiers disappear? The splash of red in it was the vermilion dot that he saw recede into the greens of the Malabar. And, without doubt, the genie in the bottles, released from the bottles, have begun their capers! The acorn had been split with an axe!

All he can sense now around him is the insistent cawing of seagulls and the words he had heard in Calcutta the night before they departed for the hills.

'Mr Edward Lear, the Viceroy's artist employed to paint the Kanchenjunga.'

It was Evelyn Baring introducing him to a grim-looking gentleman who had recently acquired a large collection of botanicals produced by the finest artists of the Company School.

'Ah, the painter of the mighty Kanchenjunga,' the gentleman had said, sipping champagne.

'I was under the impression that Mr Lear only wrote nonsense and created funny drawings to entertain children.'

Evelyn had smiled and walked towards the door to greet another guest.

He hears Giorgi saying triumphantly, 'Mr Lear. The boat has arrived.'

Lear looks up. An iron-hulled sailing ship is slowly making its way up the harbour, the bright blue letters *'Ceylon Star'* reflected on the still grey-green sea glinting in the sun. He raises himself and sees the letters breaking into a million pieces on the moving surface of the water. Another journey, another discovery. Suddenly, he feels the first drops of rain. Soon, the drizzle will turn to driving rain. Giorgi holds up the umbrella.

'Non c'è rimedio. There is nothing to be done when it rains.'

THEY SIT IN AN UNLIT room with a large window overlooking a grove of coco palms where the shadows are so deep that even the red hibiscus flowering in the bushes appear purple, almost black.

Edward Lear and Lockwood Kipling are at the latter's *bungalow* in Victoria, in the heart of the city of Bombay. Yet, Lear feels as if he is on a remote island. Only a faint clatter of wheels reaches his ears.

Before he walked out of Giorgi's room at the hotel on Queen's Road earlier that day, he saw him lying on the bed, his left arm placed over his forehead and very still. Pale and listless, he had barely stirred from bed since they arrived in the city a day before. Giorgi's sudden illness in Ceylon had made Lear decide to return sooner than he had planned. Peering through his door before entering, he saw him propped up against the pillow, reading the same letter repeatedly. Nikola's illness, which began six months ago, was getting worse, and there was little hope of recovery. He had only seen him look like this nearly thirteen years ago when he had heard him utter, '*E voluntà di dio.*' He was sitting on a chair in the apartment in Rome, holding a letter that had arrived from Corfu.

Elisabetta, his only daughter, had not recovered from a raging fever, and in less than a week, was gone. Later that evening, he heard Giorgi sobbing. '*Morta quella pupetta,*' over and over again. 'Only Nikola remains to care for me. I grow old and feeble.' He had stood straight, his back to the window, his face pale with grief.

'Nikola is young and strong. He will recover.' Lear touched him on the shoulder.

Realizing that his words would provide him little comfort, Lear leaned towards the back of the door to pick up his walking stick and hat.

'I'm afraid I have to leave, Giorgi. Cannot keep Mr Kipling waiting. I sent him a note yesterday saying that I would be at his place by three. Lie down, and if you need anything, call the boy downstairs. He is an attentive young lad.'

It is 9 January 1875, only two days remaining before they set sail for Brindisi. Not enough time left to attend to matters still pending. First, he has to cash his last one hundred at the Treasury and then pay Lockwood Kipling a visit. Northbrook expects a letter from me explaining my sudden decision to return, he thinks, looking up at the swirling, feeble January sun. Only last month, a letter from George Howard, his friend in London, had arrived saying that he would be honoured if Lear made time to meet Lockwood Kipling, who would soon be setting sail for Lahore. The famous Lockwood, principal of the JJ School of Art, had made Bombay his home, arriving in this bustling city when he was merely twenty-eight. He had only very recently agreed to take up a position as principal of the Mayo Art School in Lahore and would leave Bombay in the spring, the letter said.

Stepping out, Lear began his slow plod down Queen's Road. Although his weak knees were beginning to act up again, he was able to pick up pace as soon as he felt the bracing sea air on his face. On both sides, the newly installed gas lamps stood erect like soldiers from the Roman legion. Two natives were using a hand pump to flush out dirty brown water from below one of the lamps. Young men, in shabby breeches, their grease-stained shirts torn in places. One of them smiled as Lear stopped to look at the lamps.

Very much like the ones in Piccadilly, he thought, letting his fingers run over the ornamental cast iron that was beginning to show signs of rusting. The men stared at him as he continued down Queen's Road, pausing to turn left at the Glenn Pharmacy. Lear remembered the directions that the manager of the hotel had offered to get to Victoria.

As he stepped out of the impressive carved doors of the Treasury half an hour later, he felt the sharp sun striking his face. He rested on a bench before resuming his walk. Seeing the back and forth of carriages, he regretted not calling for a carriage. But he could spy the sign 'Victoria' painted in bright blue. Taking the side lane, he moved cautiously. Only a few handcarts and pull carts stood in front of the shops on either side.

As he walked, his thoughts went back to Giorgi gazing at a picture of a girl with a small, round face and a head full of curly hair. Elisabetta, *mi cara figlia*.

'Our bodies are designed for pain,' he remembers telling Giorgi the day after he had placed her little scarf on the table next to his bed. 'Every little fibre, muscle, every bone, part of an imperium of pain. And with those bodies in tow, each one of us moves through life.'

It took nearly a full year to pull Giorgi out of his grief, but he often spoke about how much he missed his beautiful daughter who loved to read and draw.

Lear found an eager-looking Lockwood waiting for him at the front gate. A jovial man nearly twenty years his junior – with a broad forehead and receding hairline, beard more luxuriant – and darker than his. There was a kind of fierceness beneath the joviality, Lear thought, as they shook hands.

Certainly tall, the famous Lear was not as corpulent as Lockwood had expected him to be. With round-rimmed eyeglasses, dark, oversized overcoat and a beard, and hatted and booted, he looked every inch the poet of nonsense who had made a career writing about and drawing strange creatures, birds, flowers and people! Only his solid cane seemed a tad uninspired. It was just before Christmas that he had received a letter from his brother-in-law – Edward Burne-Jones – saying that Lear wished to pay him a visit before he left India.

Lear's hastily scribbled note had reached him the day before.

'It was Howard, your friend I believe, whom I met years ago. Not sure where in London. Burne-Jones introduced us, but I quite forget where, though. Alice – my wife – adores Jones and will most likely remember where we met.'

Lockwood's words stumble out of his mouth fitfully as he leads Lear through the sitting room into the study. 'Unfortunately, she had a prior engagement this morning at the Art Club. With the children being far away in Portsmouth, she keeps herself busy outdoors, and I mostly spend my time here in this room.'

Lear sits, staring at the dark walls covered with paintings and lithographs. Towering shelves nearly touching the ceiling are thickly stacked with books.

'That is Alice.' Lockwood points to a framed photograph on the wall. It is of the young Lockwood perched on the edge of a table while his wife, Alice, sits on a chair holding a book on her lap. Her strikingly beautiful profile is turned away from the viewer.

'The photographer insisted that she have the tip of the left middle finger tucked inside the book.' Lockwood begins to wipe the frame somewhat absent-mindedly with his handkerchief.

'One day without dusting, and you are left with a patina of fine grey. Settles on every inch of every exposed surface. One of the pleasures of living in the heart of Bombay. Not much difference, I imagine, from living in Kensington.'

His sparkling white teeth flash as his face breaks into a wide smile.

'Howard and I have been friends for years,' says Lear, but he does not mention Burne-Jones. 'In London, people are marvelling at your architectural ornamentation. I was honoured to visit Crawford Market soon after my arrival in Bombay over a year ago.'

Lear walks down the length of the wall facing the window without the aid of his cane. Adjusting his eyeglasses, he turns his face towards the paintings that hang on the walls.

'That was one of the first places I saw. The friezes above the entrance of the market, and the fountain nearby erected, I believe, quite recently, too, were striking, very unusual.'

The carved animals and gargoyle-like figures, the river goddess surrounded by flora and fauna of infinite variety had intrigued him.

'I am glad they did not escape your notice. My two little ones, Rudyard and Trix, adore your limericks. But the animals are their favourite drawings. My little boy often tried to copy the funny kangaroo. His favourite was the very lifelike and colourful parrot.'

A young native woman walks in with a tray of tea and some sandwiches. Lear helps himself to one.

'I am very worried about my manservant, my travelling companion, Giorgi. The diarrhoea in Ceylon took a terrible toll on his health, and now, his son is very ill back in Corfu. I left him at the hotel.'

'Diarrhoea! Very common here. If he has been in India for a year and suffered the air and food, he will, no doubt, recover in due time.' The bemused expression on Lockwood's face takes Lear by surprise, but he remains silent.

The conversation turns to Ceylon.

'Do you regret not being able to see much of Ceylon?'

Lear is slow to respond. He cannot stop thinking about Giorgi. The almost skeletal body hidden under a white cotton sheet was nothing like the tall, gaunt man he had known for all these years, so unresponsive that he had not uttered a single word when he walked out of the door.

But Lear is curious about Lockwood.

'What prompted the decision to move to Lahore, considering that you are so highly regarded here? I imagine it is not for pecuniary reasons.'

Lear's eyes fall on the densely knotted and elaborately designed carpets on the floor and the fine throws on the furniture. Lockwood picks up the last sandwich from the plate and pours himself a second cup of tea.

'Ha, that is quite another story. The Gothic Revival in Bombay, well, sadly, it has become – for lack of a better word – a *mania* in Bombay. The other being the Public Works Department's dreadfully misguided architectural design that appears to have taken over the city. Most of my students are new converts to this godawful *Revival*! I feel that there is very little for me to do here. *Bungaloathsome* – that's what I call it, the uninspired architecture you now see all around.' Lockwood's voice is serious but in a mocking way.

'A man after my heart.' Lear's ear picks up the well-crafted nonsense word. He wants to tell him about the unattractive

'Anglo-Saxonism' he had witnessed in Simla but finds himself wanting to learn more about Lockwood's work in Bombay.

'Time to dust off the old Bombay from my shoulders. Punjab would be the ideal spot for working with rural artisans – terracotta, wood carvings, brassware, textiles. I began as a ceramics expert, and since I have been in India, have become enamoured of terracotta design.'

'Why, of course, you were in Simla, where you did a drawing of a woodcarver – that was just a few years ago, was it not?'

Lockwood nods.

'I imagine that you have an affinity with the Brotherhood painters. Many of your landscapes – that I must confess I have not actually seen – but I am told by Burne-Jones, are largely inspired by Turner.'

'Yes, my interests lie mainly in watercolours and oil, that is when I can afford oil and know there will be a buyer. But mostly, my drawings are with ink on paper, washes and sepia. Routine business for a draughtsman and lithographer of my calibre.' He was quite certain that Lockwood knew about his short run as the Queen's art teacher.

'What will chronic poverty not do to an artist! Sadly, that is the lot of so many in our times – and then, there is Morris.' Lockwood pauses. 'But William Morris has done well for himself. He has discovered the trick, I imagine.'

For the first time, they both laugh out loud.

The conversation meanders while the sound of insects chirping fills the room. Lockwood's eyes gleam when Lear brings up the story about his discovery of natural dyes in Malabar.

'An unexpected gift from India, I should think. New discoveries are to be expected for someone who has literally travelled the length and breadth of the country.'

He gestures to Lear to follow him through the door that leads to the garden.

'Reeves, Roberson, Rowney and Winsor and Newton are the colourmen of our times. In an age mesmerized by gilded pigments produced in factories, they are certainly a novelty. Sadly, you find most artists these days becoming sceptical about returning to what they call "old" traditions. This is the age of progress. No looking back, they say.'

The air outside is so fragrant that Lear first thinks it must come from the incense stand that he had seen on the table as he walked in through the door.

'Ah, the fragrance that you detect comes from the *saptaparni*, a local tree that gets its name from the funnel arrangement of four-nine leaves arranged around a branchlet. It gets more powerful as the sun loses its intensity. And something more interesting – its wood makes the finest coffins in these parts, so most European houses have the tree in their gardens.'

'Most interesting.' The gathering darkness soon covers the trees. He cannot tell on which trees, among the many he saw, these flowers had bloomed. But the scent is overwhelming.

'You are a much-travelled man, Mr Lear. A single man, with no family to take care of. No children waiting to be sent off to schools in distant England.'

'Sometimes I wished I *had* a family. Verily, my manservant has been with me for nearly twenty years, and he is, without doubt, a jewel, almost family. I am truly fortunate.'

As they reenter the study, Lear realizes that some of the lamps have already been lit.

'One needs money to travel. Plenty of it, more than an artist can afford.'

The silk carpets gleam in the soft light.

As Lear begins to talk about his long fourteen-month itinerary in India, tracing his travels on trains and *jampans*, Lockwood's eyes light up.

'You are a lucky man – to have Northbrook as your patron.'

The steaming cup of tea emits a beautiful aroma.

'The Himalayas! Nature at its sublime best! Fortunate to be making Lahore my new home. Close to that ethereal range of mountains.'

Lear finds himself talking about the Kanchenjunga – and how elusive it had been when he first glimpsed it in Kurseong and how often he had fretted over getting it right in his sketches. He avoids mentioning the incident of falling from his sketching stool.

Lockwood notices the gleam in Lear's eyes.

The conversation moves to the sights of Gwalior, Delhi, Calcutta, Tanjore and the Malabar. 'I regret not being able to visit the Ajanta Caves, which I believe are not far from Bombay. The prayer halls and magnificent frescos – all discovered by accident fifty years ago. Certainly worth a visit, but perhaps not in this lifetime.'

Lockwood offers Lear a chair.

Ceylon did not seem to interest or intrigue Lockwood very much. Just when he is ready to share some details of Kandy, the servant walks in to inform Lockwood that a Mr Teale is waiting for him in the garden.

Lockwood excuses himself and leaves.

Getting up from his chair, Lear feels a strange fatigue wracking his body. Wonder if Giorgi has fallen back into slumber. Hope he will be able to have a bite to eat for supper. Just days away to sail; he needs to recover some of his strength back.

On the marble-topped table is a book with the title engraved on its spine in silver that immediately catches Lear's attention: *Manners in Bengal*. Picking it up, he walks up to the window where there is a little more light. Filled with delicate hand-coloured lithographs, page after page. *Twenty four Plates Illustrative of Hindoo and European Manners in Bengal: Drawn on the Stone by A. Colin from Sketches by Mrs Belnos*. Under the title is the picture of a bare-chested Brahmin priest resting under a tree by a pool, holding a stick in his hand. Lear's hands are a bit unsteady. He skips the pages. Holding a heavy, hardbound book in his hand seems difficult these days.

He gradually works backwards, turning over the pages slowly. The picture of two young women by the banks of the Ganges, one bending and offering flowers to the river, the sky awash in a blank space marked by a few strokes of very pale grey, with a temple in the background. The other woman stands behind her, holding a small pot in her right hand, with the fingers delicately grasping the base and her left hand propping up the right elbow. Such poise, such stillness, a perfectly meditative moment, almost like an interregnum between doing, thinking and feeling the world around. He pauses for a moment and closes his eyes.

Something very startlingly unusual catches his attention. At the far right of one of the pages is a man – a bare-chested priest looking up at the rising sun, with his right hand lifted in a sign of benediction. Just below him, half submerged in the flowing waters of a river, is a dying man, whose lips barely touch the spout of a vessel being held by another priest. His soon-to-be widow is drying her eyes with the edge of the garment wrapped over her shoulders. Their dark bodies are painted in deep brown and the rest in a wash of pale indigo, grey and white.

A Dying Hindoo Brought to the Ganges.

Lear is startled.

The man's ashen face – highlighted by the dark lines around his mouth – his lifeless limbs falling into the waters.

Lear himself reentering the dark room in Kandy to find Giorgi lying on his bed, the light from the lamp casting deep shadows around his cheeks and eyes. He does not respond when Lear calls out his name. Dr Rudd's anti-diarrhoea pill appears to have brought some relief, which is why he decides to step out to walk to the Kandy Library. As the sun goes down the horizon, Lear realizes that it will get too dark for him to find his way back. He hurries back to Giorgi's room. The poor man is moaning, almost inaudibly. Seeing Giorgi's face, he does not waste a moment; he rushes out again and hurries to Dr Rudd's house. When they return, Dr Rudd looks at Giorgi's face and says, 'We have to take him to Colombo. I am not sure if anything can be done for him here in Kandy.'

The rains begin and lightning flashes across the skies.

That night, both he and the doctor sit by his bedside, and the next morning, as the dawn breaks through the distant hills, their cases are taken out and Giorgi is carried to the train station. He cannot take his eyes off Giorgi as he is propped up in the rail carriage. The same listless face, the same unmoving lips. Through the entire journey on the train, Lear holds his hands and wipes his watery eyes. The mountains sweep past, the foliage racing by in flashes of intense green. A few spires of distant temples are visible through the tops of trees. Lear's body feels the dull weight of unquiet desolation.

As the train gathers speed, he remembers the words he had penned in Rome in his diary soon after he read Giorgi's letter saying he was very sick in Naples and without any money. Although he had sent him twenty pounds, he was informed that Giorgi could not be traced to the house where the money had been sent. And when the trouser-mending Giorgi did finally show up at the door a few weeks later, his joy was indescribable. 'His plain fidelity is delightful,' he had noted that evening when he sat up late watching Giorgi reading his book.

At Queen's House in Colombo, Dr White arrives and asks Lear to leave the room. Sitting outside, he hears temple bells ringing in the distance. A few fireworks break the silence of the darkening skies. Then, Governor Gregory comes up to him.

'He is to be taken to the hospital.' Patting his pale hands, he adds, 'He should be well. Do not worry.'

What if I lose Giorgi, what will I do? Does he even know I am here? No words have come out of his lips since they left Kandy. Where will I go? What will I tell Nikola? Fireworks light up the sky. He sees a man climbing the tower in the darkness. He remembers the river below, fearing that the slippery banks are too treacherous to walk on without having Giorgi hold his arms. Giorgi's face reappears as it did, peering down at him the moment he opened his eyes that cold morning in Kurseong.

'Mr Lear, I am so sorry it took so long. I had to sign some papers – official ones.' Lear is startled to hear Lockwood's voice as he enters the room. Hastily, he puts the book back on the table. Lockwood sees the book on the table but remains silent. Lear notices Lockwood walking up to the corner of the room to open a carved mahogany box and draw out a scroll.

'I wish to share with you something from Calcutta that you may be aware of, although I cannot imagine either Evelyn Baring or Northbrook being in the least interested in these items of art.'

It is a brightly painted watercolour on cheap paper of a fat cat – with a giant lobster in its mouth. Out of its narrowly set fish eyes, the cat stares at him as if he had interrupted its meal.

'A satirical, comical portrait of the Hindu priestly caste.' Above the large eyes, the caste mark on the cat's forehead stands out.

'How playful, how cleverly executed. No pretensions to high art and to tonal differences. Part of my collection of folk art – I have about ten procured recently from Calcutta. These inexpensive pictures – executed with swift brushstrokes on cheap paper – are collectibles, usually bought by the English residents of Calcutta.'

Collectibles? Lear is struck by the bold primary colours, but what draws him to the painting is the sheer temerity of the drawing.

'The anonymous artists who make them are usually from villages, many drawn to the city to make a living. Hungry artists suffering from famine and loss of their crops. Making simple paintings and drawings – they are good at it. The new art of lithography has been a heaven-sent skill. The hand-coloured prints are quite the rage in Calcutta. Just look at the colours! The startling alertness of the artists – the innovation of simple, unlettered people who have the only thing left to them in this world – their expansive imagination.'

'I wonder what Morris would think of these paintings.'

Lear smiles as he bends down to gaze at the smile on the face of the cat.

'Have not the slightest clue,' is Lockwood's response, but seeing his expression, Lear knows what he is thinking. 'Certainly not something you can incorporate into a wallpaper design!'

Lockwood hands him another scroll. Lockwood whispers, almost under his breath, 'Kaali, the defiant Black Goddess.' A red tongue sticking out of the mouth, neck garlanded with a string of human skulls, and one of the four arms holding a sword and another one a severed head, the painting reminds Lear of the figure he had encountered that winter day in the dark recesses of the Buddhist shrine in Darjeeling.

'The Goddess of Time!'

Time! Was the figure the same as one of the outrageously ugly gods he had seen pious Hindus worshipping in a temple close to the railway station the morning they left Calcutta? And here she was, again, the Dreaded One – Time herself! A bare black leg stepping delicately on the chest of a prostrate pot-bellied man with a crested moon attached to his top locks. Clad in tiger skin, he rests his head under his left arm. His eyes are shut. Red flowers with giant red pistils adorn the Goddess's feet, her large eyes glaring at the viewer.

The closest he ever came to contemplating Time figured as a fearful human form was when he had stepped into Lushington's study to find the marine sandglass sitting silently on the table. He had thought, gazing at the hemp ropes looped around its wooden base, that these were 'Time's hoops'. Reflected on the convex globes was his own face, contorted beyond recognition. But here, Time is present as the *look* itself – the gaze of the person who sees her. The severed heads hung around the deity's neck have their eyes shut, as if the darkness of the room has readied them for a late afternoon slumber on a hot day when the birds in the trees outside have ceased chirping.

Another flash of memory strikes him. It was a cold December afternoon in Calcutta – the day before Christmas Eve, in fact, when, walking alone along the canal, he had lost his way. It was a few days after his arrival in Calcutta when the sudden eruption of a host of scarlet-coated government domestics at Howrah Station had taken him by surprise. With a force that amazed him, they propelled the two out of the railway station, into a steamboat to be ferried across the river, conveyed by a horse-driven carriage to the imposing Government House, eventually to be led into a large, beautifully furnished room. The general fuss of viceregal hospitality! The first time he felt free to wander around was when he was taken by Miss Baring to the open expanse of the Eden Gardens, where he spotted a contingent of crows feeding on the carcass of a goat. That evening, he had ventured out on his own without telling Evelyn, and after taking a road by the side of a canal, found himself unexpectedly in the midst of a bustling Calcutta *bazaar*.

The December sun had begun to set as the skies turned a vivid red, with streaks of orange and yellow. He had been on the road for not more than an hour, or so he thought, as he had left his watch on the mantelpiece. But looking around, he knew he had strayed. Innumerable eyes stared at him – out of small makeshift shops and low houses with tiled roofs that line the narrow, winding lanes. Women standing outside small roadside altars, men squatting and selling clay pots – and just around the bend, two women and a man, sitting on low stools and painting with crude brushes on sheets of paper. The light was so dim that all he could see were a few pots of paint, a few brushes dipped in old tin cans, and sheets of cheap paper laid out on a straw mat. A mythic serpent surrounded by lotuses had uncoiled itself in green, blue and pink. A goddess sitting under its many-headed hood held a tuft of grass. A band of grey elephants trooping down a forest filled with green parrots.

He had looked ahead and wondered: Did I walk down that road?

Seeing him screwing up his eyes and holding his eyeglasses in one hand, a young girl had come up from the shadows and pointed her finger in the direction of two coco palms, saying 'Gorment House.'

When he later told Evelyn what had happened, he was visibly annoyed. 'I was not intending to. I was captivated by the reflections on the canal and kept following them till I took a turn without knowing it.'

'So did Joseph Hooker in Darjeeling, I imagine,' Evelyn had said, eyeing the elephant-shaped paperweight that sat on Lord Northbrook's empty desk.

When Lear finishes relating the story of that cold evening in Calcutta, Lockwood laughs. 'The Theseus of Calcutta – emerging from the labyrinth, the minotaur dead at his feet! While painters in Calcutta sit on hovels with their paintbrushes and itinerant singers dance in ecstasy with their anklets on, Ophelia is made to float downstream with half-closed eyes, her diaphanous white dress soaking wet.'

The shadows lengthen outside in the grove, and Lear looks anxiously at his watch.

'I am so glad you could make time to visit me. Your carriage is waiting outside on the front porch.'

After handing him the painting of the cat, rolled up tightly with a string, Lockwood accompanies Lear to the porch. The air is now almost full of the almost-cloying aroma of the *saptaparni* flowers. Lear inhales deeply one last time before getting into the carriage. In front, across the horizon, he sees the red and orange fading through the skies. On both sides of Queen's Road, the lamps are being lit. He looks over the ocean – a seething mass of dark grey with the last remaining streaks of light skipping over the surface. The dark mountains visible from the ship that took them from the harbour in Colombo to Bombay, the very mountains of the

Malabar that had appeared during his first visit in pulsating colours of blue, green, opal and yellow, just slid by silently this time. The trees, the skies, the distant hills and the fishing nets had vanished in the darkening night. On the deck of that ship lay an inert Giorgi, barely able to utter a word.

On reaching the hotel, Lear walks into Giorgi's room and sees him sitting up in his bed reading the newspaper.

'A play in Calcutta showing the atrocities of an English planter on an Indian girl has elicited the red eyes of the Government,' repeats Giorgi. 'That is the *only* newsworthy bit in the *Times of India*, I am afraid.'

Lear is reassured. Giorgi is on the mend.

Walking back to his room, he opens his notebook and writes:

January 9
Wrote to Evelyn Baring, telling him I had drawn on the Viceroy for two hundred pounds and why: also to the Viceroy telling him of my decision to go back, which I know is the best course of action, given the circumstances. Picked up photographs from Shepherd & Bourne and paid twenty-four pounds. Got my eighth hundred cashed at the Treasury and have taken my two places to Brindisi. So much, therefore, is decided. I go.

A seagull shrieks somewhere outside the window. The waters splash noisily and then seethe somewhere in the darkness. Two shadows swing with the swish of the *punkah* – the twin black angels on the walls – and between these shadows loom two faces – the Mahakaal with his fangs bared and Kaali with her pitch-black face and fearful eyes. Stepping on someone or being stepped on – such are the world's fearful symmetries. The majestic Kanchenjunga, with its perilous slopes, casts a glow that moves like the flash of a shooting star. From another window, Lear glimpses the street lamps being put out, one by one, and feels his sixty-odd years pass in the wheezy shudder of the windows facing the dark waters. Giorgi has fallen asleep, and is, in fact, snoring softly.

As he turns away from the open window, Lear's eyes fall on a grasshopper. A grasshopper in a room? Very odd! He bends down slowly to have a closer look at the creature. Unlike the last time when he saw the beetle in the bushes, this is just an ordinary garden grasshopper, the three pairs of legs held still under leathery hindwings. Lear holds his breath, expecting it to transform itself into a being with beard and eyeglasses! But nothing happens. A ticking chip suddenly fills the air, and almost instantly, it flinches and gives a mighty leap, flying out into the darkness. Not a creature of his savage imagination but a fellow from the grasses, bushes and trees that grew outside. He takes off his eyeglasses to look. But there is no fairyland frog, with protruding eyes and webbed feet, waiting in the corner for its next meal.

'Liberty! A gentleman who has been wielding a gavel all his life will be delighted to know that I am finally free,' he murmurs, looking at the two tickets on the empty desk.

'Have to be up bright and early. The ship leaves at nine. I reckon some stories have to end, sometime, somewhere, even if the journey continues.'

Afterword

At the invitation of the then Viceroy, Lord Northbrook, Edward Lear, the English artist and poet of nonsense, who had made Italy his home for over twenty years, travelled to India in November 1873 with his manservant, Giorgi Kokalis. As he traversed the length and breadth of the vast subcontinent, Lear kept a journal that was published nearly seventy years later – as *Edward Lear's Indian Journal,* edited by Ray Murphy and published by Jarrolds, London.

Between first encountering the hardbound edition of the *Journal* at the British Library in 2013 and receiving, in May 2020, my friend Steven Nuss's first reactions to words that I had jotted down describing Lear sitting on a stool to draw the Kanchenjunga, was an interregnum of sorts that, in retrospect, appears to embody the story that emerged in this novel. Steven wrote: *'I love the sense of delay… well actually the very real delay in making the first mark on the paper… there is this suspended action that nevertheless propels things forward (when WILL he draw??) the intense feeling of quiet, the vast and intimate spatial imagery through which you toggle. Again, the silence, or muted nature of the scene which is broken by the creak of the stool and the seizure only heard in the head… and still waiting and wondering when the hand will make a mark on the paper.'*

The story of Lear's journey opened with the drama of his deferrals – powerfully mirrored in Steven's simple question: 'When will he draw?' Significantly, my own writerly journey began not when I first leafed through the pages of the *Journal* but nearly eight years later – with the question that my colleague, Sarah Braunstein, a fiction writer, raised when I first confided to her that although Lear's *Indian Journal* haunted me, I had absolutely no idea what to do with them. *'Fascinating as they are, the journals are little more than fragmentary observations, incomplete stories, riddled with gaps and silence.'*

'Turn it into fiction, historical fiction' was her advice on a particularly chilly, sunny morning in Kalimpong, a Himalayan town located not far from Kurseong, a colonial outstation that Edward Lear had visited nearly a hundred and fifty years before to sketch the mighty Kanchenjunga.

'I am no fiction writer. I do critical, literary, historical scholarship,' was how I had responded to Sarah's suggestion.

Barely three months had passed since that exchange when the world appeared to slip into an abyss. During the three months of the pandemic lockdown, I found myself literally imprisoned in a small apartment in Kolkata, thinking obsessively about Lear. What was one to do with the *Journal*? Turn it into short fiction? A novel? Perhaps even a prose poem?

In May 2020, cyclone Amphan surged through the city with the fury of an interstellar explosion. From my apartment window, I witnessed the drama of thunder and lightning unfolding in the darkening skies, the wild winds tearing down mercilessly the branches of fifty-foot-tall trees. Then a strange calm descended. But after a few hours, the 'eye' of the great storm slipped across the sky, following which the winds surged again, leaving behind a trail of downed power lines and shards of broken roofs. It took another hour for the winds to ease up.

True to the spirit of the cosmic drama that I witnessed that day, the first pages of the story began to take shape – *in media res* – at that throbbing cusp of danger, relief and renewed fear, each one folding into the other. I imagined Lear gazing at the half-defined outlines of the majestic Kanchenjunga looming across the skies, the tip of his pencil quivering over the sheet of paper, unsure if he would be able to get anything down on paper.

I had an opening!

From that point onwards, the story began to move, at times stuttering, then pulsating and racing ahead. Characters unnamed in the *Journals* began to come to life as flesh-and-blood individuals; the railway platforms from where the two alighted from trains echoed with clangs, shouts and songs; the dying fires in the fireplaces of the cold and dank *dak bungalows* hissed and crackled.

As the story of Lear's travels crystallized, I also became dimly aware of its half-concealed, subterranean layer. For the first time, I sensed that this extraordinary man – a world traveller, poet and painter known for his wild imagination and unconventional humour – was also an individual perplexed and shaken by his troubled past. How would I capture this new terrain of buried memory and desire that appeared to lie beyond the words that I had encountered in the *Journals*? Were the long ellipses, unfinished sentences and fragments more than what they seemed – inevitable gaps resulting from the exigencies of travel?

Just when I thought I had to discard the mantle of literary analysis in order to exercise my literary creativity, Virginia Woolf's *Mrs Dalloway*'s masterful narrative came to mind. One could excavate Lear's buried memories, untie the knots, loops and tangles, opening up the gaps and allowing the silences to speak. Woolf's style provided the path for braiding the private and the public. Once I had turned *that* invisible key, there was no looking back. The more I followed Lear's itinerary of travel, the more I was able to explore Lear's world of memory – of a difficult childhood and his unfulfilled desire for a wife, including the unreciprocated longings for a close friendship which he thought he had found in Lushington. Through this process, I also began to discover the different ways in which the archival work I had done earlier fed – almost in a capillary manner – into the novel, helping build its historical base *and* its dramatic interest. To better grasp that story's relation to Lear's personal life, I also turned to Peter Levi's biography of Lear and to Jenny Uglow's *Mr Lear: A Life of Art and Nonsense.*

Throughout this process, I was fortunate to receive timely suggestions, comments and queries regarding the narrative style and content, particularly from my colleagues at Colby College, namely Paula Harrington, Tilar Mazzeo, Mary Ellis Gibson and my agent Book Bakers. Without their input, I would not have had the impetus to keep writing. After uncountable meetings on Zoom, after puzzling through questions posed by an online audience attending a talk organized by Loreto College, Kolkata, and after months of frantic fact-checking and revising, reordering, modulating and even discarding entire chunks of narrative, *The Viceroy's Artist* came into being in its present form.

As distant as Edward Lear may be in time and place, to me he appears as a strangely familiar figure, the 'odd' man in a bowler hat who inspires, by the sheer dint of his audacious courage and fortitude and by the wondrous sweep of an unhindered imagination, curiosity and compassion for the world.